BOOKS, BOXES & WRAPS

Binding & Building
Step-by-Step

Marilyn Webberley
& JoAn Forsyth

Illustrations by
Marilyn Webberley

to Faye with love & joy!
Marilyn Webberley

Bifocal Publishing   Kirkland

First edition Published 1995
Printed in the United States of America
10 9 8 7 6 5 4 3 2 1

ISBN 1-886475-00-8

Library of Congress Catalog Card Number 94-96690

Printed on acid free paper

Bifocal Publishing, PO Box 272, Kirkland WA 98083-0272

This book is dedicated to the creative spirit within us all.
May it help spread joy and delight, laughter and
inspiration after the work is done.

CONTENTS

BOOKS, BOXES & WRAPS is an outgrowth of a university course I taught. The first day of class everyone was given handouts containing small drawings and very brief notes. Students had to cut, collate, and stitch this into a small booklet which slipped into a non-adhesive cover they also made. All the required projects for the quarter were included.

Every two or three quarters I revised this booklet. By fall, 1986, it had expanded to over 30 pages and was stitched in four signatures as a Four Needle Binding. By now, I liked this booklet so much I thought of printing some on special paper and making them for Christmas gifts!

I was so excited that I called Jo to share my great idea. Her response was, "You don't want a booklet. Write a book!"

From my perspective, it would have been hard to come up with a worse idea! I had no interest in writing a book. In the next few months Jo called two or three times to say, "Think about it. How about a book? . . . I will help you."

At this time we were both aware that information on simple book making was hard to find in either libraries or book stores. Months later we began.

Since that time, I have had children graduate from high school and college, and both of us have had children marry and have children of their own.

Looking back, there were times of great enthusiasm mixed with times of none. There were times when we worked long hours, six and seven days a week, and there were times when neither of us worked on the book nor had any interest in finishing it.

This book would never have been completed if it weren't for the One who said, "Finish it. There is good information for people here." And the continuous flowing grace that moved through the many obstacles that followed.

There were so many obstacles, that I was recently asked if this project was destined to never be. It's not like that. These obstacles gave us the opportunity to learn many things about ourselves.

It brought a chance to become clear and steady with the task, to persevere, to practice seeing everything as a lesson where one has the chance to see the truth from within, follow that truth, and become stronger. We both took that chance and acted on that truth.

Much grace and many blessings go with this book.

Marilyn Webberley
Kirkland, 29 March 1995

ACKNOWLEDGMENTS

Grateful appreciation and thanks go to my students
and teachers who were the inspiration that began this project;
to Jo Forsyth for encouragement, insight, contributions toward the research, writing, and
revising this book, and for team teaching with me to test projects and instructions;
to Sandra Kroupa for filling several carts with books for us to browse through
in the University of Washington rare book library as this project began;
to Don Guyot for patiently answering all my questions in person and by phone;
to Stan Knight for cover calligraphy and book design assistance;
to Eileen Canning for watercolor-marbled design on cover;
to Mary Danielson for proof reading an earlier version of this book;
to Andrea Hammer for editing suggestions;
to Barbara Getty and Dolores Johnson for proof reading;
to Steve Colello for proof reading and final editing;
to Michael W. Moore for computer assistance;
to Ceci Miller-Kritsberg for organizing information about
the authors, how to use this book and back cover pages;
to Marie Pauson for her assistance as printing consultant;
to my creative friends at Menucha who sampled projects and shared ideas;
and to the others who helped bring this project to a close:
Sally Ashford, John Baxter, Mac Baxter, Olav Martin Kvern,
Melodie Hurlen, Edye Colello-Morton, and Fran Sloan.

And once again to all who placed pre-publication orders,
thank you for your belief in this project and for your patience.

Thanks to my husband, Gary, for his constant advice;
I am now taking it. I'm going painting!

Marilyn Webberley

HOW TO USE THIS BOOK

Before you begin your first project, take a few moments to familiarize yourself with this book. It is laid out like a workbook, and contains invaluable tips and information that you'll want to use while you're creating your book, box or wrap. Because a number of the projects require many of the same steps to be done, we decided not to reiterate those steps for each project. Doing so would have made the book much too challenging to carry around! We decided to localize the instructions in three places: in special sections at the front and back of the book, and in the "General Information" sections at the beginning of each chapter.

At the front of the book are two short sections worthy of note: "Thoughts on Binding Books" gives a brief overview of the creative process of bookmaking — it presents historical as well as practical and aesthetic considerations. Next, "Suggested Tools" lists all the tools needed to make the projects in this book, along with instructions for their use.

Each chapter begins with snippets of historical information, and gives the general instructions necessary to make the kinds of projects contained in the chapter.

At the back of the book, in "Binder's Tool Chest" you will find knots and closures, suggestions on working with paper, measuring, pasting, sewing, mitering corners, and labeling covers. This section also gives detailed information about materials, including a list of adhesives, an extensive chart of various papers, a list of supply sources, and a glossary of bookmaking terms. As you work, you may refer to these sections as often as needed to assure the best possible results.

For even more information about methods and materials, the Bibliography recommends helpful books, articles, and catalogs.

THOUGHTS ON BINDING BOOKS

CREATING A BOOK draws together a variety of skills, from visualizing layout to choosing an appropriate style of lettering. Whether made of palm leaves, clay tablets, metal plates, or bound paper leaves, all books demand that you think about the connections between form and content; that is, between how something is put together and what it says.

Creating a book means, for example, thinking about the dynamic possibilities inherent in traditional formats. Historically, books are put together in four different ways. They may be *scrolls*, or rolls, of vellum, papyrus, silk, etc. They may be folded like an accordion. They may fan out, like a peacock's tail before collapsing back into place. Or they may take the form of the codex. The word codex derives from the Latin *caudex*, which means the trunk of a tree, a tablet of wax-covered wood used for writing or a code of laws or statutes. Codex (pl. *codices*) now generally refers to a form of manuscript book. Whichever format you choose to work with depends largely, as it always has, on the materials you have available to you as well as on what you want to say.

Format, then, involves the sizes, shapes, and materials of the leaves as well as the method of binding. But discussions of format are somewhat complex because so many mutually influential elements are involved. A format, for example, may be passive or dynamic, depending upon its content. A passive, or traditional shape is quiet and unassuming. A dynamic shape, on the other hand, may exaggerate width, height, or both. A fragile format might be derived from delicate materials and techniques; whereas a more rugged, sturdy format can be made to withstand a child's constant use. The purpose of the book will influence these various expressive qualities and be influenced by them.

Creating a book means using the possibilities and restrictions of the binding itself, also a significant element of its format. In some binding structures, for instance, the spine's flexibility will critically affect the layout, as some bindings open fairly flat with no loss of inner margin. Others, such as edge sewn bindings, do not. In some bindings, endpapers – *paste downs* – serve as structural bonds that hold the book block to the binding. In others, however, they serve as a transitional step but have no structural duties. In these, a *fly leaf*, whether patterned or plain, might act as a form of framing, a quiet space before one enters the text. Endpapers might be used to complement or accent the binding and text.

Finally, in some book forms – such as fold books – they might disappear altogether.

Creating a book means thinking about reading. Traditionally, books encourage a kind of linear reading, whether the eyes move from right to left, left to right, or top to bottom. But increasingly books accommodate a more random reading. They may also emphasize the tactile experiences of unusual surfaces and three-dimensional qualities. Regardless of these differences, all books involve turning pages, and turning pages brings movement into play, and with movement, rhythm. Harmonizing this rhythm is possible, and continuity can evolve through some kind of uninterrupted sequencing. Books unfold in time and allow readers to work through time, either literally or emotionally. And, as the page is turned, books allow for surprises.

Finally, creating a book means considering which, if any, conventions of the printing trade are to be adapted to your handmade book. A hallowed sequence in book content has evolved over the years in the printing trade, yet parts of this sequence may or may not apply to the handmade books you will find in this manual. For most handmade books, a title page and colophon are usually sufficient, for often the small size of a handmade book makes a table of contents unnecessary. A title page is usually a right-hand (*recto*) page or a double spread. A colophon is a short inscription that may describe the papers, mediums, binding information, edition size, attributions, dedications, year, and/or anything else that distinguishes the book. Colophons usually include the author, scribe, and binder. Sometimes designed in a special shape, a colophon is placed on a separate blank page or at the bottom of the last text page. In commercial books today, the information in a colophon usually appears on the back of the title page.

Much has been passed down about books and bookbinding, yet much remains to be discovered, rethought, or invented. So this is a book not only about making books, but about enlarging your sense of what a book is and what it does and what it might do. By including boxes, folders, and wraps, we hope to stimulate you to explore the subtler ways that content and form are married – and why.

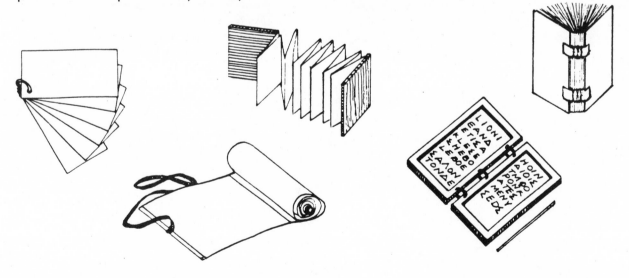

SUGGESTED TOOLS

ACE BANDAGE

  Use an elastic bandage to hold pressure around a piece while adhesives are drying. Two or three inches wide is a convenient size. Ace is a brand name.

AWL

  A metal tool with a sharp point that is used to make holes. Hardware stores have awls with thick shafts which make big holes. Bindery suppliers have a narrow shaft style which works much better. Make your own awl by inserting a needle into a wooden handle from a hardware or craft store. Use pliers to hold the eye end of needle over a stove and heat. Gradually force the heated end into the handle. Substitute a wine bottle cork with plastic top for the wooden handle. The plastic end prevents the needle from pushing through the rear end of the cork. Use a sewing machine needle or darning needle and push or burn it into the cork. Hold the needle in place with instant-bond glue if necessary. Trim length of cork if necessary.

BRUSHES

  Those used for pasting are described on p. 239.

CHISEL

  A wood chisel, beveled on one side, is used to make slits in bindings and boxes for closures and flat binding tapes; 1/4" and 3/8" are useful sizes.

CLAMPS

  Quick Grip Mini Bar Clamps are a locking clamp ideal for clamping parts together while drying adhesives or drilling holes. They have soft, pliable pads to protect surfaces, but board scraps should also be used between clamp pad and surface to avoid dents.

CLIPS

Use clips to keep parts aligned
when sewing or pasting.

Place board scraps
between clip and
surface to avoid dents.

Bulldog clips are made
of heavy gauge metal.

Spring clips or
French Clothes Pins
are plastic coated wire.

FOLDERS

A folder is a smooth, flat tool used for folding, creasing, and slitting paper and for
smoothing surfaces after pasting. Folding tools are usually carved from bone and are
sometimes available in bamboo.

Both a slim pointed style and a
broad rounded end of medium
width are useful. Buy folders
from binding or art supply
stores.

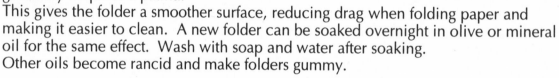

With use, a bone folder
gradually acquires a patina.
This gives the folder a smoother surface, reducing drag when folding paper and
making it easier to clean. A new folder can be soaked overnight in olive or mineral
oil for the same effect. Wash with soap and water after soaking.
Other oils become rancid and make folders gummy.

Reshape a chipped folder with a file or knife and smooth with fine sandpaper.

Plastic folders are less sensitive to paper surfaces and not carefully finished.
  A dull table knife, letter opener, tongue depressor, or spoon is an acceptable
substitute.

FOLDING GAUGE

In Japan, a wooden gauge is used to accurately fold accordion pages.

A wood block is cut about 1/2"
thick and about 1 1/2" wide.
The ends are beveled with a
45º angle. The folding gauge
is moved along the back side of
a paper strip. The block length

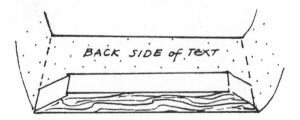

BACK SIDE of TEXT

determines the fore edge folds.
Make a mark at each end of
the gauge as it is moved
along the bottom edge of
the strip. Line up bottom
edges of paper and make
folds at these marks.

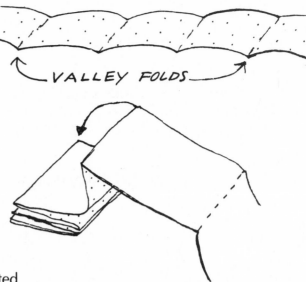

When strip is turned over, these
valley folds become mountain folds
and mark each double page spread.

Render art work before making
center fold. To form center folds,
bring folded edges together, one
by one. Finish folds with a folder.

A scrap of binder board can be substituted
for the wood block. Cut corners square for accuracy.

HAND DRILL

A drill is used to make holes in thick book blocks. An assortment of bit sizes is handy.
Buy extra. Small sizes break easily. An electric drill can be substituted. Directions
for use are on p. 244. Buy drill and bits at a hardware store.

KNITTING NEEDLES

Roll paper beads on knitting needles.
A dull knitting needle point can be used as a scoring tool.

KNIVES

Several styles are useful. Buy at a hardware, wallpaper, or art store.

A blunt, round-end, smooth-edged
table knife is good for scoring. It is
also useful for prying and slitting.

Utility knives with retractable,
replaceable steel blades are useful
for cutting heavyweight papers
and boards. They should fit the
hand comfortably.

A knife with disposable
snap-off blades is useful
for light, delicate cuts.

L SQUARE

This is a carpenter's metal tool that is useful
as a guide for right angles and as a cutting edge
when trimming fore edges or squaring boards. Substitute with a right triangle.

MALLET
A hammer with a wooden, plastic, or leather head that is used to drive a chisel or awl when making holes. Substitute a hammer with a broad, padded head.

NEEDLES
Binding needles are made in England with polished eyes to reduce wear on thread. Buy them from binding suppliers.
Substitute #3-#00 cotton darner needles or crewel embroidery needles.

NEEDLE-NOSE PLIERS
Use pliers or tweezers to pull closure parts through slits in boards.

PRESS, BOOK
A simple book press is easy to make; 12" x 15" is a versatile size.
Use two pieces of 1/2" shelving or 1/2" plywood. Assemble boards with four carriage bolts, about 5" long with washers and wing nuts, through holes drilled in each corner as shown.
A handle on the top board makes it easier to raise the top to put in a book.
Place scrap binder board between the pressing boards and the binding.

Substitute *Quick Grip* Mini Bar Clamps, p. 1, and boards for a book press.

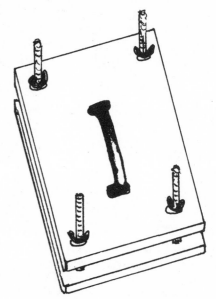

PRESSING BOARDS
Mat-finish, smooth plastic laminate counter-top
boards or sink cut-outs make good boards for pressing work while drying. Other choices are 1/4" plastic sheets, smooth hardwood boards, plywood, or tempered masonite sealed with paint or varnish.

Pressing boards should be larger than object being pressed.
Standard sizes are sold by binding materials suppliers.

RAGS OR SPONGES
It is important to keep work surface and fingers clean when pasting.
A damp rag or sponge helps to clean fingers and to wipe up spills.

RULERS
An 18" transparent plastic ruler with grid marks is useful for general measuring and aligning boards when making cases.

SANDPAPER OR EMERY BOARDS
Edges may be sanded to smooth a burr from binder board or to modify the fit of a board in box making, Do not expect sanding to solve cutting errors.

SCISSORS

A medium-sized pair with pointed tips is useful for general purpose cutting of book cloth and other materials.

SHARPENING STONE

A stone with both fine and medium grade sides is useful for sharpening dull knife blades. Buy these at hardware or cutlery stores.

SPACER

This device is used in case and box making to measure space between boards as placement lines are drawn and boards are mounted. Make a spacer from the same board and covering material as the project.

Board = 3" X 6", cut one

Covering cloth = 3" X 6", use 3 to 7 layers according to project

Paste all layers of cloth to board and smooth well with folder. When dry, make a clean cut along the long edge.

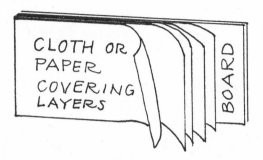

SQUARE CARD

This device is easier to use than a ruler for measuring small dimensions.

It is made from mat or illustration board that is white on both sides.

Lay out an exact 3" square. Divide the square into 4 equal smaller squares. Rule dimensions, so they are all in the same position front and back, on both sides of the card. Be sure it is exact and square.

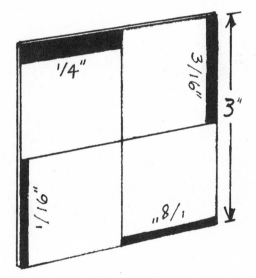

STRAIGHT EDGE

A straight edge is used for cutting, tearing and scoring. Steel is best although aluminum will work if care is used. A length of 24" to 36" will take care of most paper lengths. Buy at art supply stores.

TRIANGLE

A triangle with one leg at least 8" in length can be substituted for an L square. Use it to check right angles where necessary. Buy at an art supply store.

WEIGHTS

Weights are used for pressing bindings and boxes while drying.

Wrapped bricks, chunks of marble, containers of lead shot, rocks, or sand can add weight on top of pressing boards. Use a zip lock bag for a container. See *Pressing While Drying* and *Using Weights*, p. 241.

PALM LEAVES
& SCROLLS

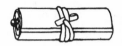

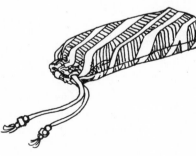

In China the earliest surviving inscriptions, which date from 1,300 to 1,027 B.C., were written on tortoise shells and animal bones. Characters were scratched into these surfaces and then rubbed with black or red ink.

People wrote on what the environment provided: stone, clay, wood, bark, palm leaves, bamboo strips, silk rolls, papyrus, hammered metal sheets, leather, and parchments.

As the need grew to hold information together, the book was born. Clay tablets and scrolls went into jars, palm leaves were strung together on cords and so forth.

PALM LEAF BOOKS

The Palm Leaf Book is one of the earliest book forms. Although few things written on perishable materials have been preserved, Pliney records that Egyptians first wrote upon the leaves of palm trees about the First Dynasty at the beginning of the Bronze Age. The earliest Indian manuscripts seem to belong to the fourth century A.D., although legend places them earlier in time.

Palm leaves were cut to the desired length and rubbed smooth. The area for holes was marked on each leaf. The text and illustrations were added. Holes were made in each leaf, and the book was strung together. Small books had one hole in each leaf. Larger books usually had two, one near each end of the leaf.

The writing tool played a part in designing letter forms. In northern India, a brush was used. In the south, a stylus scratched letters into the surface which was then rubbed with ink and wiped away, leaving the ink visible in the incised areas. Brush written forms in the north became more angular with horizontal lines above letters. Eventually, these lines became long enough to run the entire length of a word or an entire line of writing. Further south, letter forms became rounder since long horizontal lines made with a stylus cut palm leaf fibers.

VENETIAN BLIND PALM LEAF BOOK

Books strung through two holes turn like a Venetian blind.
The cover boards can be plain or covered.

Materials:
Book block, heavyweight paper
Cover boards, mat or binder board
Board cover material, optional
Sturdy cord, grosgrain
  ribbon, linen tape, etc.
Optional embellishments,
  beads, shells,
  bells, feathers, etc.
Adhesive

PLAN DIMENSIONS,
  traditionally wider
  than tall, yet most
  shapes will work.

MAKE UP text leaves.

MARK POSITION and
  make holes before
  drafting leaves, p. 243, 244.

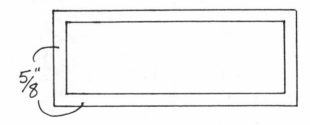

CUT COVER MATERIALS
  Cover Boards, cut two
  For overhang add 1/4" to each dimension
  Height = book block height
  Width = book block width

  Cover Material, optional, cut two
  H = cover board height + 1 1/4"
  W = cover board height + 1 1/4"

  Paste Downs, cut two
  H = cover board height less 1/8"
  W = cover board width less 1/8"

5/8"

APPLY ADHESIVE to board and center on back side of cover material.
  Turn and smooth in place with folder, p. 240.

MITER CORNERS and paste down turn-ins on both boards, p. 245.

ADD ENDPAPERS. Brush adhesive on exposed board and edges of endpapers.

Center endpapers on boards, press in place and smooth with folder. Dry boards overnight under light pressure, p. 241.

THREAD CORD through collated covers and leaves. Use one long cord as shown, or two short ones. Make knots in ends of cord adding beads if desired, ending knots, p. 226, 227.

FAN PALM LEAF BOOK

Materials:
Same as Venetian Blind Book, p. 9

Follow *Venetian Blind Palm Leaf Book,* p. 2, using only one hole in cover and each leaf. Locate hole closer to one end of the leaves than the middle.

MAKE CORD just long enough for leaves to fan out or to become two side by side stacks as shown. Experiment with proper length before tying off cord with a square knot, p. 226.

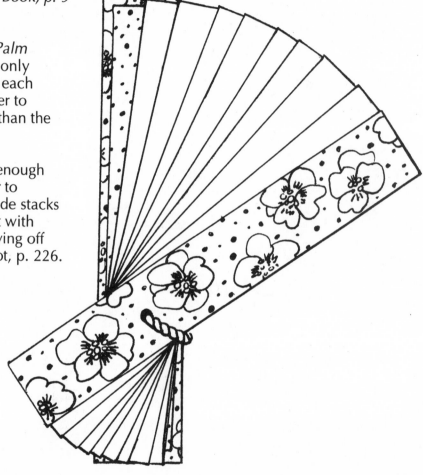

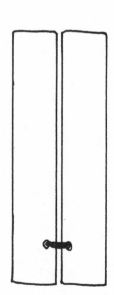

The British Library in London has a beautiful 18th Century Palm Leaf Indian Manuscript with sandalwood covers strung in a fan shape.

METAL PLATE BOOKS

Metal plates were used for record keeping world wide. Copper, bronze, lead, and occasionally gold or silver were used. The metal was hammered thin and made into plates or long strips which were then engraved. Plates were held together with a metal ring which passed through a hole in each plate. The long strips were curled into rolls.

A seal with the owner's name was attached to the ring. Records of ownership were easily changed in metal and forgeries were not unheard of.

Covers were not needed for metal books. However, with paper pages, a cover gives protection and a finished appearance to the structure.

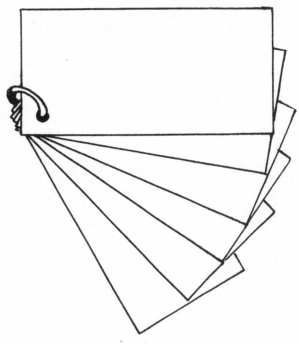

METAL PLATE FORMAT IN PAPER

Materials:
Book block, heavyweight paper,
  lightweight board, or combinations of the two
Ring for binding,
  Split rings, found in Marine Hardware stores, notebook rings,
  curtain rings, all come in a variety of sizes and weights
Cover boards, wood veneer, or mat board, p. 255.

PLAN DIMENSIONS. It will look best if 2" or larger.
  Make up book block leaves.

CUT COVERS.
  Cover boards, cut two
  Height = book block height
  Width = book block width

MARK AND make holes before drafting contents, p. 244.

USE A ring large enough to allow pages to flip easily.

PEG BOOKS

Peg books are a variation of the Metal Plate book style which pivot around a peg, forming a fan shape when open. Peg books can be round, square, or rectangular; long and narrow, or short and fat.

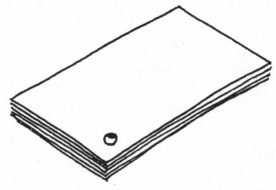

INDEPENDENT COVER

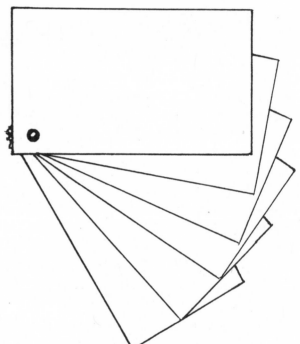

Materials:
Book block, heavyweight paper
Cover paper, heavier or same weight,
  can be contrasting color or texture
Wooden dowel, twig or bamboo stick
  1/8" diameter (must be 1/4" to
  1/2" longer than spine thickness)
Two beads with holes to fit dowel ends,
  p. 229 and p. 20
Instant Bond Adhesive

PLAN DIMENSIONS, best if 2" x 3" or larger.

MAKE UP book block leaves.

CUT MATERIALS.
  Cover Boards, cut two
  Height = book block height
  Width = book block width

MARK AND make holes before drafting contents.

TRIM PEG to match spine thickness plus extra length for end beads.

INSERT PEG through collated covers and leaves.
  Use instant bond adhesive to attach beads to ends of peg to keep peg in place.

WRAP-AROUND COVER
FLUSH COVER FORMAT

Materials:
Same as Independent Cover Peg Book,
    p. 12, except:
Cover, lightweight board, or
    paper bond

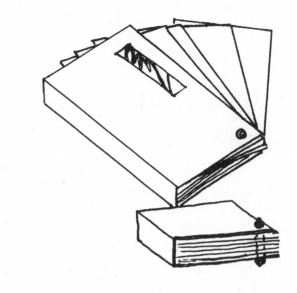

PLAN DIMENSIONS, best if
2"x3" or larger.
Make up book block, p. 12.

CUT COVER.
   Height = book block height
   Width = 2 times book block width
           + spine thickness + ease

Measure for spine thickness as
described on p. 110.
Amount of ease space in folds
depends on paper weight, see
Folds take up space, p. 28.

SCORE COVER fold lines.

MARK AND make cover holes
   using a book page for a pattern.

Follow *TRIM PEG* and
INSERT PEG, p. 12, to finish book.

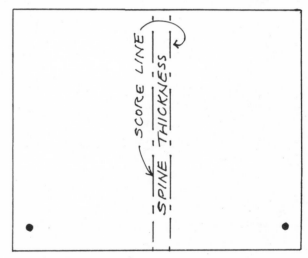

OVERHANG COVER FORMAT

CUT COVER.
   Height = Height + 1/4"
   Width = 2 times page width + spine thickness
           + 3/8" for overhang + ease

   This gives 1/8" overhang
   on all edges. Position hole to
   accommodate extra space at spine.

CIRCLE BOOKS

Circle books and creativity go together.
These books can combine a variety of papers, textures, colors, and weights.
Paper can be handmade in small embroidery hoops or easily cut from larger sheets.

PLAIN BOARDS, TWO HOLES

Materials:
Book block,
  heavyweight paper
Cover, heavyweight paper or
  board, matching or contrasting
  color and/or texture
Cord, long enough to spread
  pages out for viewing
Beads, shells, or other optional
  decorations

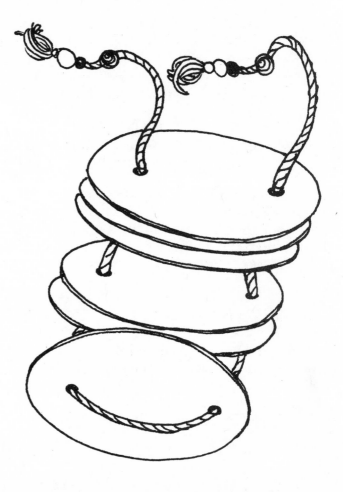

CUT CIRCLES to make up book
  block. Draw around a glass or
  similar object, or draw them
  with a compass and cut out
  with scissors, p. 236.
  A circle cutter can also be used.

CUT COVERS the same diameter
  as the book block pages.

MARK HOLE positions at least
  1/4" from edge, across from
  each other.

MAKE HOLES before drafting pages,
  p. 244.

COLLATE AND string on cord.
  Experiment with the cord.
  Braid multiple strands of embroidery thread, perlé cotton, raffia, or ribbons into a
  single cord, p. 230. Twist sewing thread into a single cord, p. 231. Coordinate
  cord colors with text paper colors.

  Finish cord ends with knots and beads, etc.
  Decorative ending knots can be found on pages 227 and 228.
  Directions for making beads from paper or clay are given on page 229.

COVERED BOARDS, TWO HOLES

Materials:
Same as Plain Boards, Two Holes, p. 14 except:
Cover boards of mat or binder board
Plus:
Decorative paper for board cover material
Endpaper paste downs
Adhesive

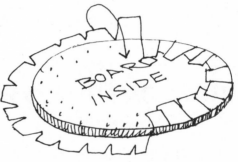

CUT COVER
   Cover Boards, cut two
   Circle = page size

Cover Paper, cut two
   Circle = 1 1/4" larger diameter than boards

Endpaper Paste Downs, cut two
   Circle = 1/8" smaller diameter than boards

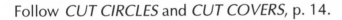

Follow *CUT CIRCLES* and *CUT COVERS*, p. 14.

DRAW COVER board position on inside
   of cover material with 5/8" margin all
   around.

SPREAD ADHESIVE on cover boards.
   Position boards on cover material.
   Turn and smooth with folder, pp. 239-240.

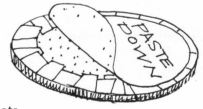

CUT TURN-INS around edges as shown.
   Leave an uncut space of about
   1/8" at board edge.

PUT ADHESIVE on inside edge of board as shown in dots.
   Lift turn-in over board edge, overlapping sections for a smooth fit.
   Repeat for other cover piece.

SPREAD ADHESIVE on bare board area and edges of endpapers. Set endpapers in
   place, smooth with folder, and dry under light pressure, p. 241.

MAKE HOLES in cover and text when dry, p. 244. Be sure cover material is firmly
   attached and dry before making holes with a drill.

Follow *COLLATE AND string on cord,* p. 14, to finish.

STRUNG ON A LOOP, ONE HOLE

Materials:
Same as Plain Boards,
  Two Holes, p.14
  or
  Covered Board,
  Two Holes, p. 15

Follow *CUT*
CIRCLES and
CUT COVERS,
p. 14. Finish as in
Plain Boards, p. 14,
or *Covered Boards*, p. 15,
making only one hole in pages and boards as shown.

COLLATE PAGES and cover. String on cord. Make a loop loose enough for pages to turn without binding and tearing. Plan this with book open and separated into two sections with a small space between. Tie a loose knot to test loop size; change if necessary. Finish with an overhand or square knot and any desired decorations.

STRUNG ON LONG CORD, ONE HOLE

Materials:
Same as above

Follow *CUT CIRCLES*
and *CUT COVERS,*
above.

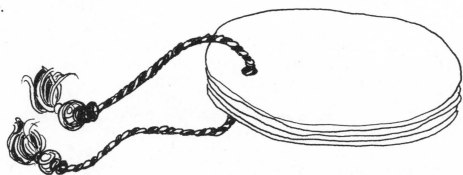

STRING ON long cord and follow *FINISH CORD ends,* p. 14.

CLAY COVERS STRUNG ON A LOOP

Use a polymer clay such as *Fimo* or *Sculpy* that hardens when baked in an oven. The clay surface can be decorated. Use an interesting tool, stick, or rubber stamp to press a pattern in the surface before baking. Gold Leaf will stick to the surface. Put it on before baking and burnish it with a cotton ball or silk cloth when cool. The surface may be painted with acrylics after baking.

ROLL OUT clay with rolling pin.
 Cut with knife to fit pages.

MAKE HOLES before baking.

DECORATE CLAY, optional.

STRING ON loop as before.

LARGE CIRCLES OR HEARTS FOLDED IN HALF

Materials:
Handmade rounds or hearts from
Twin Rocker Mills
Variety of artist papers

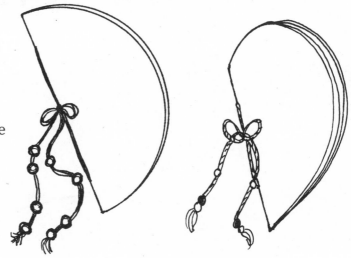

ALTERNATE ARTIST papers, cut or
 torn, to match size with handmade
 shapes for variety, p. 234.

INSERT ONE inside another after
 folding and sew through the fold
 using butterfly stitch, p. 91.

BEGIN AND end sewing pattern
 at outside hole of choice.
 Embellish as desired.

LARGE CIRCLES STACKED

PLACE SEWING holes to one side.
 End sewing on top side at hole
 of choice and embellish as desired.

SCORE ALONG sewing line if necessary.

SCROLLS

The scroll was one of the earliest forms of the book. It appeared in different parts of the world at about the same time and was made from the materials at hand: strips of birch bark, leather, papyrus, silk, or many sheets of paper joined together. Sometimes separate sheets of paper were mounted on silk.
Scrolls were rolled for storage.

In some cultures, scrolls or hand rolls were used for scriptures as well as letters, stories, poetry, and paintings.

Writing or painting was done on one side only. A roller was often attached to one or both ends. In some cultures, a cloth or paper cover was attached to the beginning end, and a flat cord was added to wrap and hold the scroll closed.

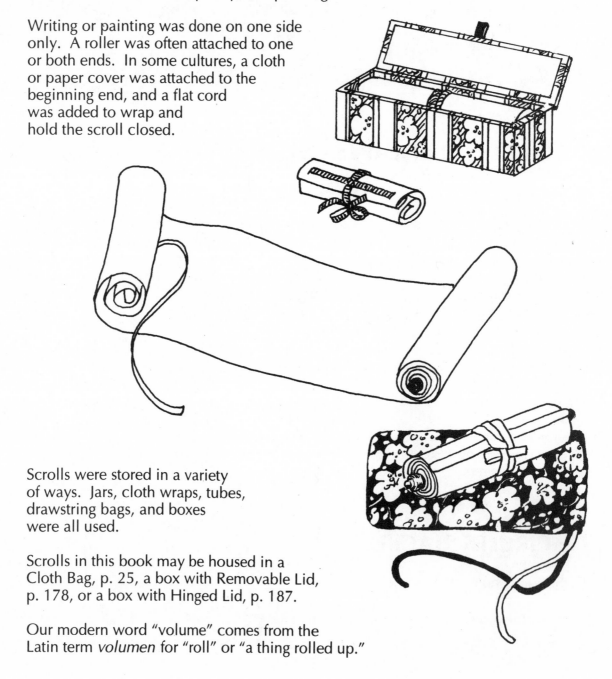

Scrolls were stored in a variety of ways. Jars, cloth wraps, tubes, drawstring bags, and boxes were all used.

Scrolls in this book may be housed in a Cloth Bag, p. 25, a box with Removable Lid, p. 178, or a box with Hinged Lid, p. 187.

Our modern word "volume" comes from the Latin term *volumen* for "roll" or "a thing rolled up."

VELLUM OR PAPER SCROLL

Edward Johnston recommends this scroll in *Writing, Illuminating and Lettering.* He favors "a rather narrow, upright parchment" (p. 320) and suggests putting it in "a neat japanned tin case which may be obtained for a few shillings" (p. 321).

Materials:
Vellum or medium
  weight paper
1/4" ribbon of a length that
  is 2 times scroll width plus
  distance around rolled
  scroll plus enough to tie

CUT SCROLL.
  Allow extra length for folded bottom edge. Top edge may be plain or folded with ribbon woven through a pattern of slits. Paper needs to be cut with grain parallel to opening edge.

FOLD BOTTOM edge up twice.
  Make folds about 1/2" wide.

MAKE SLIT in center and
  3/8" to 5/8 from each end,
  p. 235.

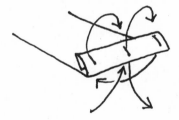

LACE RIBBON as shown.
  Untwist if necessary and pull ribbon snug. Place one end of ribbon on each side of long stitch, as shown, and tie.

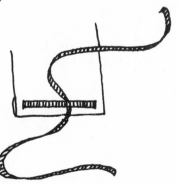

ROLL SCROLL from top to bottom.

WRAP RIBBON ends around scroll and tie.

ROLLER MOUNTED SCROLLS

The procedure drawings are for languages reading left to right.

SCROLL WITH ADDED COVER PIECE

Materials:
Scroll paper
Cover paper, matching or contrasting papers
  need to roll easily and have grain direction
  as indicated
Wooden dowel for roller, in proportion with
  scroll size, 1/4" longer than narrow dimension
  plus space to add optional end knobs
2 end knobs, details and alternatives
  presented below
Thin wooden stay for opening edge
Flat cord,
  enough length to wrap rolled scroll
4 times
Adhesive

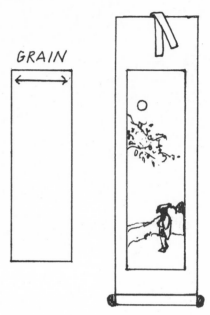

GRAIN

CUT PAPER for scroll to size needed. Scroll paper
    dimension must include 1/8" - 1/4" to attach to cover
    piece plus enough extra paper to wrap roller once at the
    other end. Be sure all edges and corners are cut square.

CUT ROLLER.
All sizes include rolling ease space.
    Simple Finish
    Roller length = narrow dimension of scroll + 1"
    Dowel ends are sanded smooth for a soft edge
    with the wood stained, painted, or sealed.

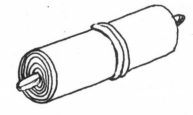

    Wooden Knobs
    Roller length = narrow dimension of scroll + 1/4"
    Keep knobs in proportion with dowel. Small
    drawer pulls with screws, found in hardware stores,
    will work. Use an awl or drill to make holes in center
    of dowel ends and screw in knobs.

    Polymer Clay
    Roller length = narrow dimension of scroll + 1/4"
                    + space needed for clay at each end
Form clay around dowel ends. Remove clay from
    dowel and bake. When cool, clay can be painted
    with acrylic paints. Use Super Glue to hold knobs on dowels.

PAINT OR seal to finish the wood and polymer clay ends.

Paper Knobs
Roller length = narrow dimension of scroll + 1/4"
     + space needed at each end for paper knobs
Use long paper strips. Wind tightly and smoothly around dowel ends.
Use a thin layer of adhesive on underside, at each end of strip.

The paper knobs are rolled directly on the roller ends.
They can be made in a cylinder or tapered style, p. 229.

Kraft paper will look like wood when
rolled and varnished. Kraft paper
can be painted with acrylic paints.

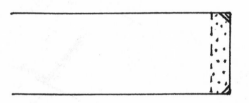

ADD ROLLER to scroll end.
   Be sure scroll edges are square.
   Wind scroll bottom edge around
   roller once and lightly mark distance
   on scroll with pencil. Trim off corners at an angle.
   Brush adhesive in area marked for roller, as shown in dotted area.

Place roller along edge and roll
paper around roller once.
Press paper to roller with fingers.
Carefully smooth in place.

CUT COVER piece.
   Length = enough to wrap rolled scroll 1 1/4 times + 5/8" to cover stay
   Width = narrow width of scroll.

ADD STAY to opening edge.
   Score and fold a line 5/8" in from opening edge on inside of cover.
   Cut off angle at both corners as shown.

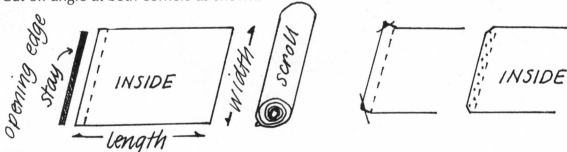

Brush adhesive along edge formed by fold, shown with dots.
Place stay along crease.
Fold flap over stay and lightly smooth in place. Turn over and smooth again.

ADD COVER to scroll.
Unroll beginning of scroll and mark a line 1/8" - 1/4" along opening edge on inside of scroll.

TURN COVER outside up.
Apply adhesive to a 1/8"-1/4" wide strip to edge opposite stay, see *Pasting In Limited Area*, p. 240.

TURN COVER inside up. Line up cover and scroll edges along a straight edge. Press adhesive edge of cover piece over opening end of scroll. Smooth with folder.

TURN FACE down and dry under light pressure with waxed paper barrier.

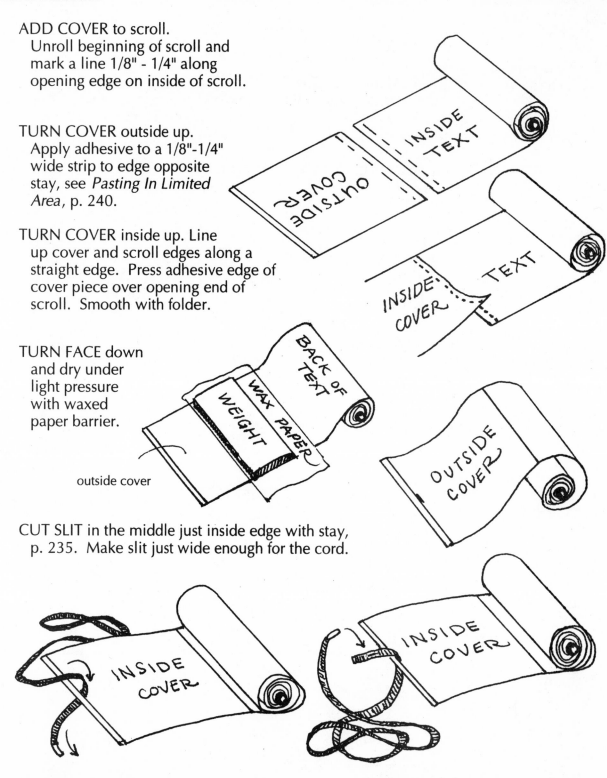

outside cover

CUT SLIT in the middle just inside edge with stay, p. 235. Make slit just wide enough for the cord.

THREAD CORD through slit from inside to outside of cover. Tips for threading cord are given on p. 76. Leave a short end on inside of cover as shown.

MAKE SLIT in cord close to **short** end. Thread other end **of cord** through slit and pull snug **around** stay. Untwist if needed.

FINISH END by pulling short end through slit to inside. Trim end, unravel a little, and paste to inside of scroll. Cover with a small piece of matching paper pasted over the end.

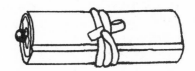

ROLL SCROLL tightly.
   Wind cord around scroll 3 1/2 times
   to measure length. Cut off extra length.

WRAP SCROLL 3 times without overlapping cord and tuck in end as shown.

SCROLL WITHOUT SEPARATE COVER PIECE

Materials:
Scroll paper
Wooden dowel for roller
End knobs
Stay
Flat cord
Adhesive

CUT SCROLL paper.
Length = needed length for contents
            + enough extra to wrap scroll 1 1/4 times
               (for closing edge)
            + 5/8" (to wrap stay on opening edge)
            + enough to wrap roller once
Width = desired width

Follow *ADD ROLLER, ADD STAY,* p. 21, and *CUT SLIT,* p. 22, to finish.

SCROLL BACKED WITH CLOTH OR PAPER

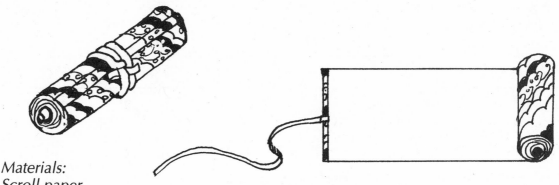

Materials:
Scroll paper
Backing material
Wooden dowel for roller
End knobs
Stay
Flat cord
Adhesive

CUT SCROLL paper.
Length = needed length for contents
         + enough extra to wrap scroll 1 1/4 times
         (for closing edge)
         + 5/8" (to wrap stay on opening edge)
         + enough to wrap roller once
Width = desired width

CUT BACKING material a little larger than scroll size on all sides.

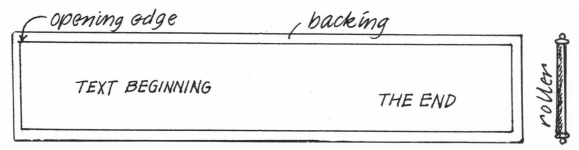

BOND SCROLL with backing material, p. 239, 241.
  Trim to match scroll size after bonding and drying.

DRY UNDER weight.

Follow *ADD ROLLER, ADD STAY,* p. 21, and *CUT SLIT,* p. 22, to finish.

STORAGE BAG

This bag is designed to hold long, narrow shapes like scrolls and adaptations of palm leaf styles.

Materials:
Fabric
Cord, ribbon, or tape
  Tying cord
Thread
Beads, optional

1/4" seam allowance is used for all seams. If fabric ravels easily, use wider seams and adjust measurements.

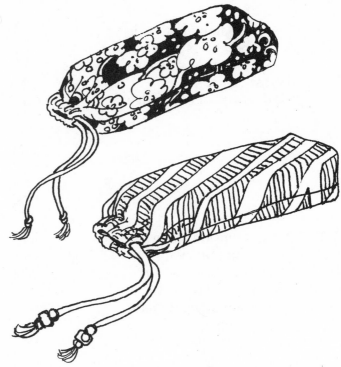

FIGURE SIZE of fabric for bag with a scrap of paper wrapped around widest part of contents. Add 2" for seams and ease.

Measure height plus any end knobs. Add 3 times thickness measurement to height measurement plus 1 1/2" for seams and cord casing.

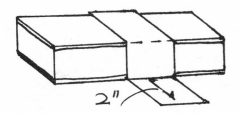

CUT CORD.
Length = length of fabric casing
        + 14"

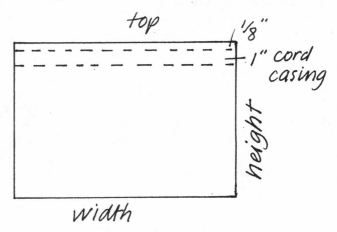

FINISH CASING edges first,
so cord opening won't fray.

FOLD IN 1/8" along both side
edges at top. Press with iron.
Fold in once more, as shown,
and press again.
Stitch down 1" of each edge.

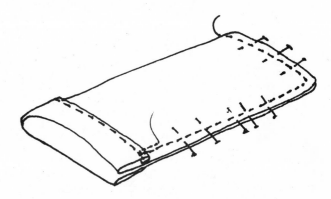

FOLD 1/8" to inside along
top edge and press with
iron. Fold 1/2" over again
to form the cord pocket.
Pin and stitch along folded
edge as shown.

FOLD BAG together with inside out.
Pin edges together as shown.

Sew seam down length
of bag and across bottom.
Begin sewing at casing seam,
keeping casing open.

Double stitch seam at
beginning and end or tie
thread ends with square knots.

TURN BAG right side out.
Thread cord through casing.
A safety pin pierced through
cord helps in threading
cord through casing.

ADD DECORATIVE beads or knots to cord ends if desired.

ACCORDION BINDINGS

Scrolls were often awkward due to the inconvenience of rolling and unrolling to find a desired place in the text. A normal Egyptian papyrus scroll used about twenty papyrus sheets , each nine inches wide, to make a scroll about 15' long. Many were much longer. The text was written in a series of columns.

Gradually the practice of folding scrolls into fixed lengths became popular, forming the accordion style.

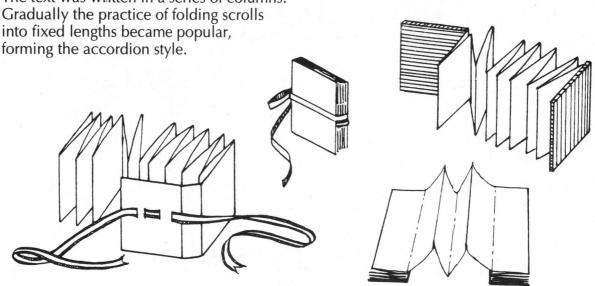

Accordion panel strips may be bound in many different ways and use a variety of paper weights and types. They lend themselves to creativity and invention. Covers can be separate or hinged. They may be held in a small folder or wrap-a-round cover. Explore *Folders & Soft Wraps*, p. 141, for ideas. Unusual shapes can be folded into accordion strips, p. 37. A narrow accordion strip can be used as a hinge to hold pages for additional material such as photographs, pp. 47, 48.

GENERAL INFORMATION

FOLDING ACCORDION strips back and forth from one end to the other rarely works. Folds get out of alignment, and the strips become crooked and twisted. Two methods are given which will make folds quickly and accurately. Corners of the strip must be square or folds will not be accurate.

Each panel or section is a page. The two panels adjacent to a valley fold make up a leaf or a double spread. The valley fold is the spine edge. When width and number of panels is known, the length of strip is easy to figure.

Folds take up space. This amount must be figured in the total length.
Heavy papers require more folding ease.
Fold a dummy to see how it will work out.

Not all papers fold well. Fibers break along the folds of many papers forming an irregular pattern which simply does not look good. Experiment before cutting supplies for project.

FIRST METHOD allows visual boundaries to be set in advance. Art work is then rendered before the strip is folded.

Use the *folding gauge*, described on p. 2, to mark the front side of strip only. This will insure proper placement of renderings on each panel. When the art work is finished, the gauge is used again to mark and fold as described on p. 2. The end of strip is trimmed or lengthened after folding to form desired length, p. 30.

SECOND METHOD is used when panels must be narrow or when a predetermined panel width is not necessary. This method uses the entire strip and evenly divides the space into equal panels. Number folds lightly, in pencil, to avoid confusion later. Practice on a strip of paper to get the idea.

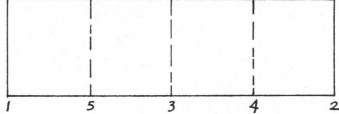

FOLD STRIP in half,
1 to 2, making 3

FOLD INTO four equal panels,
fold 2 to 3, making 4
fold 1 to 3, making 5

Turn strip over, after making the four equal panels, to divide panels with folds made in the opposite direction, valley versus mountain or peak folds.

DIVIDE PANELS in half:
fold 2 to 5, making 6
fold 1 to 4, making 7
fold 2 to 4, making 8
fold 1 to 5, making 9

To make a strip with 16 panels, 8 mountain folds and 7 valley folds, turn the strip made above over and continue to fold for the in-between folds.

fold 2 to 7, making 10
fold 2 to 6, making 11
fold 2 to 8, making 12
fold 1 to 6, making 14
fold 1 to 8, making 15
fold 1 to 7, making 16
fold 1 to 9, making 17

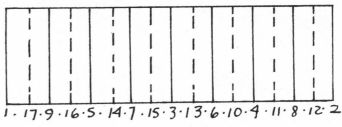

THIRD METHOD aligns panel strip with straight edge, p. 5. Measure and mark panels carefully. Place triangle against straight edge near fold line so that scoring tool rests on desired fold line. Accuracy is more difficult with this method, but it is sometimes the best way to fold.

JOINING: Short strips can be joined together in several ways to make up a long accordion strip. Choose method to suit materials.

If the paper is always doubled on the same edge, spine, or fore edge, this edge will be thicker when closed.

OVERLAP PANELS for joins.
Adhere new section on the front or back to make up strip.

Length of sections to be joined can vary. Trim a bit off joining panel edge to prevent binding.

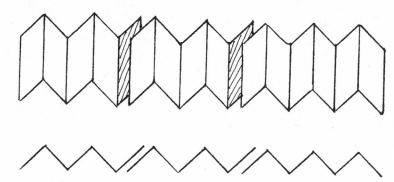

CUT HINGES for joins.
Adhere hinges as narrow as 1/4" to hold strips together. Wider strips can become a decorative part of the whole. Any proportion that works is fine.

Explore contrasts of color and texture rather than hiding the joins. Add extra strips for design or to balance bulk.

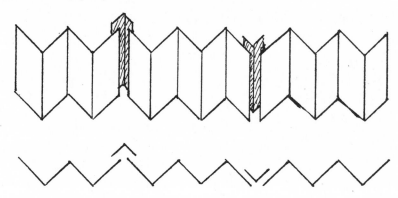

FOLD HINGES for joins.
Fold narrow hinges on one edge of panel and paste to the next section. Alternate hinge placement to distribute bulk evenly.

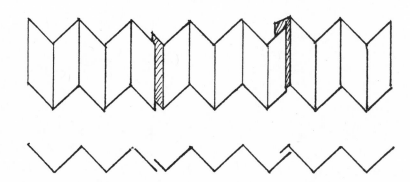

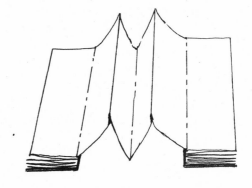

TIP PASTE edges for joins.
   Join either spine edges or fore edges.
   Margin is lost when spine edge is
   joined. Either way the accordion
   will not lie flat when open.

CLOSURES: Closures are often
   added. They can be made from
   a variety of materials and work
   in several ways.

Ties
Fasten ribbon, tape, etc.
between back cover and
last panel and tie on front.
Ties can be placed inside both
covers and tied at each side.

Loop
Make a loop at one end of
ribbon or cord. Place between
cover and last panel. Wrap
book and pass ribbon through
loop. Finish with half hitches.

Button, Bead, Twig, or Shell
Macramé a cord or braid ribbon
or raffia with a loop on one end.
Add a button, etc. to the other end.

Bone Clasp
Follow *Bone Clasp Closure*, p. 194.

Long Cord Wrap
Place long cord between last
panel and cover on one side.
Make cord long enough to
wrap book 3 1/2 times.
Wrap and fasten like a scroll, p. 23.

Hinged Cover
To make hinge, see p. 43. Hinges can
be made with ribbon, tape, or cord.
Measure spine thickness as shown on p. 110.

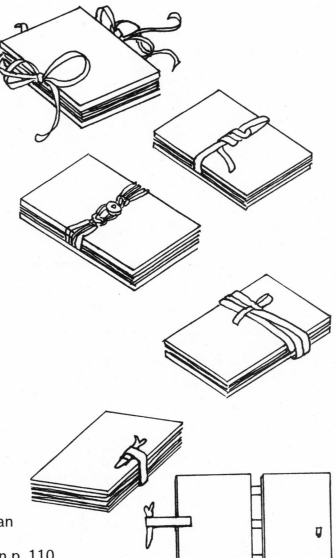

Follow MAKE CLASP *closure strip,* p. 220,
to make and mount clasp closure and anchor loop at fore edge.

SEPARATE COVERS

Materials:
Accordion strip, any paper weight
Cover boards, weight compatible
with strip
Material to cover boards if desired
Closure if desired
Adhesive

MAKE UP strip.
  Begin and end with valley folds.

CUT MATERIALS.
  Cover Boards, cut two
  1/16" overhang on all sides
  Height = accordion strip height + 1/8"
  Width = panel width + 1/8"

  Cover material, cut two
  5/8" turn-ins on all sides
  Height = board height + 1 1/2"
  Width = board width + 1 1/2"

DECIDE CLOSURE placement if used. Thick closures can interfere with turn-ins and
  cause lumps in paste downs. To avoid this, draw closure outline on board and follow
  Recess Area For Label, p. 246, to peel away several layers of board. This becomes the
  inside of board.

TURN COVERING material underside up. Center board and pencil outline. This
  should give a 5/8" margin on all sides.

SPREAD ADHESIVE lightly on outside of cover boards and position on cover material.
  Turn boards and smooth with folder and protective paper, pp. 239, 240.

MITER CORNERS and turn in, p. 245. Add closure if one is used.
  Filler can be added if desired to avoid ridges caused by turn-ins, p. 112.

CHECK BOTH boards and accordion before mounting strip to boards.
  Beware of upside down covers or text when a directional pattern is used
  on cover boards.

ATTACH FIRST and last panels of strip to cover boards.
  Spread adhesive lightly on exposed board area and on edges of panels and place in
  position. Smooth with folder and protective paper.

  Press until dry using waxed paper barriers to protect interior from adhesive moisture,
  pp. 240, 241.

FLUTTER BOOK

An accordion book wrapped in a single cover sheet was popular in China during the 10th through 13th centuries. Since the pages are not attached at the spine, they can easily fall free and flutter in the wind. This was called a Flutter Book.

Materials:
Text paper, lightweight
Cover paper, heavyweight paper,
  or paper bond
Adhesive

MAKE UP strip.
  Begin and end strip with mountain folds.

CUT COVER in one piece.
  Turn-ins are a part of the cover
  Height = accordion strip height
          + 1 1/2" (for 5/8" turn-ins)
  Width = 2 times panel width
          + spine thickness
          + ease for folds
          + 1 1/2" (for 5/8" turn-ins)

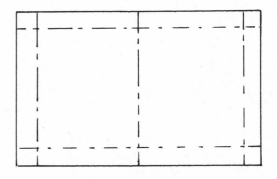

SCORE AND fold spine line. Score
  two lines if needed for thickness.

SCORE AND fold head, tail, and
  fore edge turn-ins to match
  folded book block.

REMOVE NARROW wedges from
  turn-ins at spine folds and
  cut modified miters to
  avoid binding, p. 245.

SPREAD ADHESIVE lightly on
  fore edge turn-in of front cover
  and attach edge of first panel
  to turn-in.

Repeat for back cover.

Press until dry.

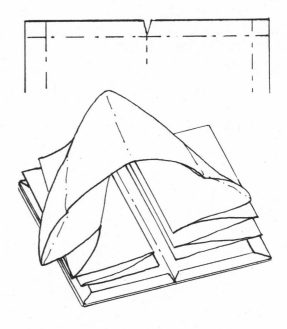

THROW-OUT ACCORDION IN CASE BINDING

A butterfly stitch through the first or last valley fold holds a short strip in a Case Binding. One end of the strip is free.

Materials:
Accordion strip
Endpaper paste down
Case binding, p. 111
Hinge, p. 256
Adhesive

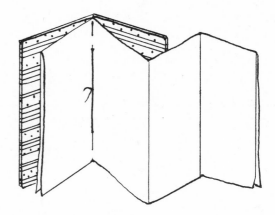

MAKE UP strip.
  Fold strip carefully.
  The two panels facing stitching are equal.
  The rest must be narrower, or they will extend beyond the edges of the adjacent panel.

  A French fold will give more body to lightweight paper. Paper is folded in half lengthwise before it is folded into panels, as shown above. The French fold works best with a short strip. Careful folding is needed.

  Make long fold first. Open long fold to add perpendicular cross folds.
  Reverse half of each cross fold.

Follow procedures given in *Single Signature Case Binding,* pp. 109-112. The accordion replaces the single signature and flyleaves are omitted. If case is covered with book cloth, the same book cloth can be used as paste downs. Then no hinge is necessary. The cloth becomes both the hinge and paste down.

  Be sure right side of paste down faces accordion when stitched.

  Be sure strip is placed with overhang at spine edge so cover will lie flat when closed.

WRAP-AROUND COVER

A small size accordion with 2 3/4" square panels is a good size for the Slip Case on p. 158.

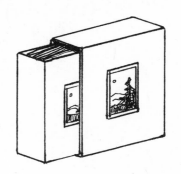

Materials:
Text strip and cover, heavyweight
   paper or Bristol Board

MAKE UP accordion strip.
   Cut strip with extra length at beginning for covers and spine thickness. Folding ease is hard to judge. A safe practice is to make cover ends generous, then cut and fold to size after text panels are folded and spine thickness is established. After folding is completed, trim extra length.

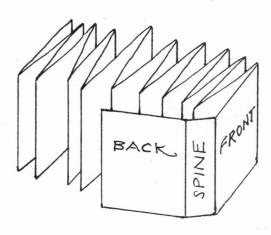

COMPRESS LIGHTLY to measure for spine thickness, p. 238.

MAKE SLIP case for book if desired, p. 158.

RIBBON CLOSURE VARIATION

THREAD RIBBON through slits in back cover panel to wrap-around and tie on the front.

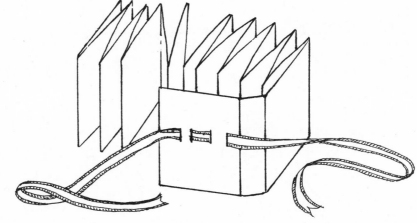

HANDLE CLOSURE VARIATION

This is a fun book for a small child to carry.
The accordion strip can be bonded with Tyvek
to make it sturdy.

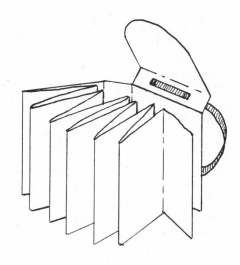

Materials:
Text panel strip and cover,
*   heavyweight paper, Bristol board,*
*   or paper bond*
Ribbon or tape for handle
Small Velcro patch
Instant Bond adhesive for Velcro

MAKE UP accordion strip same as
    Wrap-Around Cover, p. 35.

CUT HANDLE panel.
    panel is added to outside of back cover panel
    Height = 1 2/3 strip height + spine thickness
                (extra becomes front flap)
    Width = back cover panel width

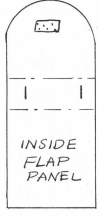

FOLD HANDLE section.

CUT CURVE on flap.
    Add slits for ribbon handle, p. 235.

ADHERE OUTSIDE of flap panel to inside of back cover.

ATTACH VELCRO patches, using instant bond adhesive,
    to inside flap and outside front cover.

THREAD RIBBON or tape
    through slots.
    Instant bond can be used
    to join ends together on
    underside of flap.

UNUSUAL FORMATS

By using a common edge, like paper doll chains, many shapes can become accordion strips. Asymmetrical shapes face each other in pairs.
A rectangle or square added to the shape will
extend and reinforce the common edge.

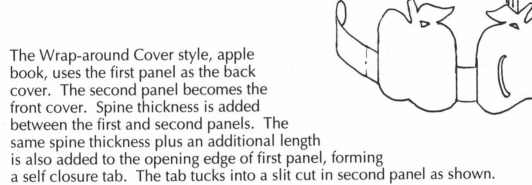

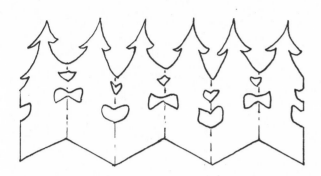

The Wrap-around Cover style, apple
book, uses the first panel as the back
cover. The second panel becomes the
front cover. Spine thickness is added
between the first and second panels. The
same spine thickness plus an additional length
is also added to the opening edge of first panel, forming
a self closure tab. The tab tucks into a slit cut in second panel as shown.

NON-ADHESIVE COVERS

This booklet is a delightful format for a short note or card.
Horizontal and vertical wraps can match
or contrast. Materials and construction
are simple. The project makes a good
learning tool for young children
involving measuring, folding,
cutting, and no mess.

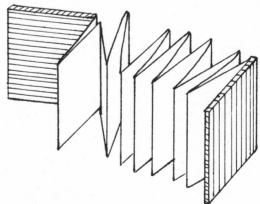

Materials:
Text paper medium weight,
 e.g. Canson Mi Teintes
Cover paper same as text
Cover boards, e.g., mat board

Alternate material suggestion for mini books:
use manila folders for boards and gift wrap for covering

MAKE UP accordion strip.
Include a blank panel at each end to slip into covers and hold accordion in **place.**

CUT MATERIALS.
Cover boards, cut two flush with strip
Height = height of strip
Width = width of one panel

Horizontal wrap cover paper, cut two
Height = board height
Width = 2 times board width
+ an overlap of more than half board width

Vertical wrap cover paper, cut two
Height = 2 times board height
+ an overlap of more than half board height
Width = board width

SCORE PAPER along board edges if necessary, p. 234.
Fold up and crease paper over board edges

WRAP BOARDS horizontally with overlap on inside.

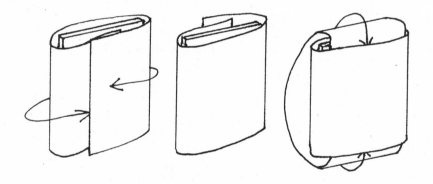

WRAP BOARDS vertically to cover overlap.
Carefully tuck ends into top and bottom, covering board edges.

INSERT BLANK end panels
carefully between cover
wrap and board.

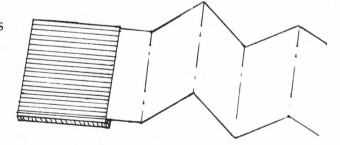

SPINE INSERT VARIATION

With the addition of a simple spine insert joining the two cover boards, the entire book makes a standing display. This also makes a nice cover for a paper back.

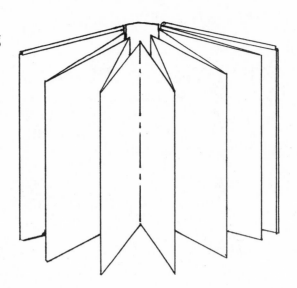

CUT SPINE insert.
   Height = board height
   Width = spine thickness + 2 flaps
          to extend across 1/3
          of board width

SCORE SPINE thickness down
   middle of insert and fold.

CUT TAPER on head and tail sides
   of insert to aid in insertion into cover.

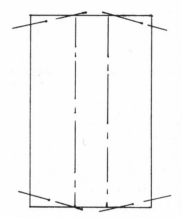

SLIP INSERT between cover wrap
   and boards at spine edge of book.

OTHER NON-ADHESIVE COVERS

School Book Cover, p. 119, or non-adhesive covers with tabs, pp. 95, 127 also work for accordions.

The first and last panels of the accordion slip into the non-adhesive cover.

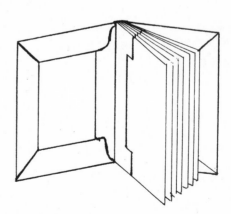

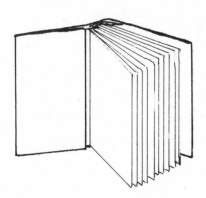

For added stiffness, an insert of the same or heavier material can be placed in the non-adhesive cover before accordion is added. The insert will not show.

TRIANGLE BOOKS

EQUILATERAL TRIANGLE

This book is based on a 60º angle, forming an equilateral triangle. It opens well in all directions and turns into a spiral when hung.

Materials:
Text paper, medium to heavyweight
Cover boards, weight compatible
* with text weight*
Cover paper for boards optional
Adhesive
Closure if desired

MAKE A practice book first. When strip is folded ,there will be a gap between each point along strip edge for folding ease. When folding by aligning edge without scoring, this happens automatically. However, if scoring before folding, ease must be left at the points.

MAKE UP strip with square ends and a consistent width.
  Strip edge must be carefully aligned before creasing each time a fold is made, otherwise the whole stack will be askew when folding is finished.
  Score folds when using heavyweight paper.
  Make strip a little longer than needed to allow for ease used in folding.

Trim to size after folding.

Use a 30º/60º Δ:
Trim strip end along Δ with 60º angle at the bottom edge.

Turn Δ to score along edge if needed.

Fold cut end to top edge.

Crease with folder.

Flip strip over and score or fold up aligning edges. Crease with folder.

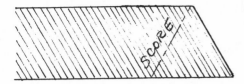 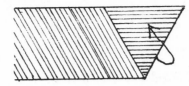

TURN UP
ALIGN EDGE
CREASE FOLD

Continue flipping strip and folding until finished.

 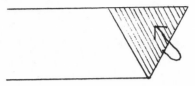

TURN UP
ALIGN EDGE
CREASE FOLD

TRIM ENDS of strip to angle in opposite directions. This allows both covers to be
  attached on the same side of the strip. Carefully trim extra length. First and last
  triangles attach strip to covers.

MAKE PRACTICE layout
  to avoid errors.
  Page sequence is complex.
  To establish page sequence,
  close strip and lightly mark
  A, B, and C with pencil as shown.

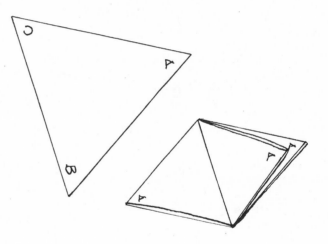

Lift point A and continue marking
  all fore edge points with A as shown.

Close book. Turn so B is at fore edge.
  Open and mark all B fore edge points.

Repeat for C.

CUT MATERIALS.
  Cover Boards, cut two
  flush with triangle edges or with a 1/16" overhang on all sides.

  Cover Material, cut two
  Cover Board size + a 5/8" turn-in margin on all sides.

BRUSH ADHESIVE on one board and center on material, p. 239.

Follow *SMOOTHING SURFACE AFTER PASTING,* p. 240.

Repeat for other board.

MAKE MITERS. Brush adhesive on board edges and turn-ins.
Turn edges following *MITERING TIPS*, p. 245.

PREPARE ANY desired closure or hinging.
Add to book between triangle paste down and board.

BRUSH ADHESIVE on exposed board and edges of end triangles.
Carefully position on boards, aligning boards one on top of the other.
Be sure any pattern faces the same direction on both boards.

DRY COVERS under weight with waxed paper moisture barriers, p. 241.

ISOSCELES TRIANGLE

Based on a 45º angle, this book forms an
isosceles triangle. When open, it forms
beautiful shadows but has a front and back
feeling. Used in a square format,
it makes an unusual book for the
Origami Fold Box, p. 162.

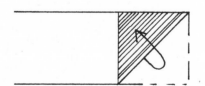

Materials:
Same as Equilateral Triangle,
p. 40

MAKE UP strip.
Use 45º Δ if needed.
Fold right end to top
edge, align and crease.

Flip strip over and fold end over, align lower edge, crease.

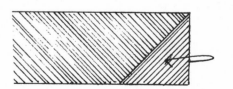

Flip strip over and fold end down, align bottom edge, crease.

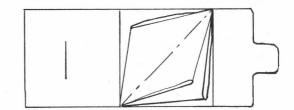

Continue to flip strip over for each new
fold, two triangles to top edge then two
triangles to bottom edge, until all folds
are made.

Leave last triangle unfolded for a square
base. Trim off extra length beyond base.
Mount in cover if desired.

HINGED COVERS

Materials:
Same as Equilateral
  Triangle, p. 40
Closure, tape, ribbon, or
  cover material strips

 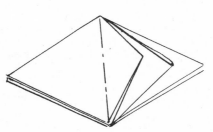

CUT HINGES, cut number desired
  Length = spine thickness
              + about 1/2" to fasten under triangle paste downs
              + ease for folds + overhang
  Width = in proportion with spine length

MAKE HINGES.
  Cover material hinges use
  a strip of material two thirds
  wider than finished width.
  Strip is folded in thirds and
  pasted together.

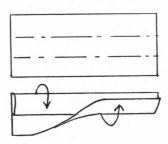

  Paste hinges to boards before
  attaching accordion strip.

  Dry under weight with waxed
  paper moisture barriers, p. 241.

WINGED ACCORDIONS

Winged accordions have two panels of equal size forming covers, which enclose a series of panels one half their width. The narrow panels have tabs fastened in two alternating patterns which appear to fold together like interlocking fingers when the book is opened.

BOARD COVER

Wings may be a contrasting color or texture.
Fold out flaps added inside back cover board conceal back panel paste down.

Materials:
Panel strip, wings, fold out flap
  and closure band, medium
  to heavyweight paper
Cover board, weight compatible
  with panel strip paper
Optional cover material
Adhesive

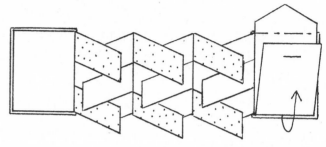

DETERMINE NUMBER of wing sets needed.
  Mountain folds determine the number of wing sets the book will have.
  The illustration below shows three mountain folds, thus three sets of interlocking wings. The number of wings per set is a personal choice. An odd number usually looks best. Here three wings have
  been used for each set.

CUT MATERIALS.
  Panel Strip, cut one
  Height = wing set height
  Single panel width = 1/2 wing width
  Length of panel strip = the number of
        wing sets + 2 (one for each cover paste down panel)

  Wings, cut number needed
  Height = number of wings per set divided into panel height
        (in illustration, height = 1/3 panel height)
  Width = 2 panels (the distance between 2 valley folds)

  To allow for folding ease, measurements may need to be *slightly*
  less so wings will interlock without binding. A gaping space is
  not charming. Experiment to see what works.

  Optional Fold Out Flap section, cut one
  only the flaps will show, writing will be done on paste down
  Height = 2 1/3 times panel strip height
  Width = paste down panel width

Cover Boards, cut two
1/16" overhang on all sides
Height = paste down height + 1/8"
Width = paste down width + 1/8"

Cover Material, cut two pieces
5/8" turn-ins on all sides
Height = cover board height + 1 1/2"
Width = cover board width + 1 1/2"

Follow *THIRD METHOD,* p. 29, to score and fold panel strip.

RENDER AND collate wing pieces.
　　Carefully mark the paste area on back of each wing piece.

MOUNT WINGS in top row first. Spread adhesive lightly on a wing piece and attach
　　to panel strip. Mounting wings across rather than down provides the proper spacing.
　　When top row is completed, mount wings on opposite side of mountain folds, going
　　across second row. Continue in this fashion until all rows have been added.

COVER BOARDS by applying adhesive to board and centering on back side of cover
　　material. Turn and smooth in place with folder, p. 240. Miter corners, p. 245.

CUT SLIT in lower flap, p. 235. Mount flap section to back cover board. The flaps will
　　conceal the paste down when panel strip is added. A contrasting color for the flap
　　section can be very attractive. Center paste down section and press in place. Smooth
　　with folder, p. 240.

APPLY ADHESIVE to underside edges of front end panel paste down and exposed cover
　　board. Press end panel in place. Smooth with folder.
　　Mount back end panel paste down over flap panel on back cover.

DRY UNDER light weight using waxed paper barriers as needed, p. 241.

CLOSURE BAND
　　Because of the book's wedge shape, a closure is nice.
　　Width = 3 times desired finished band width
　　Length = length of a scrap of paper wrapped around closed book
　　　　　+ 3/4" overlap for tuck in

FOLD CLOSURE band into thirds lengthwise.
　　Taper one end to slip into the other end.
　　Fit the strip to book before pasting one end
　　inside the other. Be sure band will slip on
　　and off comfortably. Trim tuck in if too
　　long for nice fit.

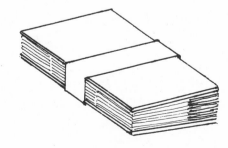

　　Other closure ideas are shown on p. 31.

SOFT COVER WITH TIES

Materials:
Strip, medium to heavyweight paper
Wings, same paper or contrasting texture or color
Cover is part
  of strip

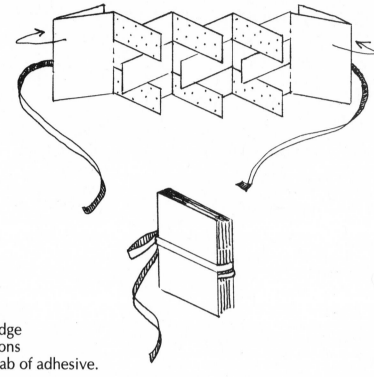

Follow *CUT
MATERIALS,*
p. 44, except:
cut strip and
fold with two
wide panels at each
end instead of one.

RENDER AND collate
  wing pieces.
  Carefully mark the
  paste area on back of
  each wing piece.

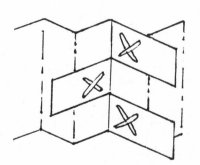

ADD CLOSURE ties inside
  cover panels. Ties can be
  extended from spine edges
  or from a slit made in fore edge
  fold as shown. Anchor ribbons
  inside cover panels with a dab of adhesive.
  Paste panels together.

DRY UNDER light pressure with moisture barriers as needed, p. 241.

CROSS STITCHED WINGS

Materials:
Same as BOARD COVER, p. 44 or
SOFT COVER above
Plus
Decorative Thread to attach wings,
  plain or contrasting, p. 242

Follow *BOARD COVER,* p. 44, or *SOFT COVER,* above, except:
Mark cross stitch hole placement. Attach wings temporarily with glue stick.
Make hoes for cross stitches and stitch in place.

EXPANDING PLEAT ALBUMS

Single sheet pages are added to a narrow, pleated accordion strip. Pleats between pages are the secret, making the spine thicker than the fore edge until material is added to the pages. Then fore edge and spine thickness become more even. Covers are mounted on end panels. Try this style for a small photo album.

SOFT COVER ALBUM

Materials:
Pages, medium to
heavyweight paper or
lightweight board
Accordion panel strip, medium to heavyweight
paper (Rising Gallery 100 works well)
Cover, same as pages, heavier,
or solid-core mat board

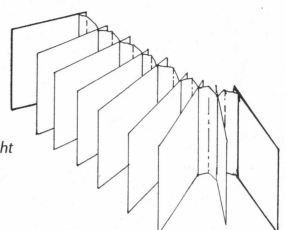

DETERMINE NUMBER of panels needed for accordion strip.
Page Panels:
Each Page requires 4 panels
> (shown as two shaded panels with an unshaded panel on each side. This is every other valley fold of panel strip. The pages are mounted at numbers 1-5)

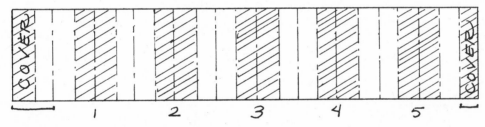

for soft cover   for case binding

Cover Panels:
Soft Cover requires 4 panels (two at each end, shown on left end of panel strip)
Case Binding requires 2 panels (one at each end, shown on right end of panel strip)

CUT MATERIALS. All parts, pages, panel strip and cover, must have square corners.
Pages, desired number,
desired size

Panel Strip, cut one
Height = page height
Single panel width = 1/2"
Length of panel strip = (4 x the number of pages + the cover panels needed at each end)
> x 1/2" (a single panel width)

Soft Cover, cut two
Height = page height
Width = page width

Follow *SECOND METHOD,* p. 29, to fold panel strip. Forget about folding ease. It will just happen as strip is folded. All panels will be slightly less than 1/2" wide. The thicker the paper, the narrower the panel because more ease space will go into the fold. Fold carefully. If the panel strip is not folded with parallel sections, the pages mounted to it will not rest over each other in a neat stack.

MOUNT PAGES.
It is tempting to paste both valley fold panels at the same time when mounting one page. This causes alignment problems which are difficult to correct. It is better to paste only one panel at a time, position the page, check to see if it is perfectly aligned. Then paste the second mounting panel to finish mounting the page.

Begin with last page. To avoid over spreading adhesive beyond valley fold panel, use scrap paper at edge of adjoining peak fold, p. 240. Brush adhesive on panel.

With back of last page facing up, place page over panel strip, aligning both head and tail, p. 56. To allow for page thickness, set spine edge just slightly away from valley fold. Press into place. Check head and tail alignment of page and panel strip again. Adjust if needed. Smooth with folder.

Using fresh scrap paper, brush adhesive on second mounting panel.
Press into place against page. Smooth with folder.

Remaining pages are added in same way, aligning each new page with head and tail of panel strip or with pages already set in place. Use moisture barriers if needed, p. 240.

Pages are mounted to every other valley fold.

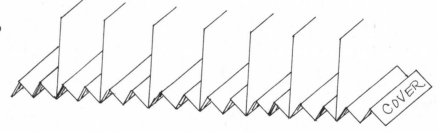

MOUNT COVERS.
Brush adhesive on end panel. Line up spine edge of panel with spine edge of cover piece. Press in place.

DRY UNDER light weight using waxed paper barriers as needed, p. 241.

CASE BINDING VARIATION
This is the previous album using the
Case Binding Cover, p. 110.

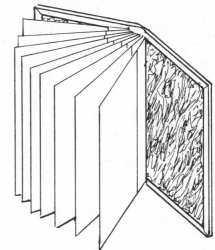

Materials:
Pages and Accordion strip,
* same as Soft Cover Album, p. 47*
Plus
Endpaper paste downs, decorative paper
Cover Boards
Covering material
Bond paper strip for spine lining
Adhesive

Follow *DETERMINE NUMBER of panels*, p. 47,
and remaining directions for soft cover album,
using case binding directions and the following cover directions.

Cover Boards, cut two
1/8" overhang at head, tail, and fore edge; spine edge is flush with book block
Height = page height + 1/4"
Width = page width + 1/8"

Cover Material, cut in one piece
5/8" turn in margins
Height = board height + 1 1/4"
Width = 2 board widths
      + 2 BT (board thickness)
      + spine thickness + 1 1/4"

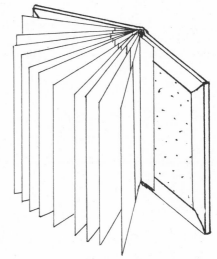

Bond paper lining for spine area, cut one
Height = board height
Width = a bit narrower than spine
      thickness to prevent binding

Endpaper Paste Downs, cut two
Decorative paper
Height = page height
Width = page width

Follow *TURN CASE covering*, and remaining directions on p. 111 to make case.

Follow *ENCASE SIGNATURE, ADD FILLER, PUT PASTE down endpapers in place* and
PRESS OVERNIGHT, p. 112, to finish book. Filler can be made of same material as
outside case covering.

STICK BOOK ALBUM VARIATION

A stick slipped through paper hinges along the spine, holds this book together. Although the hinges are vulnerable to tearing, this is a unique way to display special occasion photographs for a distinctive gift. Rising Gallery 100 makes a nice panel strip. Bonding hinge sections with lightweight, long fiber oriental paper or Tyvek will make the hinge area stronger. A variety of things from a pencil to a small branch can be used for the stick.

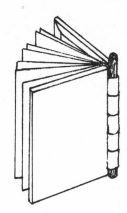

Materials:
Pages, medium weight paper
Accordion panel strip paper, same as pages or heavier
Cover boards
Cover material
Endpaper paste downs, contrasting or same as pages
Stick, dowel, chop stick, small branch, etc.
Thread
Adhesive

DETERMINE NUMBER of panels needed for accordion strip.
  Page Panels
  Each Page requires 2 panels
  Cover Panels and hinge requires 6 panels (shown as A-B and C-D)

CUT MATERIALS for book block.
  Page size, cut desired number
  Height = desired page height
  Width = 2 times page width

Panel Strip, cut one
  Height = page height
  Single panel width = circumference of stick + ease
        (measure distance with paper scrap same weight as hinge)
  Length of Panel Strip = (2 times number of pages + 6) x single panel width

Panels A-B and C-D are for hinge and cover mounting. Numbers 2 and 3 will be mountain folds mounted on cover boards.

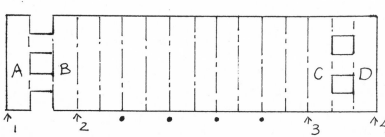

Pages are mounted to all remaining mountain folds (shown as •).

Follow *SECOND METHOD*, p. 29, to fold panel strip.

MAKE PRACTICE pattern for hinge on scrap paper to work out placement of hinge cuts.
  Draw lines for hinges (like ladder rungs) wide enough to be strong when cut.

Make at least three sections in hinge panel. The illustration shows five which is stronger. An uneven number always looks best. Transfer pattern to hinge panels.

CUT OUT the first space on hinge between panels A-B. Continue cutting out every other space on this panel.

Keep the first space for the second hinge, between panels C-D to dove tail space between A-B. Cut out the second space and continue cutting out every other space on this panel.

ROLL CUT panels around stick to curve them. Do not crease or fold. Soft curves look best.

CAREFULLY BRUSH adhesive on back side of panel B. Bring panel A over B aligning edges 1 and 2. Do not crease hinge pieces. Press A and B together. Repeat with 3 and 4 at other end of strip. Let dry.

LIGHTLY MARK strip and pages with head and tail notations to avoid mistakes.

MAKE SEWING hole template in butterfly stitch pattern, p. 91. Holes are not made in first and last peaks since these panels are used for the cover. Poke holes in remaining peaks and all pages.

COLLATE PAGES and stack upside down on right side of work space with *head to the right.*

Hold panel strip in left hand with *head to left.* Lift top page off stack, (last page of book block), and turn over so *head is at left.*

Open page and place it over panel strip with holes aligned. Clip in place and sew together. Make knot inside page. Close page and move to next page.

Using this procedure, sewn pages rest on table and only unsewn strip dangles loose. Continue until all pages are sewn.

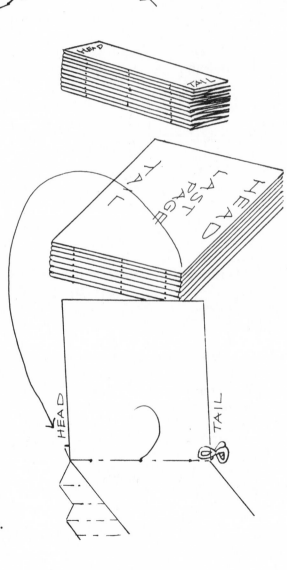

CUT MATERIALS for cover.
  Cover Boards, cut two
  1/8" overhang at head, tail and fore edge; flush at spine
  Height = page height + 1/4"
  Width = single page width + single panel width + 1/8"

  Cover material, cut two
  5/8" turn-ins
  Height = board height + 1 1/2" turn-in
  Width = board width + 1 1/2" turn in

  Endpaper paste downs, cut two
  1/16" visible board margin at head, tail and fore edge
  Height = board height less 1/8"
  Width = board width less 1/16"

PENCIL BOARD positions lightly on inside of each cover paper piece.

SPREAD ADHESIVE lightly on cover boards and position on cover paper. Turn boards
  and smooth paper with folder, p. 239.

MITER CORNERS, p. 245. Spread adhesive lightly on head and tail turn-ins
  and board edges. Lift turn-ins in place and smooth with folder.
  Dry under light weight, p. 241.

ADD PASTE downs. Spread adhesive lightly on bare boards and edges of paste downs.
  Position paste downs flush at spine edge, all other margins equal.
  Dry under light weight.

ADD BOOK block to cover.
  Use a light coat of adhesive on panel A.
  Line up hinge edges carefully with spine
  edge of front cover. Press panel in place
  with fingers. Avoid creasing hinges.
  Smooth with folder.

  Use waxed paper barriers to keep
  moisture out of book. Mount back
  cover in the same way as panel A,
  brushing adhesive on panel D.

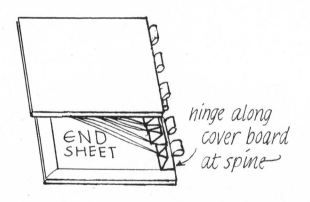

END SHEET

hinge along cover board at spine

DRY UNDER light weight using waxed paper barriers as needed, p. 241.

PUT STICK through hinges.

PAGE VARIATION

Double fold pages form three panels. The pages can be used as fold out panels where art work extends all the way across or as frame pages. For frame pages, mount photographs or art work on the third section and cut windows in the other sections.
Use medium to heavyweight papers.

Materials:
Same as Stick Book Album Variation, p. 50

FOLLOW DIRECTIONS for Stick Book except change page size.
  Width = 3 times page width
        Narrow third section slightly
        to avoid binding when folded

SEW PAGES to strip through fold between second and third sections.

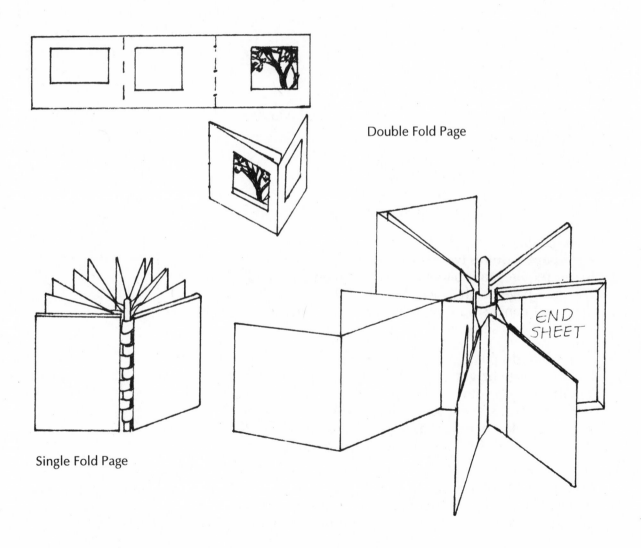

Double Fold Page

END SHEET

Single Fold Page

REVERSE PLEAT BINDINGS

REVERSE PLEAT WITH PAGES

A strong color or value contrast between strip and pages creates a striking booklet.
Use this book to display collections of interesting fabrics, papers, stamps, etc.
Each page has a spine edge tab which mounts in reverse folds cut in the panel strip.
Cover boards can be mounted like pages or the first and last pages can become the covers;
place in Non-adhesive Covers With Tabs, pp. 95, 127, or School Book Cover, p. 119.

Materials:
Pages, medium to heavyweight paper
Accordion strip same weight or heavier
Cover, heavyweight paper or lightweight
   board or make a cover mentioned above
Adhesive

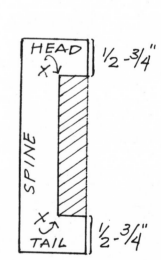

DETERMINE NUMBER of panels needed.

CUT MATERIALS.
   Page Size, cut desired number
   Height = desired page height
   Width = desired page width + 1 single panel width

   Single panel width is a visual choice.
   A pleasing balance between page and panel size is important,
      e.g. 4" x 5" page and a 5/8" wide panel
      6" x 8" page and a 3/4" wide panel
      8" x 10" page and a 1" wide panel

   Panel Strip, cut one
   Each page requires two panels.
   Cover requires four panels (two at each end, AB and CD)
   Height = page height
   Length of panel strip = (2 times number of pages + 4)
            times single panel width

   Cover Boards, cut two
   Height = page height
   Width = page width
   Without tab at spine, mount to panels A and D
   With tab at spine, mount as pages; make reverse folds
   in mountain folds AB and CD to mount to covers

Template

MAKE TEMPLATE for marking reverse fold sections in panels. Use manila folder paper
   or a similar sturdy paper cut the size of one panel. Draw a line from head to tail just
   to right of center. Mark *SPINE* on left side. Along right side mark 1/2" to 3/4" from

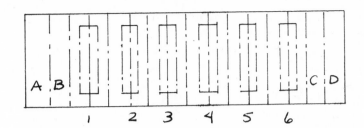

right head and tail. Distance depends on page size. Choose proportion you like. Push a pin point through pattern at corners marked X .

Cut shaded area out of pattern.

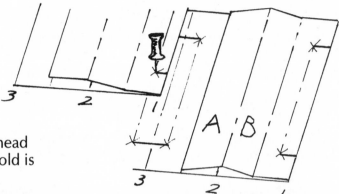

CUT SLITS in mountain folds. Do one pleat at a time. Line up *spine side* of template with valley fold; *L-shaped corners* with peak fold. Push pin point into corner to mark cut, shown as X.

Slits for pages are cut parallel to head and tail in peak fold. One peak fold is used for each page.

Use straight edge and sharp knife to cut from pin hole to peak along heavy line as shown. Cutting tips on p. 235.

The end panels, AB and CD are mounted to cover boards.

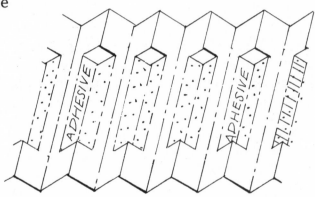

SCORE FOLD lines from pin hole to pin hole, shown by dotted lines. These lines become mini mountain folds part way across panel.

Push the original mountain fold inside this, forming a valley fold for mounting pages.

Reverse pleats ready for mounting pages

USE SAME template for marking corner cuts on page edges.

Page tab is twice as wide as the reversed pleat section of the panel strip.

Set spine edge of pattern on spine edge of page. Mark *L-shaped* corners with push pin and light pencil lines. Remove template and finish line to spine edge. Use straight edge and sharp knife to cut away corners to form tabs for mounting pages.

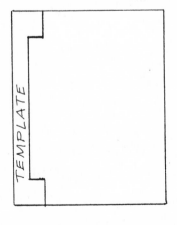
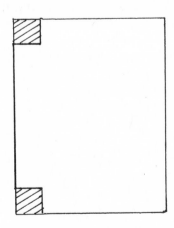
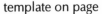

template on page   remove corners

MOUNT PAGES on strip one at a time. Spread adhesive lightly on both sides of reverse fold, pp. 239, 240.

Set last page in place, aligning page edges with strip edges. Fold panel over tab.

Place moisture barrier over CD and fold last page over barrier, front of last page facing up. All remaining pages will be aligned over this page.

MOUNT COVER. Spread adhesive on underside of panel A and stick to panel B. Repeat for CD. Spread adhesive on panel D. Carefully set back cover in place. Using panel A, repeat for front cover.

PUT BOOK block in School Book or Non-adhesive Cover made to fit it or make cover boards to be mounted on panels AB and CD.

CASE BINDING VARIATION, p. 48, can also be used for this book.

VARIATION WITHOUT PAGES

Visually this structure is much like a fan even though its ends separate. It is an unusual way to display a beautiful piece of paper.

The reverse pleat uses a diagonal cut. The cord limits how far this book will open.

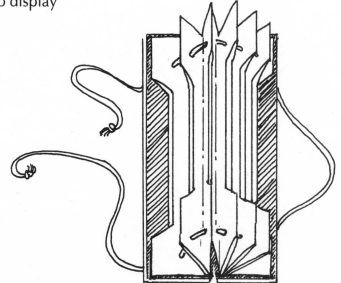

Materials:
Accordion strip, unusual paper,
  e. g. marbled, handmade, etc.
Cover boards
Cover material
Endpaper paste downs
Cord
Decorative beads, etc. if desired
Adhesive

Size is a personal choice partially dependent on requirements of paper and pattern to be displayed.

Panel Strip, cut in one continuous piece
An even number of panels are needed; the first and last are mount on cover boards

Single panel width is a personal choice
Height = desired panel strip height
Length of panel strip = desired number of panels
    + folding ease

Follow *SECOND METHOD*, p. 29, to fold sections of panel
    strip.

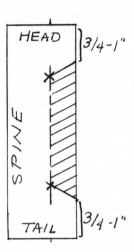

Template

MAKE TEMPLATE for placing reverse fold sections in panel strip
    mountain folds. Use manila folder or a similar paper cut the
    size of one panel.

Draw a line from head to tail just to right of center.
Mark *SPINE* on left side. Along the right side mark 3/4" to 1"
from head and tail. Add 1/2" more from head and tail at
center line, X. This will form the diagonal cut line as shown.

Pierce template with a push pin at corners marked X. Cut
shaded area from template so diagonal can be traced on the strip.

MARK REVERSE pleats.

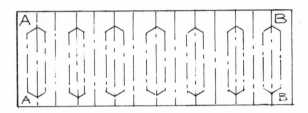

Follow *CUT SLITS* and
SCORE FOLD, p. 55.

CUT COVER materials.
    Cover Boards, cut two
    1/16" overhang on all sides
    Height = panel strip height + 1/8"
    Width = single panel width + 1/8"

    Cover Material, cut two
    5/8" turn-in
    Height = board height + 1 1/2"
    Width = board width + 1 1/2"

    Endpaper paste downs, cut two
    Height = slightly less than board
    Width = slightly less than board

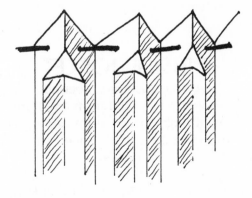

Follow *TURN CASE covering,* p. 111, and continue with the directions to mount
    covering material to boards. This will be two cover boards rather than one as shown.

SPREAD ADHESIVE on underside of panel A.
  Mount on cover board with an even margin on all sides.
  Repeat with panel B on back cover board.

CENTER MARK for holes near head and tail of template.
  Mark hole positions on one cover.

Follow *EDGE SEWN binding holes,* p. 244, to make holes. Use a drill with bit large enough for cord. Fill empty side of structure with scrap while making holes or temporarily wrap the thickest part from head to tail so cover won't tip while drilling.

MAKE HOLES through covers and folded panel strip.

Cord Length = 2 times loosely extended strip + distance between cover holes
         + enough for knots and visual needs

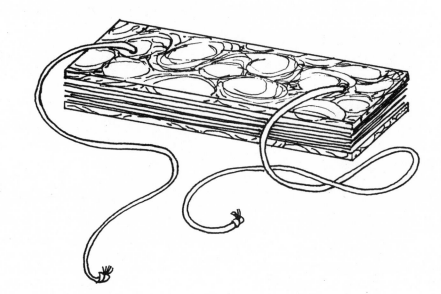

Cord goes in
one set of holes,
travels across back
cover board, and
out the other
set of holes.

SURPRISE BOOKLET
No sewing or pasting is needed.
This booklet is folded from a rectangle.
All eight pages or divisions are viewed
on the same side of the sheet, so it is
easily copied or printed.

Cut windows in the pages for a surprise
peek inside, which has also been
decorated in the illustration.

Materials:
  Paper, light or medium weight

FOLD SHEET along length to form AA.
This becomes the head of the booklet.

FOLD SHEET across middle
forming BB.

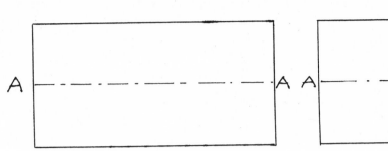

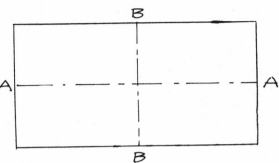

BRING BB to meet the fore
edge, forming CC.
Open CC fold.

USE SCISSORS to cut through
fold BB along AA to X.

OPEN BB fold.

REFOLD AA.

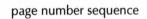

page number sequence

EXPAND BB. Fold page 2 against
page 3 and page 5 against page 4.
The fold between pages 1 and 8
is reversed as it becomes the
spine.

TO AND FRO ACCORDION BOOKLET

This form is created from a folded rectangle. The format works with even or odd number divisions in both directions. This booklet can have its own cover boards. It also fits neatly into the Non-Adhesive Cover p. 37.

Materials:
Paper, text weight to heavyweight
Cover, lightweight board
 or heavyweight paper
Closure ribbon if desired.

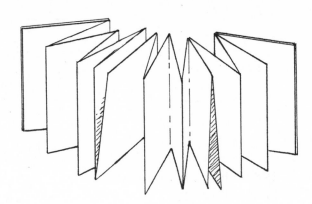

FOLD RECTANGLE into panels
 both directions, see *MEASURING WITHOUT math*, p. 237.

CUT ALONG horizontal fold lines.
 Cut first line from right to left leaving last panel uncut.

 Cut second line from left to right leaving last panel uncut.
 Continue alternating direction until all horizontal fold lines are cut.

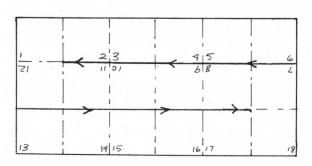

FOLD INTO accordion. At each row
 end, fold uncut panel over or under to the next row of panels. Every uncut pair forms a double page.
 Some open to the head, some to tail.

Layout reverses when crossing double panel layout. Therefore, every other row is upside down. Lightly pencil page numbers on panels to avoid confusion when rendering booklet.

CUT COVER boards flush or with slight overhang.

PLACE RIBBON ties between covers and text if desired. Two mounting styles follow. Ribbon can be centered and attached to inside back cover to tie over front. With this mounting style, the book can spread out allowing all panels to be seen.

Fold ribbon in half. Center folded ribbon at spine, attaching to both cover boards. Tie at fore edge. This allows the book to fan open rather than spread out. A diagonal ribbon mounting is shown on p. 160.
See p. 31 for more ideas.

ATTACH COVER boards. Spread adhesive on end panel and attach to front board. Repeat for back board.

EDGE SEWN BINDINGS

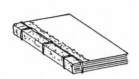

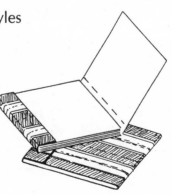

EDGE SEWN BINDINGS

Edge sewn bindings are held together with stitches along the spine. This style is thought to have originated in China. By the twelfth century, it had become the standard form of binding for most block printed books in both China and Japan. This remained so until the introduction of Western bookbinding methods in the nineteenth century.

The style was called *fukuro-toji,* which literally translates as bag or pouch binding. The book was made of single sheets printed or written on one side only then folded outwards forming double leaves with the fore edge being the fold. Paper covers were added. After the spine was stitched together, the top and bottom edge of each folded leaf remained open like a bag or pouch, forming a "pocket."

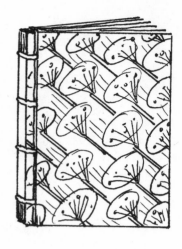

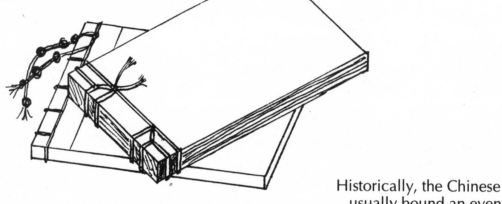

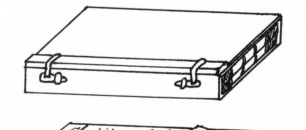

Historically, the Chinese usually bound an even number of holes. The Koreans favored an odd number of holes, and the Japanese used both, favoring three, four, and five holes.

When a large volume was bound, it was split and bound in an even number of volumes in China and an odd number, usually three, in Korea. Each book within the set had the same covering. A case was made to house the set. The Wrap-Around Case with Bone Clasp, p. 218, is a good choice for this.

GENERAL INFORMATION

Illustrations show books oriented for languages reading from left to right rather than
right to left.

PAPER: Text papers used in edge sewn bindings should be thin and flexible because
the binding method limits flexibility. There is a loss of movement immediately next to
the stitching.

FLEXIBILITY TEST: Hold several sheets of paper in one hand, along the edge. Turn the
sheets of paper over the hand holding it, as if turning a page. If paper does not lift and
turn easily, it will not open well when sewn.

MARGINS: Wide margin space is needed for binding in order to see all of page content
easily. The less flexible the paper, the wider the margin needs to be.
Thick book blocks take up more margin area as successive pages are turned.
Thus, more margin is needed along the sewing edge to view the content.

A landscape format can provide a better page size
in relation to margin needs.

Class notes can be bound with stab
stitching. However, papers usually used
are not lightweight or flexible and grain
often runs the wrong direction.
To compensate, students should use a
wider margin along the sewing edge.

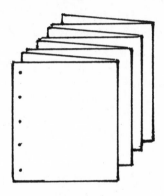

SHADOWS: Use folded fore edges with
lightweight papers to increase opacity.
When paper is doubled, the amount of
see-through quality is less.

folded fore edge pages

THREAD: Length measurements used for the traditional stitching patterns in this
chapter are based on lightweight, flexible Japanese papers and their traditional
dimensions. Variations using other sizes and papers require margin considerations
explained above and more thread for stitching.

EDGES: The book block needs to be square.
This binding form often leaves all edges exposed.
Add inner binding to secure book block while trimming, p. 64.

When lightweight papers are difficult to align, divide book block into several smaller
stacks to align. Then reassemble.
With pocket pages, align fore edges and do any trimming at the spine edge.
Even on a spine edge, torn or deckle irregularities are fine, unless they are so ragged
that they interfere with stitching.

TEMPORARY WRAP: Collate and align text. Make a small mark in upper left front corner to identify book block orientation.

Wrap a strip of paper around aligned book block. Make strip snug, hold with glue stick or rubber band. Weight each end as shown.

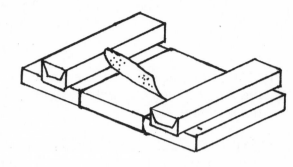

INNER BINDING: Extra inner stitches are made to hold the book block for final stitching in traditional bindings. The inner stitches do not show when the binding is finished. They make a stronger binding that will not come apart if the cover stitching breaks.

Two pairs of holes are made in area *between* finished stitching line and spine edge, near each end of the spine, about 1/8" in from stitching line works well. Plain thread is sewn through each pair and tied with a square knot. These holes are not used in final stitching.

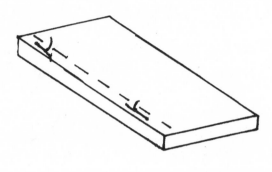

Compression for all parts of the book (end caps, inner binding, and book block with covers) must be the same for a book to lie flat, p. 238.

END CAPS: Caps of contrasting paper or cloth protect book block spine edge corners in traditional bindings. Caps cover the spine from the first stitch at head and tail and wrap the corner extending to stitching line. They work best if a book block is at least 1/4" thick after compressed for measuring, p. 238.
If lightweight cloth is used, back it with paper first, *BONDING*, p. 240.

Caps need to be tightly fitted and neatly done.

Secure book block with temporary wrap if not using inner binding stitches.

Caps, cut two
Length = stitching margin width
        + distance from end hole
          to book block head or tail
Width = 2 times stitching line margin
        + spine thickness

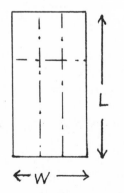

head to stitching line

head to first hole along spine

← W —→

LIGHTLY MARK cap placement along book block thickness at head and tail, where
  stitching will pass over head and tail.

PUT ADHESIVE on back of one cap. Align edge with mark, being sure width is
centered. Press thumb and index finger along adjoining edges, pressing cap edges onto
front and back of book block.

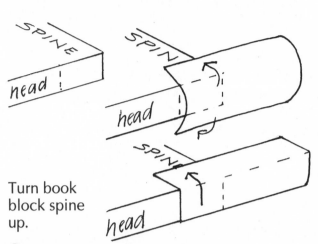

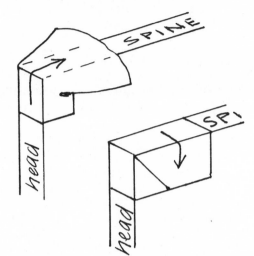

Turn book
block spine
up.

Open
free end flat
and press center against spine.

Pull remaining edges smooth over front
and back of book block. Push corner
folds flat with fingers. Repeat for tail cap.

SPINE LENGTH cap extends to cover the
  whole spine length. Follow previous direction
  adding the length needed to cover the whole spine.
  For a wider spine, line as shown on p. 78.

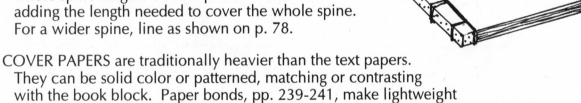

COVER PAPERS are traditionally heavier than the text papers.
  They can be solid color or patterned, matching or contrasting
  with the book block. Paper bonds, pp. 239-241, make lightweight
  papers heavier.   A case cover using binding board is described later in this chapter.

SEWING HOLE placement is part of the aesthetic unity of the book; placement the
  stitching line and placement of the holes along this line. Distances will vary with
  format proportions. Traditional stitching patterns are handsome in their simplicity and
  proportion. Experimentation with your own unique patterns is also a possibility.

SEWING TEMPLATES are useful when making holes in the cover and book block.
  Details for making templates and holes in edge sewn bindings are given on pp. 243-
  244.

HOLE SIZE for the traditional patterns in this chapter need to be large enough for thread
  to pass through three times unless otherwise stated in a diagrammed stitching pattern.

THREAD TYPE should complement and be compatible with cover materials. It may be a contrasting color. Double the thread or sew twice if thread weight is too fine to be in good proportion with the binding. More about thread can be found on pp. 242, 256.

THREAD LENGTH is roughly measured by the number of times the thread travels the spine height, the spine thickness, the stitching line distance from spine edge, the number of holes, plus knots and decorated ends, if desired.

SEWING TIPS are given on p. 242.

KNOTS are usually made inside the signature to prevent bumps in cover spine.
Tie ends with a square knot after pulling thread tight. See below for decorative ends.

PLAN DESIGN in advance for desired finish. Sewing begins and ends in same hole on same side of the book. Leave enough thread length at the beginning to tie a square knot when finished.

Hidden Knots and sewing threads:
pull or poke both ends and knot back into the hole.

Trailing Ends with decorations of knots, beads, shells etc.:
add decorations to thread endings. Finish with ending knot of choice. Square knot and other ending knots are on pp. 226-228. Fray to finish.

Traditional Patterns without exposed thread ends: begin sewing on the back of the book and come up through
a center hole.

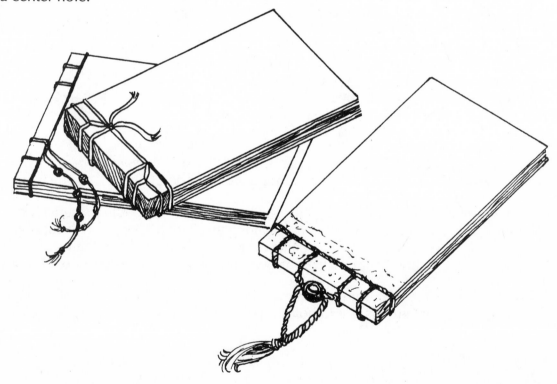

TRADITIONAL FOUR HOLE TOJI

Toji is the Japanese word for book.

Materials:
Book block complete with inner binding, p. 64
Two cover pieces, same size as book block
Cap paper, optional
Adhesive for cap papers
Binding thread

Japanese books follow traditional proportions based on their paper sizes. This often makes a book about 6 1/2" by 9".

Hole Placement
Sewing Line: 3/8" in from the spine edge
Inner Binding: 1/2" in from sewing line
Head and Tail Holes: 5/8" in from each end along the stitching line
Remaining Holes:
divide the space equally

Thread Length: a generous 3 1/2 times spine height
When this format changes, thread length will also change.

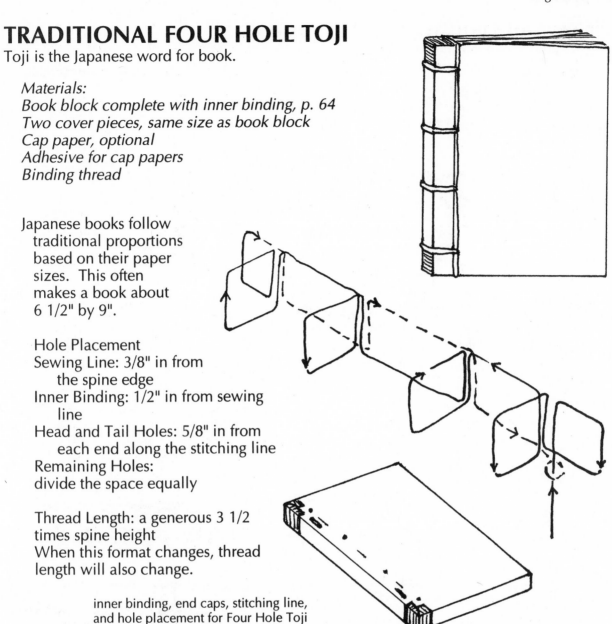

inner binding, end caps, stitching line, and hole placement for Four Hole Toji

DOUBLE STITCHED CORNERS

Add an extra hole closer to each corner, between spine and stitching line in both end spaces. Place on the diagonal between the corner and the end hole.

Make both end holes in basic stitching pattern large enough for the thread to pass through 4 times. Diagonal corner holes and all remaining holes have thread pass through three 3 times. Sew it in sequence.

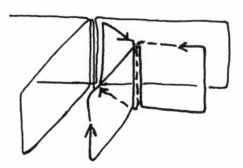

FLAX (OR LINEN) LEAF PATTERN

Materials:
Same as p. 67 except thread length:
9" spine length with 3/8" stitching margin,
measure a generous 7 times spine length

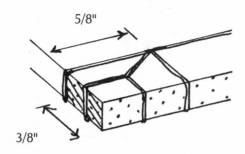

5/8"

3/8"

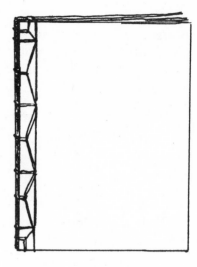

Traditional proportion; book about
9" by 6 1/2", stitching margin = 3/8"

LAY OUT standard *toji* pattern adding double
corners. Thread passes through the standard
stitching line holes 5 times and all other holes
3 times.

Add secondary pattern holes closer
to spine edge, centered between
standard holes as shown below.

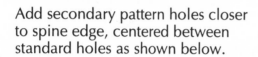

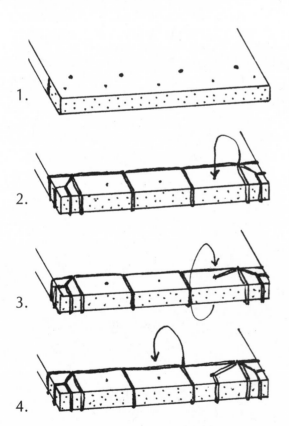

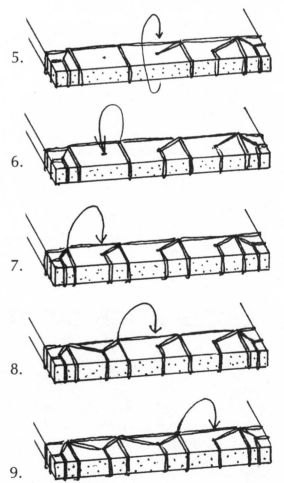

TORTOISE (OR TURTLE) SHELL PATTERN

Materials:
Same as p. 67 except thread length:
9" spine length with 3/8" stitching margin,
measure a generous 5 times spine length

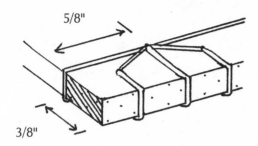

5/8"

3/8"

ADD SECONDARY pattern holes closer to spine edge. Center on each side of standard holes.

MAKE STANDARD stitching line holes large enough for thread to pass through 5 times; all other holes are sized for thread to pass through twice.

BEGIN STITCHING in the center hole of second cluster from end. Sew tortoise shell pattern, moving to next hole as in standard pattern, p. 67.

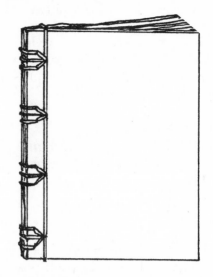

Traditional proportion; book about 9" by 6 1/2", stitching margin = 3/8"

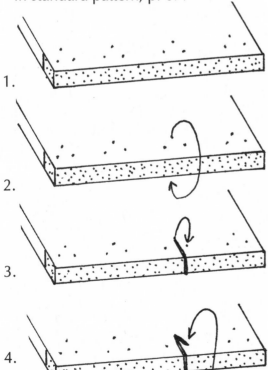

1.

2.

3.

4.

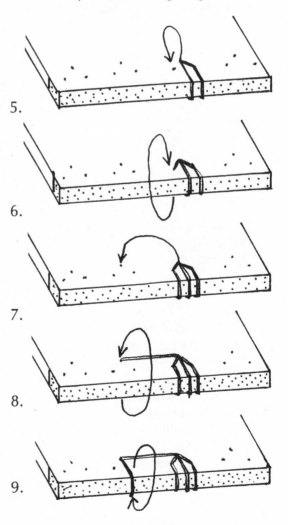

5.

6.

7.

8.

9.

DECORATIVE SPINE STRIP

A narrow strip of decorative paper to wrap
the spine can add interest.
Use with separate cover style
or spine wrap cover style.
Torn edges look nice
with some papers.

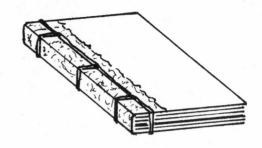

Materials:
Book block with cover and holes
Strip of lightweight paper
Thread
Adhesive

CUT STRIP to be flush with cover at head and tail
    and to extend beyond sewing holes in a pleasing proportion, as shown.

USE ADHESIVE along spine to keep strip in place while stitching.
    Edges may be left loose, but strip is more fragile when loose.

FOLDED FORE EDGE COVERS

Cover material can be lighter weight since it is
double. If stiffening is needed, insert a single leaf
between the folded cover material.

Materials:
Book block with inner binding, p. 64,
    single or folded fore edge pages
Cover paper
Stiffening paper if desired
Thread

CUT MATERIALS.
    Covers, cut two
    Height = book block height
    Width = 2 times book block width + fold ease

    Stiffener, cut two
    Height = book block height
    Width = slightly narrower than cover to fit inside and be even at spine edge

Follow *TEMPORARY WRAP* and *INNER BINDING*, p.64, to hold covers and book
block in place while making holes and sewing together, pp. 65-66.

FLIP BOOKS

Write one letter of a short message on a page.
Repeat it on the next page adding the next letter of
the message. On each following page add a letter
until the message is complete.

Try this for a special day, birthday, valentine, etc.
A small size is easiest to flip.

Materials:
Text paper, medium weight
*   e.g. Canson Mi Teintes*
Cover paper, same as text
*   or slightly heavier*
Thread

SEW WITH three or four holes depending on size of book.

THEME BINDINGS

Handmade versions of commercial covers for single sheets of paper are easily constructed.
They can be made in sections as shown or folded from one long sheet of paper. The cover
can be sewn together or fastened with commercial brads through punched holes.
This style works well for class notes, making it popular with students and teachers.

EXTENDED FORE EDGE ONE PIECE COVER

This cover is similar to *Cover In Sections*, p. 72,
where cover is cut in three pieces,
the pleat being a separate panel.

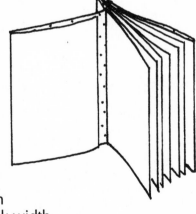
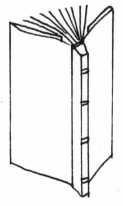

Materials:
Book block with inner binding,
*   p. 64*
Cover paper
Thread

CUT COVER in one piece.
   Height = book block height
   Width = 2 times book block width
          + 2 times desired fold back width
          + spine thickness
          + ease for 2 spine folds

Follow *THIRD METHOD,* p. 29, to score and fold.
All lines must be parallel or cover will not rest even with head and tail of book block.
Wrap around book block. Hold with clips.

PLAN SEWING pattern and make template, p. 243.

MAKE HOLES in pleat and pages, p. 244, and sew together.

COVER IN THREE SECTIONS

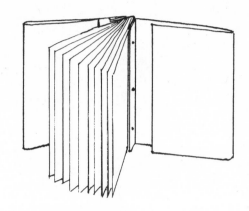

Materials:
Text pages
Cover material, paper, paper bonds,
  or cloth and paper bonds
  heavier than text pages

DETERMINE PAGE size.
  The pleat overlaps a portion of the margin
  along spine edge. Allow for pleat width
  + visual margin when designing pages, see *MARGINS,* p. 63.

CUT MATERIALS.
  Cover, cut two
  fore edge flush or with slight overhang
  Height = book block height
  Width =1 page width + 1 pleat width
          + 2 times desired fore edge flap width
          + 2 times overhang if desired

  Cover Pleat, cut one
  Height = book block height
  Width = 2 times pleat width + spine thickness

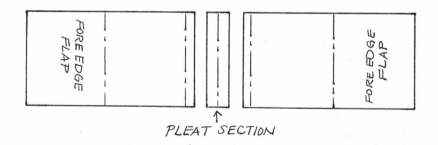

PLEAT SECTION

Follow *THIRD METHOD,* p. 29, to score and fold pleat.

ASSEMBLE COVER sections and book block. Hold with clips.
  Make holes in pleat and pages, p. 244. Finish with brads or butterfly stitch, p. 91.

COVERS JOINED TO ENDPAPERS

First and last book block pages are left blank to become endpapers when covers are joined to the book block. This Chinese binding method was often used with plain indigo paper and white thread.

Materials:
Book block, folded fore edge pages
  with inner binding, p. 64
Cover paper heavier than text
Thread
Adhesive

CUT COVERS.
  Height = book block height
  Width = book block width + 1/2"

PLACE BACK cover wrong side up
  on work surface. Align edges carefully.
  Cover fore edge will be wider.

SCORE COVER along fore edge of book
  block and fold 1/2" flap to inside
  making cover flush on all edges.

SPREAD ADHESIVE lightly on both sides
  of turn-in and adhere to page and cover.

DAB ADHESIVE between inner binding
  and spine edge to hold cover in place.

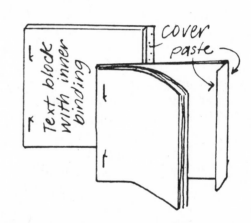

PLAN STITCHING pattern.
  Traditional Chinese hole positions differ because their parent sheet paper proportions are different. Either plain or double stitched corners are used.

  Traditional proportions for four holes:
  Head and tail holes are 5/8" from head and tail on stitching line.
  A is two times the distance from head or tail to first hole.
  B is the distance remaining between. Divided B into thirds for placement of the two remaining holes.

MAKE HOLES and
  stitch when
  cover is dry.

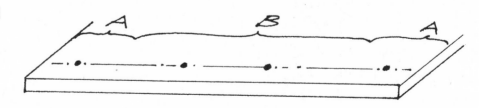

YAMATO STYLE BINDINGS

Yamato style bindings use flat tape, paper, or
fabric to hold cover and book block together.
The tape is threaded through two sets of holes
and tied with square knots.
If tape is paper, the knot is pounded flat.
Since the corners are unsupported, corner
caps are needed to strengthen the binding.

Traditionally, the cover is colorful patterned paper.
This delicate book is often used as
a guest book for weddings.

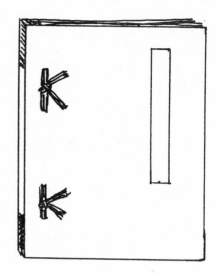

> *Materials:*
> *Text block with folded fore edge*
>   *and inner binding*
> *Cover paper, decorative pattern*
> *Endpapers*
> *Corner cap paper or backed fabric for caps*
> *Tape, cloth, ribbon, or paper*
> *Adhesive*

CUT MATERIALS.
   Covers, cut two
   Height = book block height + 1 1/4"
   Width = book block width + 1 1/4"

   Endpapers, cut two
   Height = book block height
   Width = book block width + 3/8"

PLACE DAB of adhesive
   on inner binding stitches.
   Attach right side of one endpaper
   to book block.
   Align edges with book block.

FOLD ENDPAPER fore edge turn-in
   to wrong side of endpaper, making it
   flush with book block.
   Repeat process with other endpaper.

MAKE END caps, p. 64.
   Attach to book block, p. 65.

PLACE BACK cover wrong side up.
  Score 3/8" margin along spine edge.

  Fold to inside and place 2 dabs
  of adhesive in center as shown.

PLACE TEXT block over fold,
  flush with spine, centering for a
  5/8" margin at head and tail.
  Leave a 7/8" margin at fore edge.

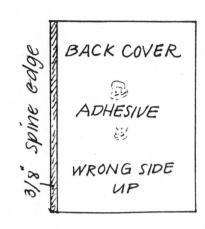

SCORE AROUND book block.
  Fold in the head and tail,
  then fore edge.

USING SCISSORS,
  trim away some
  of corner bulk
  for modified
  miter.

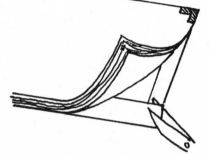

LIFT TEXT block fore edge and lightly
  brush adhesive along fore edge flap.
  Gently smooth in place.

APPLY DAB of adhesive to corner cap at each end of spine and press cover in place.
  Repeat process for front cover.

USE CHISEL and mallet to make tape holes.
  For traditional shape, 12 5/8" x 8 1/4",
  holes are 7/8" in from spine edge.
  The top and bottom holes are
  2 3/8" in from head and tail.

  The next holes are 2" closer to center.

  Place book block right side up on solid
  backing. Be aware chisel will cut into this
  surface. Align chisel with pencil mark.
  Pound hole using chisel and mallet, p. 244.

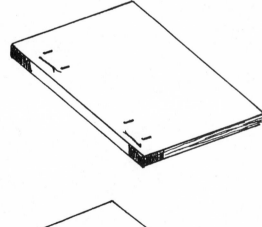

A single tie is enough for a small book.
  Divide space into thirds and tie across
  the middle section as shown.

WRAP END of cord with thin paper
or tape to help cord pass through
slits without unraveling.

TIE WITH square knot and trim ends or finish as shown below. Tie with an overhand
knot at the center, first drawing on left. Finish with a single half hitch at each slit,
shown in the remaining drawings.

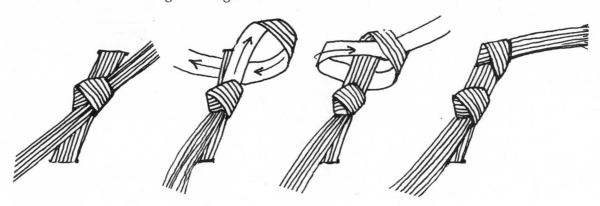

Keeping cord flat,
slip one end under long stitch following the arrows above. Pull tight as shown.

Repeat at other slit following arrows below.
Trim ends to
desired
length.

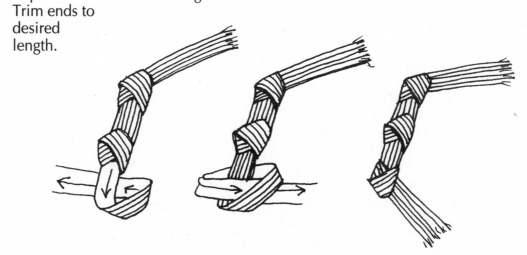

CASE BINDING, HINGED COVER

Materials:
Text block with fly leaves,
* inner binding*
Spine length cap, if desired,
* lining of 16# or 20# bond paper*
Endpaper paste downs
Binder board
Cover material, paper or book cloth
Hinge strip, p. 256
Cord or thread
Adhesive

MAKE UP book block and fly leaves. Secure with inner binding.
 Plan a wide margin at spine edge. Cover hinge uses 3/4" of space.
 The thicker the book, the wider the margin needs to be. Loss of visual space
 increases as pages are turned. Test papers for flexibility, see p. 63.

CUT MATERIALS.
 Cover boards, cut two
 Height = book block height
 Width = book block width less 1/4" for hinge joint

 Cut a 3/4" piece from spine edge of each cover board.
 This board becomes the hinge anchor and sewing area.

 Cover material, cut two
 Height = book block height + 1 1/2" for turn-ins
 Width = book block width + 2 3/4" for turn-ins, joint, and ease

 Hinge Strip, cut two
 Height = board height
 Width = 2"
 Book cloth for cover material, omit hinge strip
 Make hinge joint 3 board thicknesses + 2 covering thickness. This allows cover to
 fold back more than a 45° angle when book is open.

 Make Spacer, p. 5, using 3 boards + 2 covering thicknesses.

 Endpaper paste downs, cut two
 Height = board height less 1/8"
 Width = board width less 1/8"

Follow *END CAPS,* p. 64, or *SPINE LENGTH cap*, p. 65, to cap spine. With a thick
book block, a full length spine cap is nice. For a crisp, tailored look, lining paper is
added as shown on next page.

Lining paper for full length spine cap
Height = book block height + 1 1/2"
Width = spine thickness

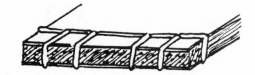

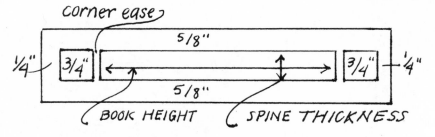

corner ease

5/8"

1/4" 3/4" 5/8" 3/4" 1/4"

BOOK HEIGHT   SPINE THICKNESS

Turn corners and paste cap to book block as shown on p. 65.

DRAW COVER board
positions on inside
of cover material
using 3/4" margins.

Use a straight edge
and right angle to
make lines square,
p. 111.

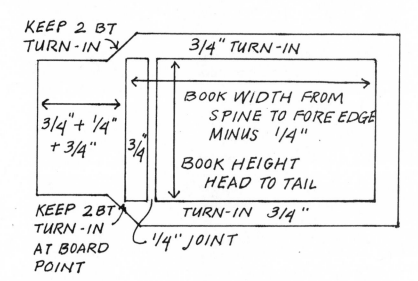

KEEP 2 BT
TURN-IN

3/4" TURN-IN

3/4" + 1/4"
+ 3/4"

3/4"

BOOK WIDTH FROM
SPINE TO FORE EDGE
MINUS 1/4"

BOOK HEIGHT
HEAD TO TAIL

KEEP 2 BT
TURN-IN
AT BOARD
POINT

TURN-IN 3/4"

1/4" JOINT

APPLY ADHESIVE to boards and mount
on cover material. Pasting tips are
given on pp. 239-241.
Do both covers.

BRUSH ADHESIVE
on board hinge area,
board thickness, and
joint space.
Set hinge piece in
place and smooth
along board
surface, down
against board thickness,

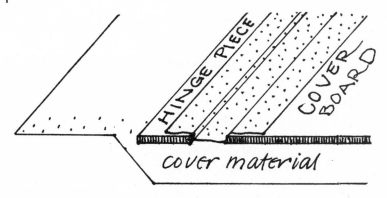

HINGE PIECE

COVER BOARD

cover material

across joint, up against next board thickness. As hinge is smoothed over
second board, be sure hinge still remains snug against inside board edges.

Follow *MITER CORNERS,* p. 245, to finish head, tail and fore edge.

FINISH HINGE. Brush adhesive on exposed hinge board, joint, and board thickness. Pull spine flap up and over, smoothing against board thickness. Smooth to hinge board, down, across joint, and up over cover board.

ADD PASTE downs. Spread adhesive on exposed board and edges of paste downs. Position on board and smooth with folder and protective paper, p. 240.

Repeat
process
on
other
board.

end paper

board

hinge   *cover material*

DRY UNDER weight, p. 241.

PLAN SEWING pattern. Make template, p. 243. Use stitching pattern of choice.

MAKE HOLES, p. 244, and stitch as planned.

JAPANESE LEDGER BOOKS IN TWO STYLES

These books are easy to make. They work well as blank books, diaries, or sketch books. Traditionally they are long and narrow, but the technique can be used to make any shape.

ACCOUNT BOOK

The Japanese characters for "Great Fortune" were often brushed on the cover.

Materials:
Text paper, medium or lightweight
Cover paper, heavyweight,
* a bond or Bristol board*
Cord
Adhesive

MAKE UP book block.
   Pages may be single sheets, French fold, or folded fore edge;
   e.g., 4 sheets of Ingres Antique can be torn into 24 folded leaves making a book
      4 1/4" by 9 1/2". Fold can be at spine or fore edge.

CUT COVERS to be flush with book block.
   For double weight use a folded
   fore edge. Covers may have
   torn rather than cut edges.

ATTACH COVERS to front
   and back of book block
   with a touch of adhesive
   along the spine between
   the hole line and spine edge,
   shown in dots.
   Align edges carefully.

POSITION TWO sewing holes about
   1/2" to 2/3" from spine edge. Make
   distance between the holes a bit more
   than 1/3 of the length of the spine.

FOLLOW DRAWINGS to sew.
   Use two cords, one for each hole.

When finished, tie each
   cord tightly across
   center of spine using
   square knot, p. 226.

Twist the two ends
   into single strands.
   Bring together
   at center.

Tie twisted strands
   together at center of
   spine with a square knot.

Finish with an overhand
   knot, p. 228,
   snuggled up
   close.
   Fray ends or
   braid as shown.

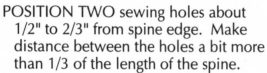

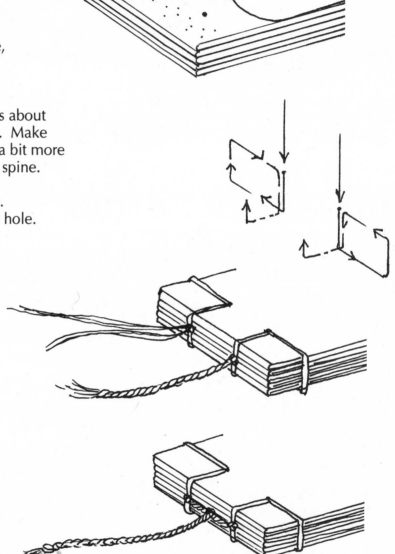

Other ending ideas can be found on p. 66 and in Knots and Closures section, p. 226.

RECEIPT BOOK

Materials:
Text paper, medium
  or lightweight
Cover paper, heavy-
  weight paper, a bond
  or Bristol board
Decorative cord
Linen thread
Bead, optional
Adhesive

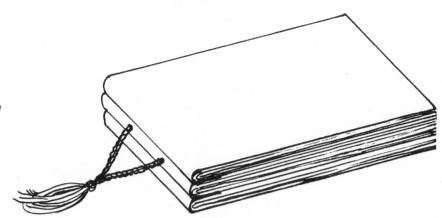

MAKE UP book block and divide into 3 signatures of equal, or near equal size.
  See *Account Book, MAKE UP book block,* p. 80, for dividing sheets of Ingres Antique
  into a book block.

CUT MATERIALS.
  Covers, cut or tear two
  Height = book block height, (narrow dimension in drawing)
  Width = book block width + 5/8", (long dimension in drawing)

  Spine piece, cut one
  Height = book block height
  Width = 1 1/8"

SCORE 5/8" turn-in at spine
  edge of both covers and
  fold to inside.

INSIDE FRONT COVER

SET FIRST signature over inside
  front cover, face down.
  Align head, tail, and fore edge.

SPREAD ADHESIVE lightly on
  inner surface of turn-in and
  fold in place. Turn-in will
  fold over signature.

FIRST SIGNATURE
(FACE DOWN) OVER
INSIDE FRONT COVER

  Repeat with back cover,
  placing last page of last
  signature next to cover.

FOLD SPINE piece in half lengthwise.
Spread adhesive on inside surface.
Center over middle section
of opened book block.
Press in place.

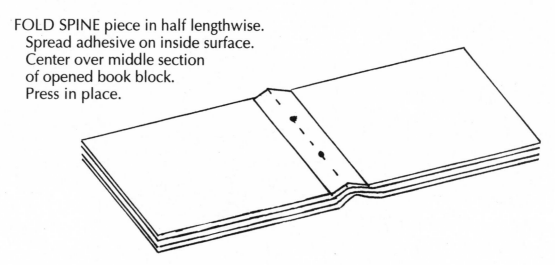

MAKE TWO holes in fold line, a little more than 1/3 of spine height apart. These holes must be large enough for decorative cord to pass through. Use drill if needed, p. 244. Traditionally, decorative cord is now added. However, when the two sets of inner binding holes are made, the decorative cord may get caught in drill. To avoid the mess, add decorative cord later.

OPEN FRONT section and place face down with cover on top and to the right.
Place closed middle section over left half of front section,
aligning fore edges at left.

Place open back section on top with
cover going to the right, as shown.
Align folds. Hold everything in
place with clips or clamps
while drilling and
stitching.

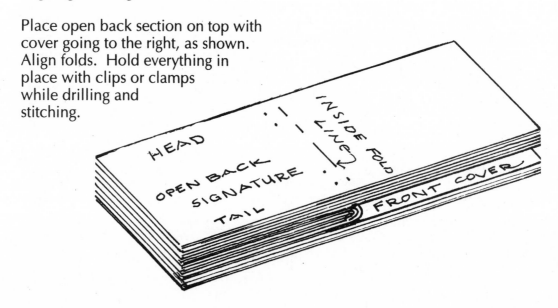

TWO SETS of inner
binding holes are pierced through all three sections. Size holes to fit the linen thread. Place all holes 1/8" in from center fold line. Make first and last holes 1/2" in from head and tail. Their companion holes are placed 5/8" closer to center, as shown.

OPEN MIDDLE section and thread decorative
  cord through holes, as shown.
  Tie with an overhand
  knot a short distance
  away from spine,
  p. 228.

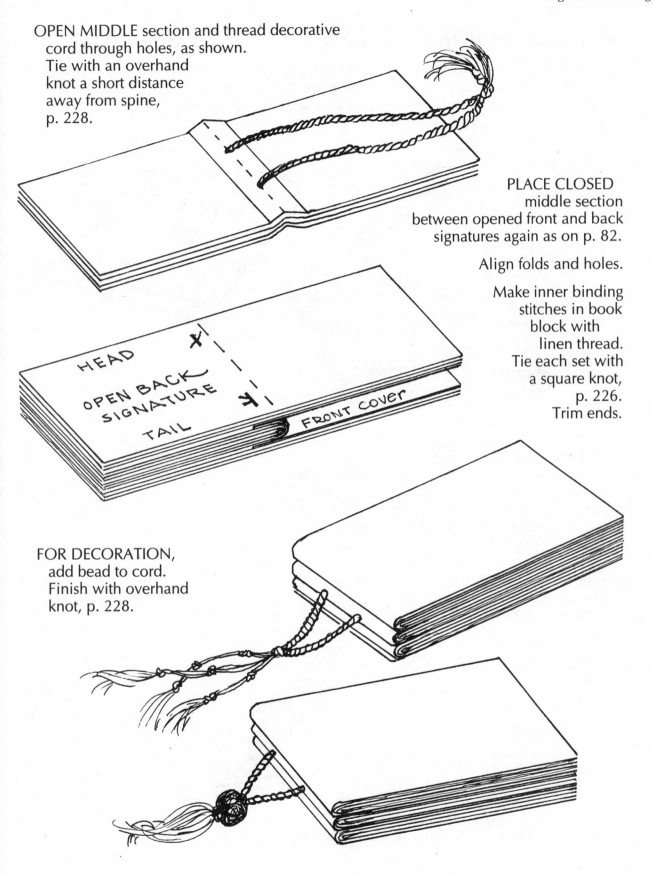

PLACE CLOSED
  middle section
between opened front and back
  signatures again as on p. 82.

Align folds and holes.

Make inner binding
  stitches in book
  block with
    linen thread.
  Tie each set with
    a square knot,
      p. 226.
    Trim ends.

HEAD

OPEN BACK
SIGNATURE

TAIL

FRONT COVER

FOR DECORATION,
  add bead to cord.
  Finish with overhand
  knot, p. 228.

MATCH BOOK COVERS IN THREE STYLES

Each style has a long cover piece which folds back over the stitching and wraps around the spine. In the first style, one long cover piece forms both the front and back cover. In the second and third styles, two covers are used, one for the front and another for the back.

ONE PIECE COVER

This cover is made from one long continuous piece.
It is stitched with face down on front of book block.
It then folds back on itself covering the stitching line, spine, book back, fore edge, and book front.
It tucks under the fold flap on front to close.

Materials:
Book block
Fly leaves, optional
Cover paper, heavier
  than text paper
Thread or staples
Adhesive

CUT COVER.
one continuous piece
Height = book block height
Width = 2 times book block width
        + 2 times spine thickness
        + 2 times stitching margin
        + 3/4" for tuck-in flap + ease for folding

MAKE UP book block and secure with inner binding, p. 64

MEASURE COVER length with a paper strip made from the same weight of paper as the cover, p. 237. Wrap strip as cover will wrap the book block, creasing at each fold. Cover ends where the tuck-in flap meets the stitching line.

PLACE OPEN cover face down over book block. Clip in place. Mark hole positions on cover.

MAKE HOLES, p. 244.

SEW TOGETHER. Use standard pattern but do not sew over the head and tail. Just sew the spine edge.

SCORE FOLD line 3/8" beyond stitching line for flap. Fold back over stitching. Score and fold remaining cover around spine and fore edge thicknesses. Trim tuck-in flap if necessary.

DAB ADHESIVE along stitches on back leaf and press cover in place.

DRY UNDER light pressure, p. 241.

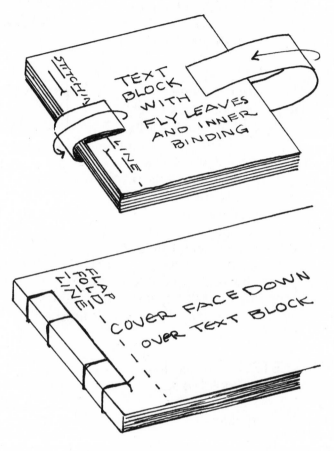

TWO PIECE COVER

This variation has a separate front and back cover. The back cover piece is placed upside down over the front cover for stitching. It then folds back on itself to cover the stitching line and spine, thus forming the back cover.

Materials:
Same as One Piece Cover, p. 84

Follow *MAKE UP book block* and *MEASURE COVER length*, above.

CUT COVERS.
  Front Cover, cut one
  Height = book block height
  Width = book block width
        + fore edge overhang
            if desired

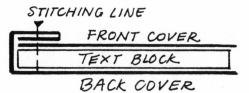

STITCHING LINE
FRONT COVER
TEXT BLOCK
BACK COVER

Back Cover, cut one
  Height = book block height
  Width = book block width
        + 3/8" sewing margin
        + spine thickness
        + overhang, if used
        + ease for folds
        + 1/4"

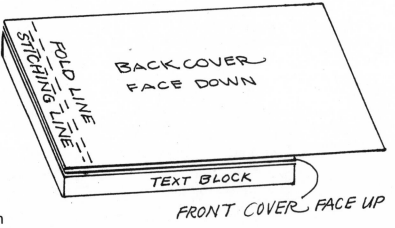

The last 1/4" is to ensure the
cover will be long enough to line
up with the top cover at fore edge.
Papers vary in folding ease. Any extra
is trimmed to size when cover is finished.

PLACE FRONT cover right side up
  on top of book block.

Place unfolded
back cover
face down
over front
cover.

MAKE HOLES,
  p. 244.

Follow *SEW
TOGETHER,* p. 85.

Follow *SCORE FOLD
line,* p. 85. This book
does not have a tuck in
flap.

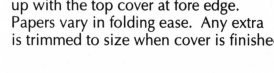

FOLD LINE
STITCHING LINE
BACK COVER FACE DOWN
TEXT BLOCK
FRONT COVER FACE UP

Follow *DAB ADHESIVE along stitches* and *DRY UNDER light pressure,* p. 85.
When finished, both front and back covers will line up at fore edge.
Trim when dry if necessary.

TWO PIECE COVER WITH INSERTS

Materials:
Same as One Piece Cover, p. 84, except:
Cover can be lighter weight since inserts are added
Cover inserts, heavy paper

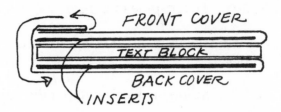

FRONT COVER
TEXT BLOCK
BACK COVER
INSERTS

CUT COVERS.
   Front Cover, cut one
   Height = book block height
   Width = 2 times book block
        width
        + 2 times fore edge
            overhang if used
        + ease for fold and
            insert

   Back Cover, cut one
   Height = book block height
   Width = 2 times book block
        width
        + spine thickness
        + 3/8" stitching margin
        + 2 times fore edge
            overhang if used
        + ease for folds and
            insert
        + 1/4" (as on p.86)

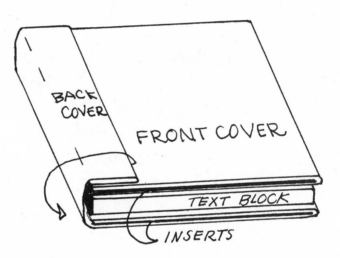

BACK COVER
FRONT COVER
TEXT BLOCK
INSERTS

   Cover Inserts, cut two
   Height = book block height
   Width = slightly less than
        book block width
        + 2 times fore edge
            overhang if used

Follow *MAKE UP book block* and
MEASURE COVER length, p. 85.
In this project, both front and back
cover fold inside to spine edge.

FOLD FRONT cover around insert.
   Spread adhesive lightly to stitching
   area of front insert and press in place
   between cover layers.
   Place front cover over book block.

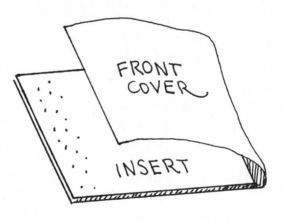

FRONT COVER
INSERT

PLACE UNFOLDED back cover face down over front cover as shown on page 86.
  Hold in place with clips.

MAKE HOLES through both covers and book block, p. 244. Stitch in place.

SCORE BACK cover just beyond stitching line.
  Fold back cover back over stitching line.
  Score and fold over spine thickness.

SCORE BACK cover fore edge using front cover fore edge as a guide.
  Fold in place.

TRIM EDGE of inside back cover flap if the flap overlaps spine fold.

FRONT COVER

INSIDE OF BACK COVER FLAP

TEXT BLOCK

FRONT COVER INSERT

USE A light coat of adhesive along
  spine edge of back cover insert
  and slip in place between spine
  and fore edge folds.

USE A light coat of adhesive
  over stitches at back of book block
  as shown in dotted area.
  Press back cover in place.

DRY UNDER light pressure, p. 241.

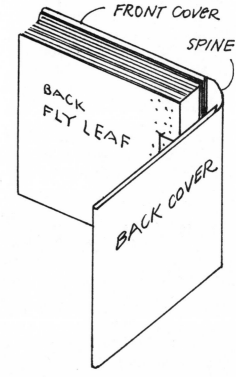

FRONT COVER

SPINE

BACK FLY LEAF

BACK COVER

SINGLE SIGNATURE BINDINGS

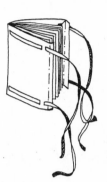

A signature is a number of leaves, traditionally eight, folded in half and inserted inside each other and sewn into a cover along the fold.

Although an octavo fold is traditional, there are many variations, p. 233.

The terms *quire* or *section* are sometimes used in place of signature.

GENERAL INFORMATION

GRAIN: All materials should be cut with grain parallel with the spine so covers and book blocks lie flat and straight, p. 232.

SIGNATURES: Estimate size and number of leaves needed for content.
Lightweight papers will make more leaves than heavyweight papers, see Folding large sheets, p. 233.
Cut or tear large sheets into smaller sizes, pp. 233-235.
Try mixing papers for variety in textures, weights, and colors.

When some edges are cut and others are not, alternate the smooth and rough edges throughout the signature.
Many papers have a different texture on each side. Place leaves with the same surface texture together, alternating throughout book block.

Be sure center fold is made at right angles with top edge of leaf.
Fold all leaves and slip them one inside of another.

Make extra leaves for changes, replacement, or practice.
Paper surface can be the same on both sides of a leaf when folded with a French Fold. This fold minimizes see-through, p. 79.

ENDPAPERS: These include fly leaves and paste downs. Their size is the same as a signature leaf. They are often a different paper and serve as a visual and tactile design link between a signature and cover.

FORE EDGE: The innermost leaf will project further than the outermost leaf at the fore edge. This edge can be left as is or trimmed to be even, p. 236. After trimming, number pages to avoid mixing them, for each leaf is now unique.

SHADOWS: Minimize shadows seen from the other side of a page by using the same line spacing, or "backing up," on both sides of a page.

Write in the same spaces on front and back sides of the page.

HOLES: Place holes in spine folds. One is placed in the middle.
Two outside holes are placed 1/2" to 5/8" from the spine head and tail.

Other holes, if used, are placed equally between these three holes.
Holes are made with any pointed tool. Be sure all holes are made in the fold. Use
clips to clamp back half of cover and signature together to minimize shifting about
when making holes, see illustration on p. 243.

THREAD: Length is twice the length of spine from head to tail plus extra for the knot.
If the thread is pierced as the needle goes through a hole the second time,
it cannot be pulled taut. Thread should be taut but not so taut as to tear the paper.

SEWING: Most signatures are sewn with thread through both cover and book block.
Tips for making holes and sewing are given on pp. 242-244.
The sewing pattern, called a butterfly or figure 8 stitch,
uses an odd number of holes.

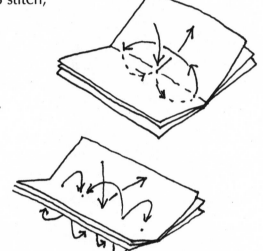

Use three holes for a spine about 6" or 7" long
and five or seven holes for longer spines.

Sewing begins and ends in the same place.
Begin sewing inside signature at middle hole by
passing through signature and cover. Move in
through next hole, up or down. If more than
three holes are used, continue along spine
moving in and out to last hole.

Return in the same manner, skipping
over middle hole. Continue on to opposite end
and back, ending at middle hole on inside of
book.

Finish by tying a square knot over the long thread that spans the middle hole, p. 226.

KNOTS: Usually the knot is made inside the signature to prevent bumps in cover spine.
Sewing begins and ends in same hole on same side of the book.
Begin wherever necessary for desired finish.

COVERS: Paper covers are usually made from materials heavier than text paper.
Cover materials should enhance rather than overpower content.
Use cover stock, paper ranging between 50 and 100 pounds, p. 261.
Paper bonds and book cloth bonded with paper can make very nice soft covers.
Bonding tips are given on pp. 239, 241.
Case binding instructions are given on p. 109.

TO SOLVE PROBLEMS, MAKE A MOCK-UP BOOK FIRST

BASIC COVERS

This cover is made with paper cut the same size and folded in the same way as the signature. It is called "flush" when the cover has no overhang.
The two parts help strengthen and support each other.

Materials:
Signature and fly leaves
Cover paper,
 heavier than text pages
Thread

MAKE UP signature and fly leaves.

MEASURE COVER width.
 Wrap a strip of paper around the
 signature from front fore edge to
 back fore edge to measure distance.
 Use paper the same weight as the
 cover material for accuracy, p. 110.

CUT COVER.
 Height = signature height
 Width = 2 times signature width
  + spine thickness

MAKE FOLD for spine at right angles
 with cover head and tail edges.
 Score fold if necessary, p. 234.

PLAN AND make holes, pp. 91, 243.

SEW SIGNATURE and cover together, p. 91.

UNUSUAL SHAPES

Any shape that will adapt to a spine fold can be made into a single signature book.

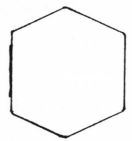

EXTENDED FORE EDGE COVERS

An extended, folded back fore edge adds strength to the edges that get the most wear. The folded flap width can vary from almost as wide as the cover to any pleasing narrower proportion.

Materials:
Same as Basic Cover, p. 92
Optional heavyweight leaf

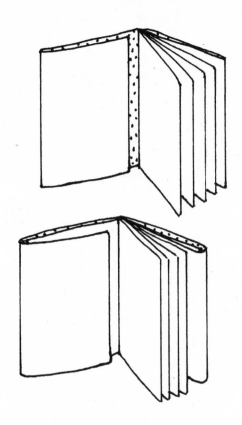

CUT COVER.
  Height = signature height
  Width = 2 times signature width
        + 2 times flap width
        + spine thickness

ADD FLY leaf of heavyweight paper to back of signature if desired to reinforce the whole structure. Tuck leaf behind flap extension.

MAKE LIKE Basic Cover, p. 92.

WRAP-AROUND COVERS

This Basic Cover variation reinforces itself as it doubles back. Material can be lighter because it is double when finished. It can be stiffened with a heavier leaf added outside the cover and the signature. This leaf, shown in black, is hidden as the cover wraps.

Materials:
Same as Basic Cover, p. 92

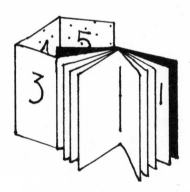

CUT COVER.
  Height = signature height
  Width = 5 times signature width

5	4	3	2	1
inside back	outside back	outside front	inside front	inside back

FRONT SIDE OF PAPER

panel 1 tucks
inside 4 & 5

PLACE FRONT side of cover material up
  when signature is sewn in cover.
  The first fold is a valley fold.
  The rest are mountain folds.

  After folding, because of ease
  needed in each fold as the
  cover wraps, the panel widths
  will all vary slightly.

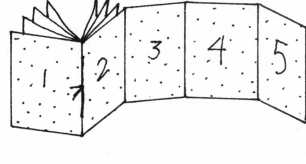

FOLD PANEL 5
  over first panel
  to complete
  cover.

Cover variations:
A decoration on panel 3 would
indicate the front of the book.
Embossing is one possibility.

Anything placed or made
on back side of panel 2
can be framed with
an opening made
in panel 3.

A tab closure variation
can be made by adding
a tab to panel 5.
Cut slits to fit tab in
panel 3, p. 235.

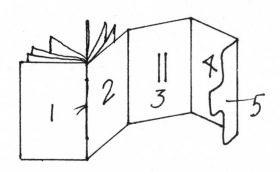

Other Wrap-Around cover books:
Accordions: p. 35, in Three Flap Folder, p. 143
Edge Sewn Bindings: Match Book format, p. 85, Peg Book, p. 13
Single Signature: Mini Book, p. 104, in Three Flap Folder, p. 144
Multiple Signature Bindings: Long Stitch format, p. 135

NON-ADHESIVE COVER WITH TABS ON BOOK

Turn-ins on all 4 edges strengthen cover edges.
Signature is held in cover by an outermost leaf
of sturdy paper sewn with the signature
and tucked under the turn-ins.

A non-adhesive cover with tabs on cover
is given on p. 127.

Materials:
Signature including fly leaves
Outer leaf of sturdy paper
Cover material of heavyweight paper
  or paper bonds

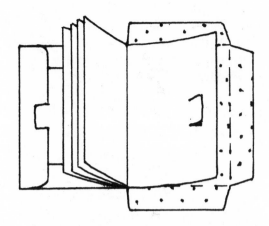

CUT COVER.
   Proportion turn-ins with size
   of cover, between 1" and 2"
   Height = signature height
            + 2 times turn-in width
   Width = 2 times signature width
           + 2 times turn-in width
           + spine fold ease

Note tab cut in outer leaf
to help hold signature in cover.
Tab goes over edge of turn-in.

ASSEMBLE SIGNATURE, fly leaves and outer leaf of sturdy paper.

Make sewing holes and stitch together, pp. 91, 243.
   SCORE AND fold turn-ins, p. 234.

CUT NOTCH from spine fold line of head
   and tail turn-ins to prevent binding. Stop
   just short of edge fold lines as shown.

REMOVE CORNER section from each
   corner for modified miter as shown, p.
   245.

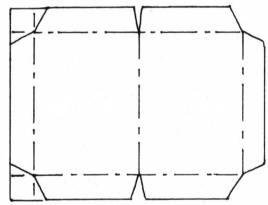

PLACE SEWN signature in cover.
   Fold head and tail turn-ins over
   outer leaf first.
   Fold fore edges last.

FIGURE POSITION and cut tab in outer leaf of signature.

CHAP BOOK COVERS

The name has its roots in the Anglo Saxon word *ceap* meaning trade. The term was used to distinguish paper bound books from leather bound books. They have long been a tradition for binding single signatures.

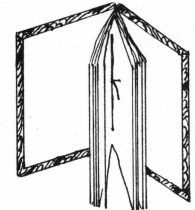

Materials:
Signature and fly leaves
Outer leaf, heavyweight paper
Cover paper, usually marbled
  or starch paper
Thread
Adhesive

CUT COVER
  with 3/4" turn-ins on all four sides.
  With small signatures make turn-ins narrower.
  Height = signature height
          + 2 times turn-in width
  Width = 2 times signature width
          + 2 times turn-in width
          + spine fold ease

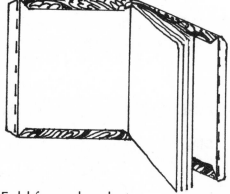

Follow *ASSEMBLE SIGNATURE,* p. 95.

CUT NOTCHES at spine fold
  of decorative cover paper.

MAKE MODIFIED miter at each corner, p. 245.

SCORE AND fold all turn-ins around outermost leaf. Fold fore edges last.

PLACE SIGNATURE in cover with outermost
  leaf under turn-ins. Align signature with
  spine fold. Close book.

paste area

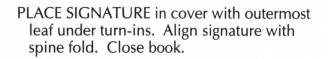

OPEN FRONT cover. Slip waxed
  paper under first leaf as shown.

Follow *PASTING IN LIMITED AREA,*
p. 240, to paste 1/4" of leaf fore edge.

  Carefully close book, pressing area
  pasted on leaf edge to cover turn-in.
  Repeat for back cover.

  Add waxed paper for moisture barrier and weight to dry, p. 241.

FRENCH FOLD COVERS AND LEAVES

This style minimizes see-through problems with leaves
and covers when using very light weight papers.
This fold also gives the advantage
of having the same surface
on both sides of a leaf.

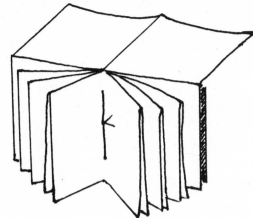

Materials:
Text papers,
  lightweight or
  other weights
Cover paper
Optional
  reinforcing
  leaf
Thread

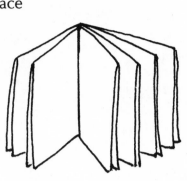

MAKE UP booklet using a French fold
  for the leaves.

CUT HEAVYWEIGHT leaf, if desired,
  to fit between cover fold layers.
  Sew signature and heavyweight
  leaf through inside half of cover only.

CUT COVER to be flush with signature.

WEAVE PAPER or ribbons through slits in cover
  layers for a decorative touch, p. 235.

CONSTRUCTION VARIATION

ADD TURN-IN flaps to fore edges of cover on outside layer only.
  Flap should be about
  1/2" wide.

  Taper ends slightly
  to avoid binding.

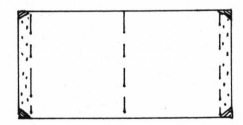

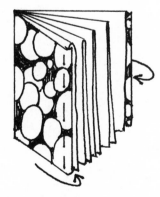

SPREAD ADHESIVE on
  back of front turn-in flap as shown. Attach to inside
  of first leaf. Add waxed paper for moisture barrier.
  Repeat for back turn-in flap. Weight to dry, p. 241.

VELLUM BINDING ADAPTATION

A non adhesive cover of vellum is found in Edward Johnston's *Writing, Illuminating and Lettering*. It is designed with fore edge overlaps for a multiple signature manuscript. This paper adaptation holds a single signature yet maintains the formal elegance of the vellum, multiple signature binding.

Materials:
Signature, completed, collated with blank
  pages to tuck under turn-ins, p. 127
Cover material, medium to heavyweight paper
Thread
Ribbon

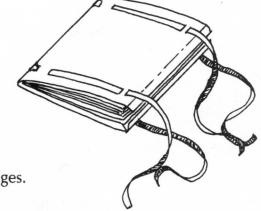

MAKE HOLES in signature. Plan for 3 holes.
  Make one hole in center of spine
  length and the others 1 5/8"
  in from head and tail.

SEW SIGNATURE with
  butterfly sewing pattern.

SLIP RIBBONS through
  thread linking 2 holes at head
  and tail on outside of signature.

CUT MATERIALS.
  Cover, cut one
  Use a 1 1/2" turn-in with a 5" to 7" spine length
  Height = signature height
          + 2 times any desired overhang
          + 2 times turn-in width
          + folding ease
  Width = 2 times signature width
          + spine thickness
          + 2 times any desired overhang
          + 4 times fore edge overlaps
          + 2 times turn-in width
          + folding ease

  Ribbon
  Length = 4 times cover width
          + 2 times spine thickness
          + any desired length beyond fore edges.
          divide length in half

Cover fore edge overhang is scored to form narrow flaps.
The flaps overlap each other, concealing the signature.

SCORE COVER lines, p. 234. Cut corners as shown. Fold head and tail first. Fold center fore edge line then second fore edge line which has now become two layers.

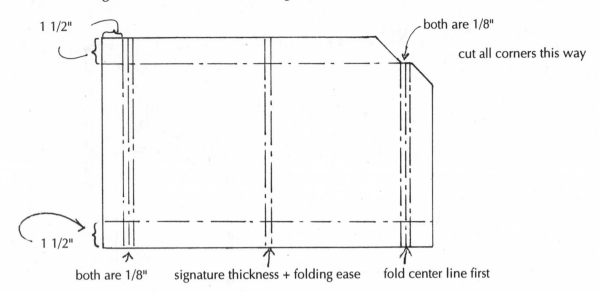

1 1/2"

both are 1/8"

cut all corners this way

1 1/2"

both are 1/8"   signature thickness + folding ease   fold center line first

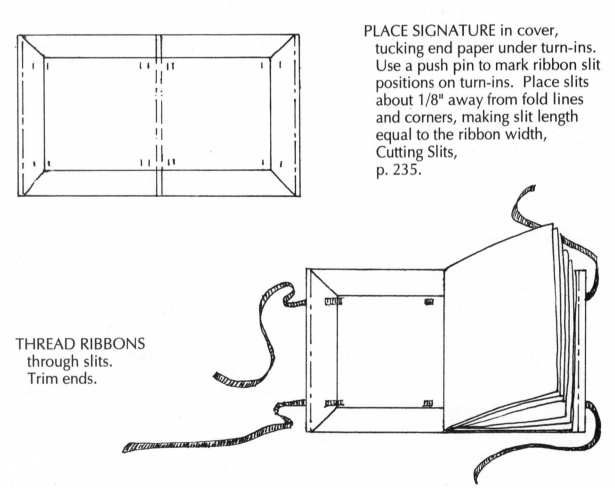

PLACE SIGNATURE in cover, tucking end paper under turn-ins. Use a push pin to mark ribbon slit positions on turn-ins. Place slits about 1/8" away from fold lines and corners, making slit length equal to the ribbon width, Cutting Slits, p. 235.

THREAD RIBBONS
  through slits.
  Trim ends.

99

PLEAT BINDINGS

SINGLE SIGNATURE WITH BEADS

This fun, decorative binding for a single signature
has beads stitched in a pleat along the spine.
Two sets of sewing holes are used, one for
the signature and the other for the beads.

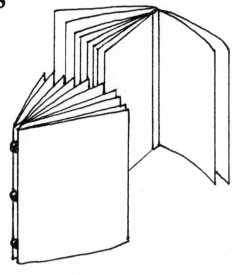

> *Materials:*
> *Single signature book block*
> *Fly leaf paper*
> *Cover paper, medium weight*
> *Beads for each sewing hole*
> *Thread*

CUT MATERIALS.
　　Fly leaf, cut in one piece
　　Height = book block height
　　Width = outermost signature leaf
　　　　　　+ 3/4" (pleat width before folding)

　　Cover, cut in one piece
　　Height = book block height
　　Width = Fly leaf width + folding ease
　　　　　　over outside of fly leaf

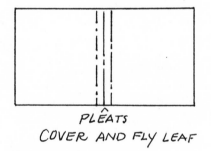

PLEATS
COVER AND FLY LEAF

MAKE SPINE pleat. Fold fly leaf in
　half to make spine fold. Crease.
　Add parallel folds, 1/4" away on
　either side of spine fold.
　Reverse center fold for pleat.

FOLD COVER the same as fly leaf.

PLACE FLY leaf inside cover piece.

MAKE TEMPLATE for sewing holes,
　p. 243. Use an odd number of holes
　for the butterfly sewing pattern, p. 91.

MAKE SEWING holes in peak fold of both cover and
　fly leaf, p. 244. Use same template to make sewing holes in signature.

SEW SIGNATURE, fly leaf, and cover together.

FOLD COVER and fly leaf back,
away from the signature.

MAKE BEAD holes in the remaining fold,
through both layers of cover and fly leaf,
using the same template.

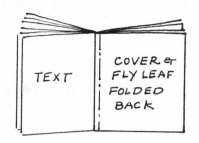

ADD BEADS with book open as shown.
Begin sewing inside back fly leaf in
pleat fold, center hole.

Move into pleat space,
pick up bead on needle,
and stitch through
corresponding front
cover hole.

Follow butterfly
stitching pattern,
adding a bead each
time the thread passes
through pleat space.

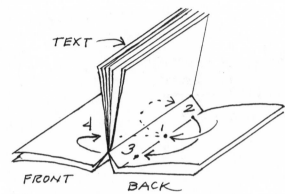

END SEWING by returning through
center hole and bead where sewing began.

Tie with square knot inside back cover.

DIVIDED SIGNATURES

This style can be used when a book block is too bulky to be one signature and not bulky enough to be several signatures. Though divided into two sections, this style is stitched as one signature. The number of pages in the two sections does not need to be equal. A pleat in the cover becomes a part of the overall design and can be as narrow as 1/4". A larger pleat can also be distinctive.

DOUBLE SIGNATURE PLEAT BINDING

An optional single leaf can be added to the peak of the pleat if desired. This leaf can be a different paper for a decorative surprise.

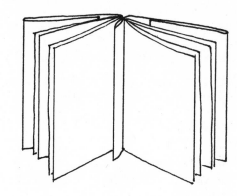

Materials:
Two signatures, text weight paper
* + an optional leaf if desired*
Cover, heavyweight paper or
*   book cloth bond, p. 239*
Thread

CUT MATERIALS.
   Cover, cut in one continuous piece
   Fore edge flush or with slight overhang
   Height = book block height
   Width = 2 times page width + 2 times pleat width + 2 times fore edge flap width
      + 4 times overhang
         if used
      + folding ease

Plead Width, at least 1/4"

Optional Leaf, cut one
Cut after cover is folded
Height = book block height
Width = 2 times page width
      less 2 times pleat width

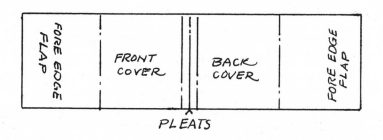

PLEATS

When book is finished, this leaf should rest even with signatures along fore edge.

Follow *THIRD METHOD*, p. 29, to score and fold cover. All lines must be parallel or cover will not rest even with head and tail of book block when finished. The center fold becomes the pleat's mountain fold. The next folds are one pleat width away from center.

MAKE UP signatures.
   Fold cover pleat, then decide width of optional leaf for the peak pleat.
   When done in this order, leaf will match width of signatures sewn in the valley fold.

MAKE THREE hole sewing template , p. 243. This will be used for all sewing holes.

MAKE SEWING holes in signature,
p. 243, and valley folds of cover.
Make holes in cover peak to match
optional leaf holes if needed.

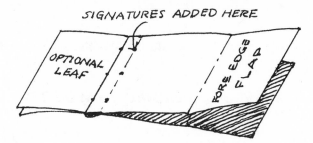

USE BUTTERFLY stitch, p. 91.
Sew optional leaf first.

Then fold covers, back lining up
sewing holes. Open signatures
and set in place, one signature
over inside front cover, the
other over inside back cover.

Align all holes carefully.
Clamp in place, shown on p. 134.

Sew cover and signatures together
all at once with butterfly stitch, p. 91.

SPLIT PLEAT VARIATION

This variation uses smaller pieces of cover
material. It cannot have a leaf sewn to the
peak since there is no fold.

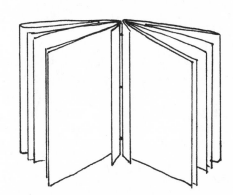

Materials:
Two signatures, text weight paper
Cover, heavyweight paper
Thread

Follow *MAKE UP signatures,* p. 102, and remaining instructions except score cover as
shown here and omit optional leaf.

Cover, cut two
  Height = book block height
  Width = book block width
         + desired split pleat width
         + desired cover flap width

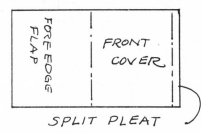

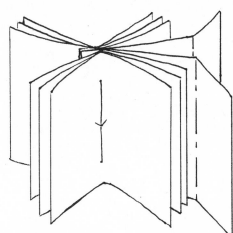

WRAP-AROUND VARIATION

Materials:
Same as Double Signature Pleat Binding, p. 102

Follow *MAKE UP signatures* and *MAKE TEMPLATE*, p. 102.

CUT COVER in one continuous piece.
  Height = book block height
  Width = roughly 5 times signature width + 2 times pleat width
          + spine thickness (between panels 3 and 4) + folding ease

5	4	3	2	1
FOLD TO INSIDE BACK	OUTSIDE BACK COVER	OUTSIDE FRONT COVER	INSIDE FRONT COVER	BACK (covered by 4 & 5)

SPINE   PLEAT

SCORE AND fold pleat between panel 1 and 2.

Follow *MAKE UP signatures,* p. 102, and remaining instructions except score only pleat folds and fore edge fold between panel 2 and 3 before stitching signatures.

CLOSE FOLDING cover over signature.
  Using the book block as a guide, score remaining folds.

Score fore edge between panels 2 and 3.

Score two lines for spine thickness, between panels 3 and 4.

Score back fore edge, between panels 4 and 5.

Panel 5 should end short of pleat to avoid binding. Trim if necessary.

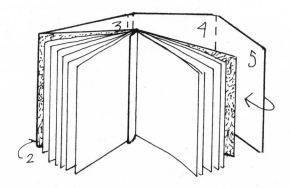

MINI BOOK WITH FABRIC BAG

If book is smaller than 1 1/2" the bag is hard to make.
Charm is lost when larger than 2 1/2".

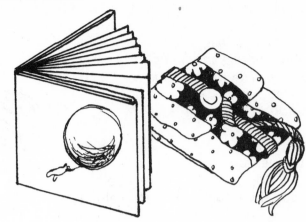

Materials for book:
Book block, lightweight paper
Outer leaf, medium weight paper
Cover, cover weight paper
Adhesive
Thread or staples

MAKE UP book block.

CUT OUTER leaf 1/4" smaller
than book block on all sides.

SEW LEAVES and outer leaf together
along the spine fold using butterfly
stitch, p. 91, or machine stitch.

If using a sewing machine, make the
longest stitch possible to avoid cutting
the paper. Pull threads to back.

Tie at each end of stitching, p. 226.

OUTER LEAF

CUT COVER.
Height = book block height
Width = 4 times book block width less 1/8"
This includes two extra panels folded
inside to the spine fold. These panels
conceal the outer leaf.

BRUSH ADHESIVE on outside of
outer leaf and attach book to
cover, centering along spine fold.
Smooth with folder.

Use waxed paper barriers to protect book
block while drying under light pressure.
Pasting help is given on p. 239.

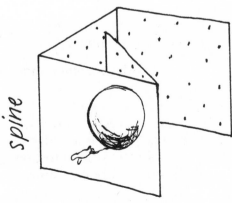

spine

FABRIC BAG FOR MINI BOOK

Bag lining can be a contrasting fabric as shown.
A ribbon and button hold the bag closed.

Materials for bag:
Fabric for bag and lining
Ribbon, 1/6" to 1/4" wide
Thread
Button

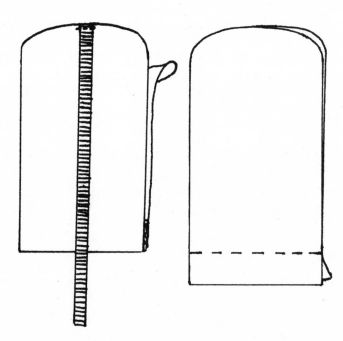

Easy measure:
Cut a strip of paper 3 times book
width. Place one end of strip along
book spine and wrap other end around
book, overlapping as shown.

Mark paper about two thirds of way across
the book. Add 1/2" to this measurement for seams.

1/4" seam allowance is used for all seams.
If fabric ravels easily, use wider seams and adjust measurements.

CUT MATERIALS.
   Bag, cut two, one is lining
   Length = 2 2/3 times book width
          + 2 times spine thickness + 1/2"
   Width = book height + 2 times spine thickness
          + 1/2" for seams
          + ease space to slip
            book in and out

Ribbon, cut one
Length = 1 1/2" longer than
            finished bag length

PLACE RIGHT sides together
   and sew end, as shown.

   Fold wrong sides together and
   press.

SEW RIBBON on open end of
   lining piece just in from edge
   seam allowance, ribbon resting
   on right side of fabric as shown.

MEASURE BOOK width from seam.
Mark width with pins on each side as shown.

FOLD FABRIC flap up at pins so that lining flap covers
one side, and outside fabric
covers the other,
shown at right.

LINING
FABRIC

PLACE RIBBON
inside. Lay extra
length along
lining fold as
shown and pin.

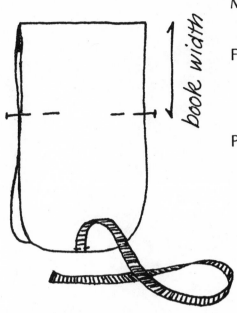

book width

FOLD LINING fabric up out of the way.
Pin outside fabric together as shown at right.
Sew outside layer, from D, just below seam,
to C at bottom fold. Remove pins.

Fold lining fabric down, covering outside
fabric and seams.

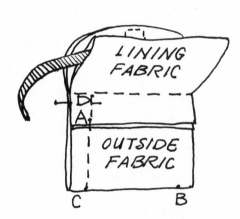

LINING
FABRIC

D
A

OUTSIDE
FABRIC

C   B

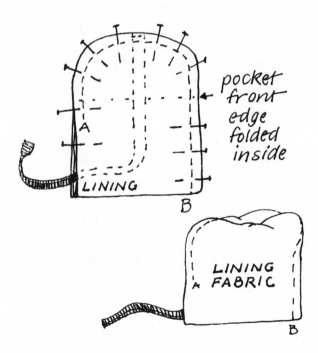

*pocket
front
edge
folded
inside*

A

LINING

B

LINING
FABRIC

B

PIN EDGES from A to B with ribbon free
inside as shown at left. Sew form A to B.
Remove pins leaving ribbon loose.

POKE IN top of flap
with fingers.
Pull ribbon to turn
bag right side out.

TURN OPEN edges under
and sew closed by hand.
Sew button to flap.

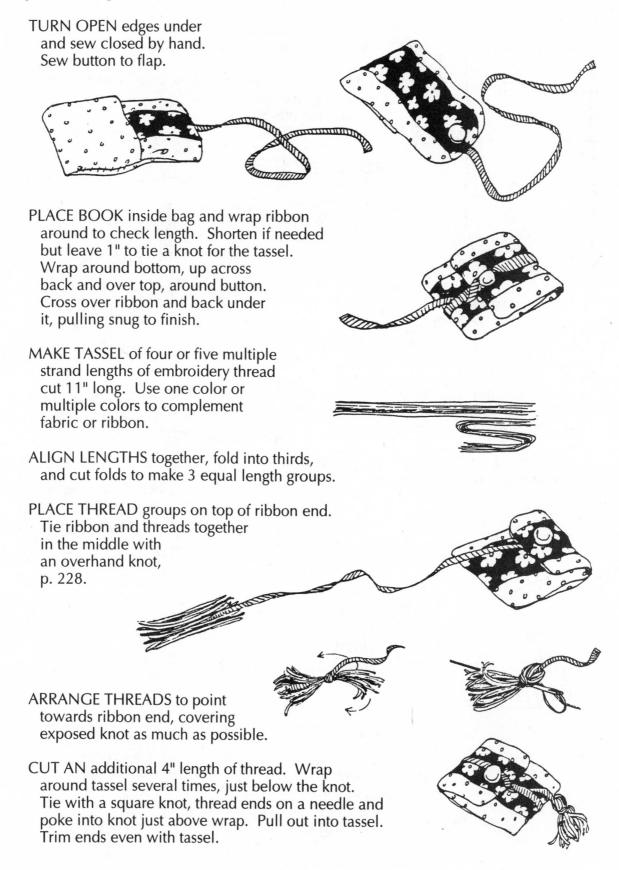

PLACE BOOK inside bag and wrap ribbon
around to check length. Shorten if needed
but leave 1" to tie a knot for the tassel.
Wrap around bottom, up across
back and over top, around button.
Cross over ribbon and back under
it, pulling snug to finish.

MAKE TASSEL of four or five multiple
strand lengths of embroidery thread
cut 11" long. Use one color or
multiple colors to complement
fabric or ribbon.

ALIGN LENGTHS together, fold into thirds,
and cut folds to make 3 equal length groups.

PLACE THREAD groups on top of ribbon end.
Tie ribbon and threads together
in the middle with
an overhand knot,
p. 228.

ARRANGE THREADS to point
towards ribbon end, covering
exposed knot as much as possible.

CUT AN additional 4" length of thread. Wrap
around tassel several times, just below the knot.
Tie with a square knot, thread ends on a needle and
poke into knot just above wrap. Pull out into tassel.
Trim ends even with tassel.

CASE BINDINGS

The case and signature are joined when hinge and endpaper paste downs, sewn with the signature, are pasted in covered boards.

SINGLE SIGNATURE CASE BINDING

Materials:
Single signature
Endpapers, paste downs
* plus optional fly leaves*
Hinge, p. 256
Binder board or similar board
Cover material, paper or cloth
Thread
Adhesive

Keep grain of all materials parallel with spine.

PREPARE SIGNATURE with end papers, paste downs, and fly leaves as desired.

Hinge, cut one
If book cloth is used as hinge, see size option on p. 256.
Width = about 2"
Length = signature height less 1/2"

COLLATE SIGNATURE with paste downs, fly leaves, and hinge. Be sure any pattern or texture is facing the right direction.

When using a book cloth hinge, sew with fabric side facing the signature.

MARK HOLE position and make holes.

SEW TOGETHER with butterfly stitch, p. 91.

MAKE CASE. When closed, signature must extend beyond boards at spine edge for cover to lie flat.

When measured and cut, boards should extend 1/8" beyond signature at head, tail, and fore edge, but not at spine edge. At the spine edge the signature should project 1/16" beyond the boards.

If signature is unusually thick, it should project more.

Caution: binder board edges are not square. Make a square corner to measure from, p. 237.

signature projects 1/16" at spine; board extends 1/8" at head, tail, and fore edge

Mark grain direction on board before cutting, p. 246.

CUT BOARDS with grain direction parallel with spine.
Cover, cut two
Height = signature height + 1/4"
Width = signature width + 1/16"

PREPARE RECESS in front board for label or design if desired, p. 246.

MAKE PAPER spacer to measure spine thickness. This is used to determine amount of space needed between boards when positioned on cover material. Set back cover board with spine edge slightly overhanging table edge. Place sewn signature on back board with 1/8" projecting at spine edge. This will leave 1/8" overlap at the fore edge if boards have been measured and cut correctly.

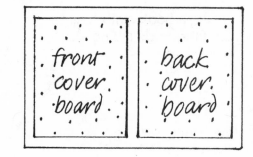

Carefully align. Add top board to match bottom board. Keeping all parts in place, wrap a strip of paper around spine edge.

Crease strip along board edge with thumb nail to mark where strip bends over both top and bottom boards. This method is more accurate than marking with a pencil.

Covering Material, one continuous piece
book cloth or paper
5/8" turn-in margin
Height = board height + 1 1/4"
Width = 2 board widths
+ spine thickness +1 1/4"

front cover board   back cover board

Spine Strip, cut one
This is not used if spine is less
than 1/4" wide.
bond paper
Height = board height
Width = 1/8" less than spine
    measurement on paper spacer

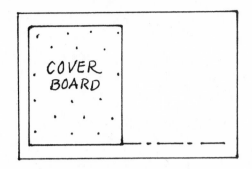

TURN CASE covering material underside up
    and draw 5/8" turn-in margin down the left
    side and along lower edge. Use a straight
    edge and triangle to make it square.

LINE UP straight edge along bottom turn-in
    line. Set one case board along corner lines.
    Draw along spine edge.

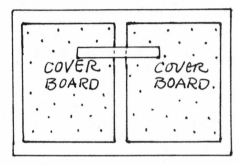

Set second board in place along straight
    edge using paper measure for placement.
    Draw along spine edge.

MOUNT BOARDS on case.
    Have plenty of waste paper ready when pasting boards, p. 239.

Brush adhesive on one case board.
With straight edge still along tail turn-in, carefully set board in place along straight
edge.

Press hand firmly in center of board; avoid
sliding hand. Press again firmly near each
corner.

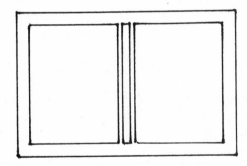

Spread adhesive on second board and set in
place. Press hand firmly, first in center and
then near each corner, being careful not to
slide hand.

Use the paper spacer to be sure gap for
spine is even and lower edges are against
the straight edge.

TURN CLOTH side up. Smooth with folder and protective paper, p. 240.

PASTE BOND paper spine strip in place, centering between boards.
    This gives a tailored look to the outside when finished.

Follow *STANDARD MITER*, p. 245, to finish case.

ENCASE SIGNATURE.
There are a number of ways to encase. One method is to hold signature together, upright centering between head, tail and boards.

Lay hinges down and trace around them.
Remove signature.

Spread adhesive in penciled area.
Reposition signature and fold
hinges down on adhesive area.

Protect signature with waxed
paper barrier and close book
to see if boards are aligned.
Adjust if necessary. Smooth
with folder and protective paper.

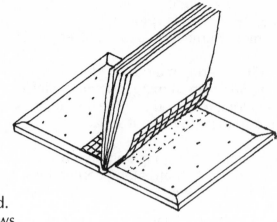

ADD FILLER to bare boards if desired.
Turn-ins can leave a ridge that shows
when endpapers are added.
Sometimes the color or pattern of
turn-ins will show through paste downs.
To even the surface and color texture,
use cover material as paste downs.

Cut filler to fit bare board area.
Spread adhesive on boards and
edges of filler.

Set in place, smooth with folder,
p. 240.

A piece of bond paper can be added
over the filler to cover any visible pattern.
Cut paper a little smaller than paste downs.

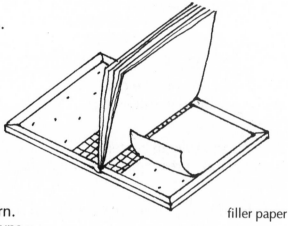

filler paper

PUT PASTE down endpapers in place.
Spread adhesive lightly on bare board or
filler area, hinge area, and edges of paste
down.

Ease paste down slowly in place from spine
to fore edge.

Smooth with folder and protective paper.
Repeat for other paste down.

PRESS OVERNIGHT to avoid warping,
p. 241. Protect signature from moisture
with waxed paper while adhesive dries.

CASING COMMERCIAL PAMPHLETS

Materials:
Same as Case Binding, p. 109,
*   using a paper covered single signature pamphlet*

REMOVE STAPLES from pamphlet.

Follow *PREPARE SIGNATURE* and remaining directions
for *SINGLE SIGNATURE CASE BINDING*, p. 109, except:
Use pamphlet as signature.
Cut fly leaves and paste down.
Pamphlet cover can be used as a fly leaf or discarded.
Use holes already in pamphlet for stitching.

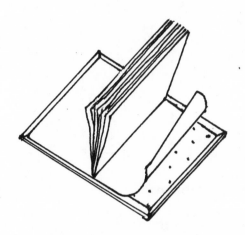

HALF AND QUARTER BINDINGS

"Half" and "quarter" are names given to binding styles that use two materials.
Traditionally, leather was the material of choice. To save money a less expensive material
was substituted. Leather was only used on parts receiving the most wear.
Full or whole bindings styles use the same covering material over the entire case.

TRY SOMETHING less traditional with wild and imaginative colors and textures.

USE PAPER patterns for proportion
  decisions before cutting.

Follow *MAKE CASE* and *MAKE PAPER
spacer,* p. 110, to measure spine thickness.

MAKE PENCIL lines on boards to
  indicate placement of first cover
  material. Boards are set in place
  along straight edge, as on p. 111,
  only here cover material is placed
  over boards. This allows the
  design to be seen while putting
  case together.

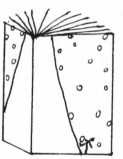

APPLY BOOK cloth first. Place
  paper overlapping cloth by 1/4".

Finish turn-ins for spine, then each additional piece of material as it is put on.

MULTIPLE SIGNATURE BINDINGS

The transition from scroll texts to codices came about early in the evolution of books. Originally the name codex, (from the Latin meaning a tree trunk or stem stripped of bark), was applied to two or more tablets of wood, metal or ivory hinged together with rings. The insides were covered with wax which could be written on with a stylus. The term was later used to describe books of this format made of either papyrus or animal skin. Papyrus codices were folded leaves usually bound by a cord laced through holes stabbed along the spine edge of the book in much the same manner as a side sewn oriental binding.

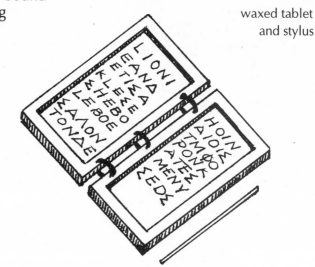

waxed tablet
and stylus

Animal skin was sewn through holes in the folds of the leaves.

For a period of time, papyrus was considered the superior material.

As a heavier more vulgar material, animal skin competed with waxed tablets rather than papyrus. Skin was used for wills, account books, and notes. When surface preparation improved, skin became superior.

Codex form had the advantage of greater convenience for continuous reading or reference, and its size could be increased at will. Several methods for sewing more than one signature together are covered in this section along with soft cover suggestions.

GENERAL INFORMATION

Brief notes on grain, signatures, endpapers, fore edge, shadows, holes, thread, sewing, and knots are given at the beginning of Single Signature chapter, page 90 and 91. These notes also apply to this chapter.

SIGNATURES SEWN WITH FOUR NEEDLES

Materials:
Four signatures of text weight paper
Four needles
Thread, 9 times spine length

RENDER SIGNATURES.
   Several pages of first and last signatures are left blank for use with School Book Cover,
   p. 119. With text weight paper, plan three pages to hold book block in cover and
   one as a fly leaf. For crisp folds, press signatures overnight under a heavy book or
   weights, p. 241.

MAKE TEMPLATE for placing sewing holes, p. 243.
   For a spine length approximately 6" long, head
   and tail holes should be 1 1/4" in from edges.

   Inner holes are placed 3/4" to 1" inside the
   outer holes. These distances will change
   with a longer or shorter spine length.
   Use your eye as a guide for proportion.

MAKE HOLES in one signature at a time.
   Open signature, align template, and
   poke holes.

COLLATE SIGNATURES.
   Stack upside down with last page on top,
   tail to left. Place on the left side of work
   area. The last signature will be sewn first.

Thread, cut two
Length = 4 times spine length
               + enough at each end
                    to tie square knot

JOIN LENGTHS in middle with
   Chinese Butterfly Knot to form
   four free ends, p. 227.

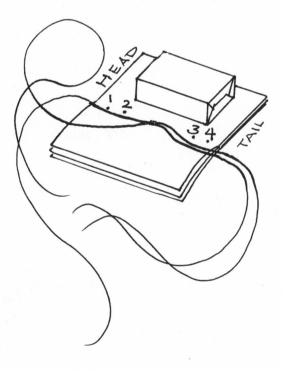

FLIP TOP signature over,
   tail to the right. Open.
   Weight back or clip, p. 134.

PLACE KNOT in center of fold.
   Thread needles on each thread end,
   two needles for head holes and two
   for tail holes.

   Sew, with head to the left, stitching
   threads 1 and 2 through holes 1 and 2;
   threads 3 and 4 through holes 3 and 4.
   Keep knot in middle.

LINK SIGNATURES together.
Close sewn signature and put next signature in sequence on top of it, with head to the left.

Line up pages and place clips or weight on back half again.

Thread from hole 1 of first sewn signature goes into hole 1 and out through hole 2 of new signature.

Thread from hole 2 of first sewn signatures goes into hole 2 and out hole 1 of new signature.

Repeat procedure with holes 3 & 4.

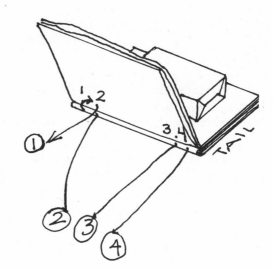

PULL THREADS snug with each new signature.

If a needle pierces a thread in sewing, the threads will not pull snug and must be redone.

CONTINUE SEWING until all signatures have been added.

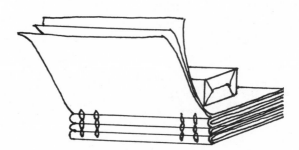

TIE OFF sewing threads as follows, threads should be inside top signature.

Remove needles. Tie threads 1 & 2 in a square knot at hole 2. Tie threads 3 & 4 at hole 3. Bring both pairs to center between knots and tie again in a square knot.

Trim threads and fray ends.

FINISHED BOOK block can be housed in School Book Cover on the following page or in Non-adhesive Cover With Tabs, p. 127.

SOFT WRAP, shown on p. 131, is a great companion for this book. The combination makes a lovely gift book or guest book for a special occasion. Coordinate materials.

SCHOOL BOOK COVERS

Remember these?
They are easily made from a variety of papers and require no adhesive.
They can be used with single or multiple signature and accordion strip book blocks.

The number of blank pages needed to hold
book in cover is determined by paper weight.
The same number of pages slip into both the
front and back cover.

Materials:
Art papers, wall papers, gift wrap,
Kraft papers etc.

Blank Pages, to hold book in cover
required at *both front and back:*
Lightweight papers require 4 pages
Medium weight papers require 2 pages
Heavyweight papers require1 page
Accordion strips use 3 panels

When paper has a tendency to break in folding, waxing before folding reduces this
tendency, p. 247.

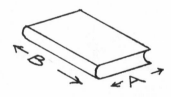

SIDE A = 4 times book block
     width plus spine thickness

SIDE B = a little more than
     2 times book block height

MEASURE AND cut cover material as shown.
  Measurement hints are given on p. 245.
  Grain direction of paper should parallel
  book block spine.

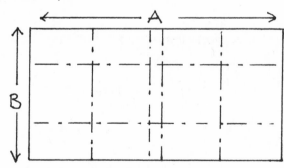

Paper will overlap when folded.
This adds strength. However,
if heavyweight paper is used,
eliminate overlap to avoid lumps.

SCORE SPINE lines and fold.

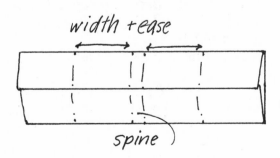

SET BOOK block against spine and score fore edge, using book block as placement guide. Allow slight ease.

CUT NARROW wedges from vertical folds to about 1/8" away from horizontal fold lines as shown. This helps cover to be smooth.

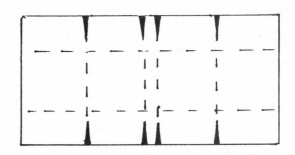

CUT SHALLOW curve from papers the weight of Canson Mi Teintes or heavier. This removes bulk from each end, allowing cover to lie flat and smooth.

FOLD COVER. Insert blank pages into first and last cover panels.

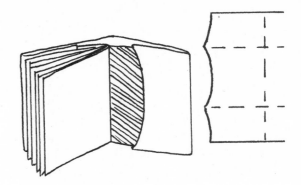

SIGNATURES AND COVER
SEWN WITH TWO NEEDLES

This style is adapted from a Japanese binding developed in the Heian period, ninth to twelfth century. It opens completely flat making it easy to use as a journal or sketch book. Cover material is visible along spine edge of each outside signature and in gutter margins, providing a decorative surprise.

When open, sewing is visible along gutter folds providing another surprise.

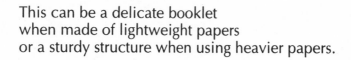

This can be a delicate booklet when made of lightweight papers or a sturdy structure when using heavier papers.

Materials
5 signatures with untrimmed fore edges
2 cover material pieces
2 end sheets
2 pieces heavyweight paper as cover inserts to stiffen covers
Adhesive
Thread, e.g. #8 perlé cotton, about 10 times spine length
Long fiber paper strip for reinforcing spine edge, optional

MAKE UP SIGNATURES.

Two parent size sheets of paper, folded into octavo size, p. 233, yields five signatures, four having three leaves each, and one with four leaves. Use the same number in each signature or make the middle one larger. Long fiber papers minimize tearing in the spine edge sewing holes.

MAKE TEMPLATE for sewing holes.

Divide spine height in thirds.
Divide each outside third in half.

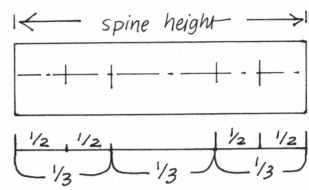

CUT MATERIALS.

Cover boards, cut two
sized to be flush with book block
Height = spine height
Width = book block width

Covering Material, cut two
5/8" turn-ins at head, tail,
and fore edges, 1 1/8" at spine edge
Height = spine height + 1 1/4"
Width = book block width + 1 2/3"
Reinforcing strip, cut two
Height = spine height
Width = 3/4"

Endpapers, cut two
Height = spine height + 1/2"
Width = book block width + 1/4"

Cover inserts, cut two
Height = a little less than spine height
Width = a little less than cover width

FOLD 1/2" strip along spine edge to the inside to make a double layer. Open, apply reinforcing strip over fold line.

PASTE 1/2" section in place on inside of cover piece.

PLACE LAST signature on inside of cover material. Wrap 1/4" of spine edge turn-in over signature edge to establish spine edge fold. Fore edge turn-in is wider than spine edge turn-in.

TRIM CORNERS of cover material off spine edge turn-in at head and tail, to fit signature as shown. Take care to keep spine turn-in even with signature length.

BRUSH ADHESIVE on 1/2" turn-in and paste to signature spine edge. Place 1/4" along the inside edge of signature as folded before. Smooth in place.

REPEAT FOR second outside signature.

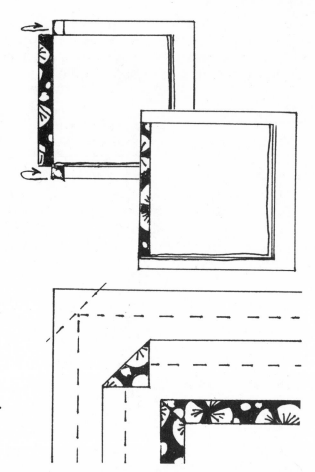

FOLD CORNERS of cover into triangles just beyond turn-in border, as shown.

FOLD IN turn-ins to book block size at head, tail, and fore edge.

POKE HOLES matching signature holes through cover material on both covers.

COMPLETE COVER after sewing.

DIVIDE THREAD in two equal lengths, about five times the spine height. Tie two ends together with a temporary knot, leaving tails 5" to 7" long. Thread two needles with the free ends and sew as show in diagram.

STITCHING BEGINS and ends inside middle signature. Follow illustrations moving in and out signatures in pattern shown. Stitch 1-8, shown as top half of column. Avoid piercing thread when reusing a hole. Double stitches will be visible inside second and fourth signatures.

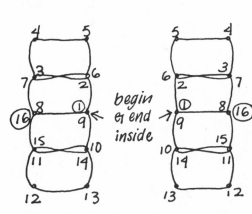

PULL THREAD taut at holes 6 and 8. Inside middle signature where stitching began at hole 8, tie short end of thread in temporary knot around a needle. This makes it easier to untie later. Stitch 1-8 in second column in same fashion, also making temporary knot around another needle when thread returns to hole 8.

CONTINUE ADDING signatures stitching 9-16, pulling thread taut at holes 14 and 16.

SLIP OUT temporary knot and tie threads with a half hitch at holes 1 and 9, p. 226.

STITCH SECOND column, 9-16, in the same manner.

Gather all threads together in middle and tie with square knot. Finish by slipping one set of thread ends under tail stitch and tie as shown. Repeat with other set of threads at head.

Trim ends even.

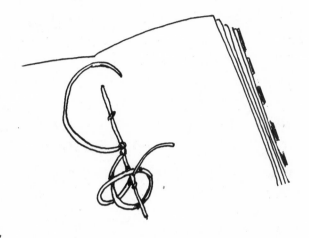

COMPLETE COVER.
End papers have 1/4" turn-ins at head, tail, and fore edge. Fold in all edges to make them 1/16" smaller than cover size.

Follow *FOLD CORNERS* and *FOLD IN turn-ins*, p. 122. The diagonal fold may be cut away to eliminate bulk, if needed.

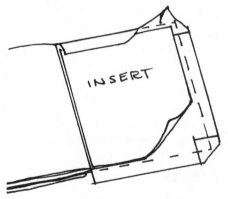

PLACE INSERTS under folded cover turn-ins before endpapers are pasted in place.

BRUSH ADHESIVE on endpaper turn-ins and attach to covers.

The spine edge will have no turn-in.

Smooth in place with folder.

DRY OVERNIGHT under light pressure, p. 241.

SIGNATURES SEWN ON TAPES

This has been a traditional method for holding signatures in a case binding. This method is attractive and works well with soft covers, e.g. Non-adhesive Cover, p. 127. When tapes are deliberately left long, they become decorative as well as structural.

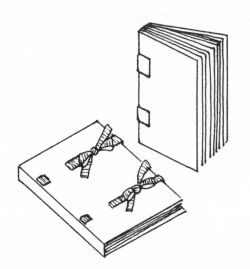

BASIC BOOK ON TAPES IN SCHOOL BOOK COVER

Materials:
Paper for Signatures, all weights
Bookbinding tape, twill tape or ribbon
Thread

MAKE UP signatures. Blank pages from the first and last signatures tuck under turn-ins to hold book block in the non-adhesive cover. The number of pages needed is determined by paper weight, see p. 119.

PLAN NUMBER of tapes to be used. This will depend on spine height and tape pattern desired in the cover. Plan and accurately draw the design on a page-size paper pattern. Later, this pattern will be used to mark the slits cut in cover. Tapes need to be long enough to wrap the spine and extend the width of a page.

Additional length is needed if tapes are to reach beyond the cover fore edge. Tapes can be as long as desired. Tie tapes as a closure; string with beads, knot, or leave plain.

COLLATE, STACK, and square signatures.

MAKE TEMPLATE, p. 243, with the following sewing hole placement:
A kettle stitch hole is placed 1/2" to 5/8" in from both head and tail.
Next holes are placed 1/2" from kettle stitch holes.
Last holes are placed one tape width plus enough ease so tape won't bind, shown on next page.

MARK HOLE placement and make holes in each signature, p. 243.

Thread length used = height of spine times number of signatures
+ enough extra for kettle stitches and knots

CUT THREAD into practical lengths. Thread wears thin and tangles if too long. Add
new thread length inside a signature as needed; use a weaver's or square knot, p. 124.

PLACE SIGNATURES upside down and to left of work area with tail to left as shown on
page 117. Flip top signature over, open with head to the left. Weight or clip in place
for sewing, shown on pp. 117-118 and 134.

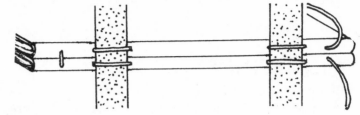

BEGIN SEWING at far right
tail hole, a kettle stitch hole.
Sew thread from outside
of signature to the inside,
leaving a few inches of
thread loose outside the hole.

Come out of signature at right side of first tape. Go in again on left side of tape.
Continue along spine in this manner until last hole on the left is reached, (head kettle
stitch hole). Move next signature into position on top of one just sewn.

Move up into kettle stitch hole on left end of this signature and out again at tape hole.
Move over tape and into signature again on other side of tape.
Continue down spine. Keep thread tension even at all times.

At last hole, (tail kettle stitch hole on right),
tie beginning thread tail to sewing
thread with a square knot.
Position next signature. Continue
to left (head) as before. At end of
third signature, use a kettle stitch
to link signatures together.

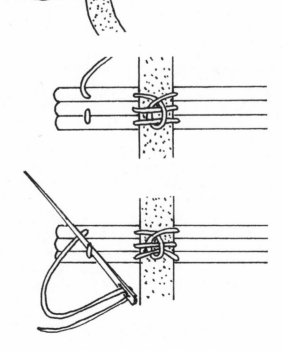

Sometimes it is easier to place tapes in
position after sewing first two signatures,
before sewing a third signature.

LINK THREADS across tapes in groups. Make
a loop every second or third signature. Pass
the needle under the crossing threads first,
then over them and under the beginning of
the loop. Pull loop tight drawing threads
together as shown.

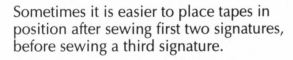

Eight signatures may be divided into 3, 2,
and 3 groupings or 4 and 4 groupings.

MAKE KETTLE stitch. Pass needle under
thread linking two lower signatures together
and over sewing thread as shown. This
forms a loop to link the new signature.

CONTINUE LINKING signatures
together with a kettle stitch at
both ends of each signature.

FINISH PATTERN with two or
three kettle stitches made over the
last kettle stitch and cut off excess thread.

PLACE BOOK in School Book Cover, p. 119.

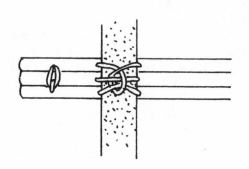

OPEN SPINE COVER ON TAPES

The cover is treated as a signature and
is sewn with the book block on tapes.

Materials:
Materials list on p. 124
Cover of heavyweight paper

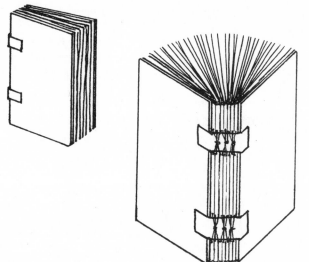

Cover, cut two
  Height = book block height
  Width = 2 1/4 times book block width

SCORE AND fold panels 1 and 2
  to fit book block flush.
  Use extra width for panel 3.

SEW BOOK block and covers on tapes.
  Sew thread ends back through first and
  last holes to inside. Tie double half
  hitch around thread to finish, p. 226.

CUT SLITS for tapes in panel 2. Position
  tape slits in line with tape sewing holes.
  Make them close but far enough away
  so they will not tear.

WEAVE TAPES in panels. Tapes can go
  through panels 1 and 2 or just panel 2.
  Weaving through both panels makes tapes
  visible inside the cover as well as outside.
  Anchor tapes inside covers with adhesive.

FINISH COVER by pasting panel 3 to panel 1.

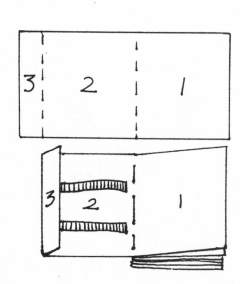

NON-ADHESIVE COVER WITH TABS

Blank pages at the front and back of the book block hold this book in the cover.
Tapes woven through slits in the cover can be used as decoration and also will help hold
book block more securely.

This cover can be used for
book blocks sewn with four
needles. With modifications
it can also be used for single
signatures.

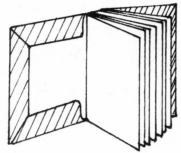

The number of blank pages
needed to hold book in
cover is determined by
paper weight.
The same number of pages
slip into both the front and back cover.

Materials:
Cover, heavyweight paper or a paper bond
Adhesive
Kraft paper to plan cover pattern

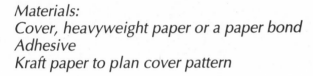

Blank Pages, to hold book in cover
required at *both front and back:*
Lightweight papers require 4 pages
Medium weight papers require 2 pages
Heavyweight papers require 1 page

PLAN COVER dimensions. The best way to solve problems of size, fit, and proportion
is to make a trial pattern. A Kraft paper bag works well for this. This pattern will be
used later for designing weaving pattern.

Make all turn-ins the same width. Turn-in size will vary with size of book block.
Anything narrower than 1" is not usually practical.

Cover Paper, cut one
   Height = book block height
         + 2 times turn-in width
   Width = 2 times book block width + spine thickness
         + 2 times turn-in width

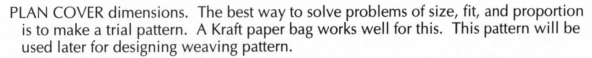

TREAT COVER paper to protect from dirt if desired, p. 247.

CUT AND fold Kraft paper pattern as directed for actual cover.
   When cover material is heavier than Kraft paper, plan for more folding ease.

DRAW LINES on inside of cover as shown.

Spine thickness is a dotted line, book width and height are solid lines.

Ease lines are dotted lines for space used in folding, about 1/16" with heavyweight paper.

Test a paper scrap to see what is needed.

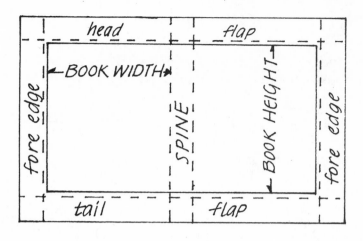

Draw lines just outside book perimeter and extend to cover's edges. Allow for ease space along spine fold lines and perimeter fold lines. Score and fold all dotted lines.

MARK CORNER miters with dotted lines at each corner, (45° angle, AB).

MAKE TABS about 1/4" wide at head and tail corners along the diagonal as shown.

To prevent binding, remove narrow wedge from fore edge turn-ins as shown on large pattern on the following page.

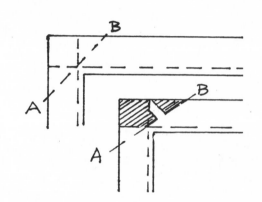

DRAW BELL shaped curve at spine head and tail. Cut line of curve only to intersection of spine thickness line and ease fold line.

Do not cut bell shape away. Fold to inside of the cover.

A single signature cover version is given on p. 95.

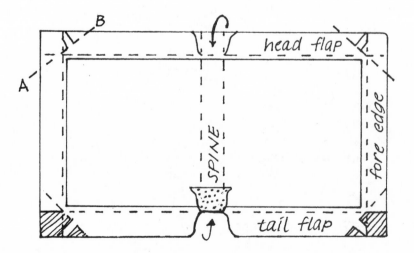

Fold bell shape in over spine as shown

PATTERN FOR NON-ADHESIVE BOOK COVER

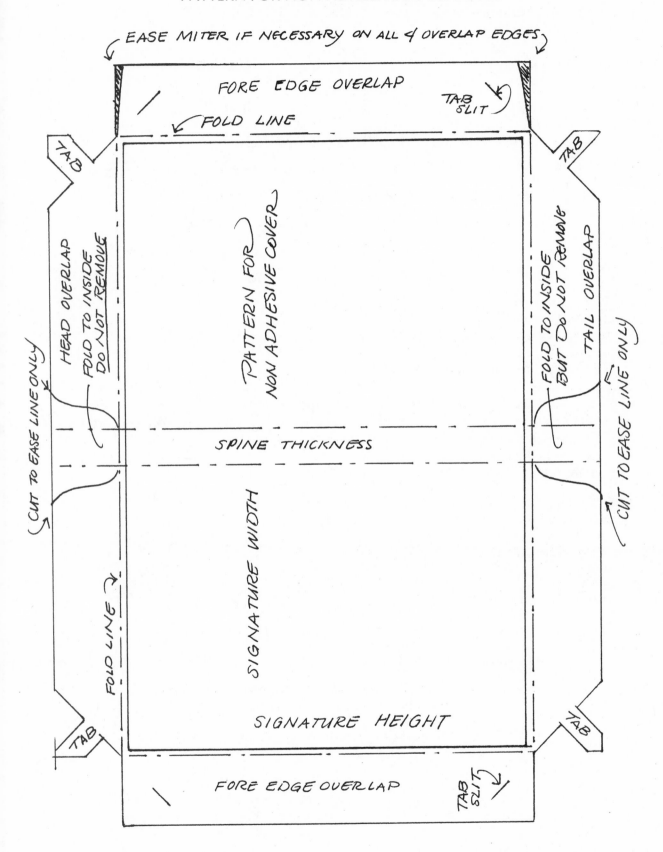

EASE MITER IF NECESSARY ON ALL 4 OVERLAP EDGES

FORE EDGE OVERLAP

FOLD LINE

TAB SLIT

TAB

HEAD OVERLAP

FOLD TO INSIDE DO NOT REMOVE

CUT TO EASE LINE ONLY

PATTERN FOR NON ADHESIVE COVER

TAB

FOLD TO INSIDE BUT DO NOT REMOVE

TAIL OVERLAP

CUT TO EASE LINE ONLY

SPINE THICKNESS

SIGNATURE WIDTH

FOLD LINE

TAB

SIGNATURE HEIGHT

TAB

FORE EDGE OVERLAP

TAB SLIT

MAKE TAB slits in fore edge turn-ins. Place book over spine and fold down pages that belong inside cover turn-ins on one side of cover. Fold in fore edge turn-in, then fold in head and tail turn-ins.

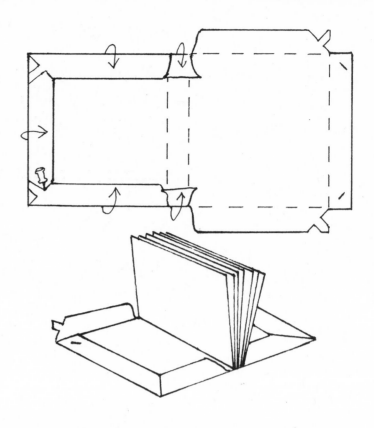

With a push pin, make a hole on either side of tab on turn-ins at corners as shown. Repeat for other side of cover.

Remove book and open cover tomake slits from hole to hole.

Follow *CUTTING SLITS FOR TAPES,* p. 235, to make slits in cover. For amore finished look, cut slits on outside of cover, p. 235. Do both front and back.

PLAN WEAVING pattern for tapes on Kraft paper pattern if desired. Cut turn-ins off practice cover. To prevent confusion, mark head and spine edges on the pattern. Line up pattern on inside of cover along solid fold lines. Slits are needed at spine fold lines plus where necessary for desired pattern.

Front and back patterns do not need to match. A difference in pattern helps distinguish front from back.

paper pattern inside cover

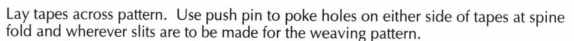

An odd number of slits finishes the tape outside the cover.

An even number finishes inside.

Lay tapes across pattern. Use push pin to poke holes on either side of tapes at spine fold and wherever slits are to be made for the weaving pattern.

Use the cover pattern and push pin to mark slit placement for weaving tapes. Make slits.

WEAVE TAPES through slits with book in cover.
A needle or push pin is useful to coax tapes through slits.

MAKE TAPES visible inside for an optional
decorative surprise. Cut book block
slits in pages to match cover slits
using cover pattern for slit
placement.

Weave cover tapes
through pages and cover.

TRIM TAPE ends to remove
fraying threads when finished.

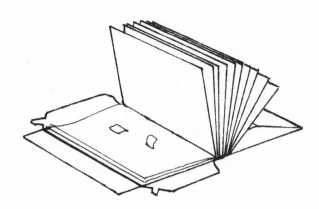

HOLD TAPES in place with a dab of adhesive. Beginning with inside back cover, dab
adhesive under each tape between outermost slit and fore edge. Press tape down with
hand, then fold book block closed over back cover. Adjust tape tension in front cover
while holding rest of book block in place with hand. Repeat dabs of adhesive for
front tapes. Close book. Dry overnight under pressure, p. 241, with spine extended
beyond the pressing boards to avoid squashing.

PAPER BACK BOOKS

Use Non-adhesive Covers for
paper back books. Slip covers
under the turn-ins to hold
book in the cover.

A SOFT WRAP FOR
BOOKS IN THIS CHAPTER

The Self Closing Folder, p. 147, made with
coordinating colors with papers or book cloth
to match a book in this chapter, makes an
unusual gift.

Nice for a guest or a wedding book.

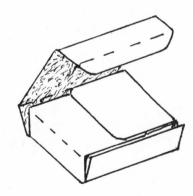

LONG STITCH BINDINGS

A visible sewing pattern on the spine holds the cover and book block together. This form of binding was used for European clerical and blank books of the fourteenth through the sixteenth centuries.

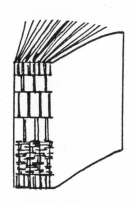 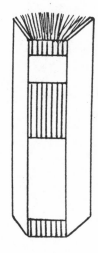

Long stitches can be interwoven with secondary patterns of multicolored or matching thread.
Decorative stitching can be added to vary sewing patterns. Stitching can be functional or purely decorative.

This style serves well as a journal or sketch book, since binding allows the book to open flat. It can be used equally by both left and right handed writers.

BASIC COVER

Materials:
Book block, several single signatures
Cover Material, heavyweight paper or paper bonds, book cloth bonded with paper
Thread, linen, perlé cotton, etc.

MAKE UP signatures, collate, and stack.

PLAN STITCHING pattern for spine.
 A series of slits are cut along the spine for stitches to pass through.
 An odd number of slits gives an overall pattern.
 An even number of slits forms a pattern with open space between every other slit.

 Top and bottom slits are 1/3" to 3/4" in from spine head and tail. The rest of the slits can be any chosen pattern.

 Draw spine shape and experiment with patterns or use one shown here.
 A thick book block and a large number of signatures give more spine pattern.

MAKE PRACTICE book out of manila file folders to take the mystery out of sewing.
 This will be time well spent. Cut up folders for signatures and for a cover. Use a single leaf as a signature. Sew with planned pattern.

MAKE TEMPLATE to fit spine measurements. Mark stitching pattern on template with
  pencil.   Be sure each line is at right angles to vertical of spine. Mark top.

These patterns are for five signatures.

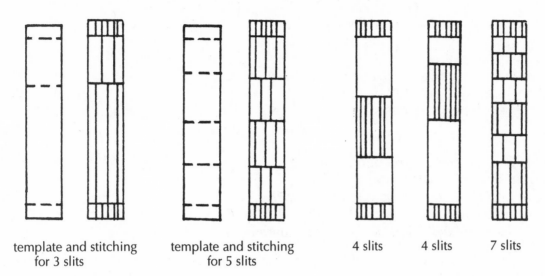

template and stitching   template and stitching   4 slits   4 slits   7 slits
       for 3 slits   for 5 slits

Cover, cut one
flush head and tail, 1/8" fore edge overhang
Height = book block height
Width = 2 times signature width
        + spine thickness + 1/4"

MEASURE SPINE thickness, p. 238.
  When signatures are not compressed enough,
  they twist and slide inside the cover. When too
  tightly compressed, the book will not close well;
  the book will gap at fore edge and the spine will
  be pinched.

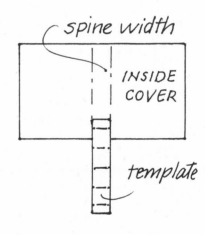

MARK SPINE with stitching pattern on inside of
  cover. Place template on spine section and
  poke holes at ends of all pattern lines. Score
  cover fold lines along edge of template.

Follow *CUTTING SLITS FOR TAPES,*
p. 235, to make slits.

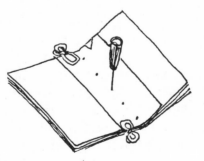

FOLD TEMPLATE in half lengthwise and
  center it in fold of open signature, align
  head and tail. Poke holes in signature
  folds as indicated by template slits.

Follow *MAKE HOLES* and *COLLATE SIGNATURES,* p. 117.

FLIP TOP signature over, tail to the right. Open and align signature spine fold with cover. Be sure both signature and cover have tail facing the same direction. Each signature will be flipped into sewing position in this way.

CLIP TWO scraps of board near fold, placing one outside the cover and one inside next to the holes as shown. Clip 3" of sewing thread inside cover between cover and signature. This end will be tied off after second signature has been sewn.

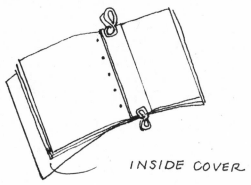

INSIDE COVER

MEASURE THREAD. The book will use about one spine length per signature, plus enough to tie a square knot. However, it is best to sew with practical lengths. Add new lengths as needed using weaver's or square knot inside the signature, p. 226.

BEGIN SEWING between cover and signature at tail hole. Bring thread into signature, outside to inside.
Go over tail at spine and enter closest slit. Return thread through same beginning hole.
Pull thread taut.

If needle pierces thread in hole, it is not possible to pull thread taut.

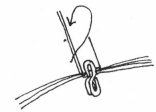

REMOVE SLACK in thread after last stitch of each signature. Pull each exposed stitch along the spine, beginning at stitch furthest from needle.

To prevent tearing at the holes, pull thread parallel with signature rather than out at a right angle to fold, shown on p. 242.

SEW THREAD out next hole and through next cover slit. Continue along spine, passing through each hole and slit in sequence.

PASS THREAD over end of spine at head and tail of each signature. This adds strength and enhances the design. When a row ends outside on the spine, go over the head or tail and back in the same signature hole and cover slit for an extra loop. When a row ends inside of signature, thread will loop over top when next signature is added.

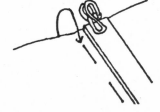

TO ADD a signature, unclip inside board and close sewn signature.
  Place next signature on top of closed one. Open new signature and clamp it to the
  closed one, aligning edges. Be sure thread end is still secured.
  Enter new signature and continue sewing.

  Thread is not visible in every space along a signature fold.
  Every other signature will repeat the same visible thread pattern.

TIE BEGINNING thread end to main sewing thread between cover and first signature,
  after sewing second signature. After thread has passed over end of spine and in
  through slit, pull slack from thread and tie with a square knot. Continue sewing until
  all signatures have been added.

FINISH BY going over spine end into a slit. Tie thread end around nearest row of
  threads, between cover and signatures, with double half hitches, p. 226.
  Pass thread under signatures to back of book and tie again around second row of
  stitches. Pass thread back under, trim and fray end.

WRAP-AROUND VARIATION
The back cover width is extended to wrap book block fore edge and end on top of the
front cover. If extension is long enough, no closure is needed. A ribbon or cord closure
is added through a slit in the flap fold.

Materials:
Material list on p. 132 with
Cover, book cloth bonded with paper, 239
Closure if desired

  Cover, cut one
  H = book block height
  W = 2 times book block width + 2 times spine
  thickness + ease + front flap width + 5/8" turn-in

  Decorative turn-in variations
  folded to the outside can be much wider than 5/8".
  They can also be trimmed at an angle. Use your eye as a guide to proportion.

SEW CLOSURE button or similar device for securing a tie to the cover before flap is
  pasted down. Handmade buttons and cords are found on pp. 228-231.

CASE BINDING VARIATION

A short spine, 3 1/2" to 5" high, is charming.
Cover can be made flush or with an overhang.

Materials:
Same as Basic Cover, p. 132,
 except cover material:
Binder board
Spine reinforcing strip
 e.g. manila folder
Book cloth
Endpaper paste downs
Adhesive

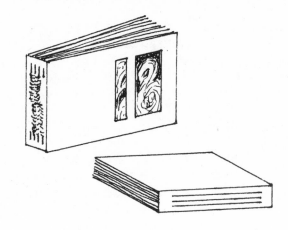

MAKE UP signatures, collate and stack.

CUT MATERIALS.
 Boards
 Overhang or Flush, one set only
 Overhang 1/8" at head, tail, and fore edge, cut two
 Height = book block height + 1/4"
 Width = book block width + 1/16"
  The book block must project beyond spine edge, see Make Case, p. 110.

 Flush Boards, cut two
 Height = book block height
 Width = book block width less 1/16"

 Case Covering
 Book cloth, cut in one piece
 Height = board height + 1 1/4"
 Width = 2 times board width + spine thickness + 1 1/4"
  measure spine thickness to determine space needed, p. 110

 Spine lining, cut one
 same book cloth as case covering
 Height = 1/8" less than board height
 Width = spine thickness measurement + 1 1/4"
  (5/8" material will lap boards on both sides)

 Endpaper paste downs, cut two
 Height = book block height
 Width = book block width minus 1/8"

 Reinforcement piece of heavyweight paper, cut one
 Height = spine height
 Width = slightly less than spine area width to prevent binding

Follow *MAKE CASE,* pp. 110-111, except: add paper reinforcement to spine.

Follow *LINE BOARDS 2 and 4,* p. 222, to add cloth spine lining before mitering corners and turning in. Set in place over paper rather than a board as shown in illustration.

Follow *BRUSH ADHESIVE,* p. 223, to mount end paper paste downs.

DRY CASE overnight under light pressure, p. 241.

PLAN STITCHING pattern for spine. When cover has an overhang, a slit line is needed for thread return over the top of the signature into the spine.

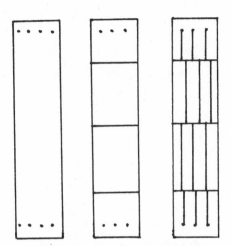

    Make slit 1/8" in from top and bottom of spine, 1/8" of the cover will be visible above and below the sewing as shown at right. A series of holes can be used in place of a slit, one hole for each signature. Placement must be precise.

    In flush cover patterns shown below, the thread passes over the edge of the cover and spine at the beginning and (or) end of each signature.

Follow *PLAN STITCHING pattern,* p. 132, to place signature holes. Continue instructions through p. 135 to stitch book block, omitting cover information.

Follow *PUT PASTE down,* p. 112, to finish book.

DECORATIVE PATTERNS FOR LONG STITCH BINDINGS

Combining different stitches makes many patterns possible.

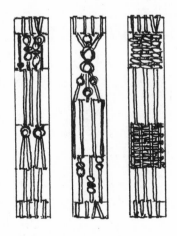

LONG STITCHES build parallel patterns as well as hold a book block in a cover.

KETTLE STITCHES are holding or transition stitches from one signature to the next.

WEAVE THREAD or add beads for decoration on covers. The pattern can be used to indicate the binding top.

    To add thread for weaving, lay a 1 1/2" length along an exposed long stitch. Weave over and under as if the two were one.

ADD BEADS as signatures are sewn in cover. They can also be added during weaving.

FALSE PATTERNS can be sewn
along the spine before primary
sewing begins. They are only
for decoration and do not
hold signatures in place.
Large cross stitches are an
example of false patterns.

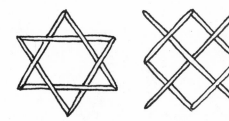

KETTLE STITCHES can be arranged in patterns along the spine, to vary a long stitch
binding pattern. They can be used on either soft or case covers. Stitching is through a
series of holes made in the spine instead of through slits.
The long stitches are not always visible when used with kettle stitches along a spine.

CALCULATE NUMBER of holes needed by adding up the number of signatures. For
long stitches, half the total is needed because two signatures usually use one set of
holes. The number of kettle stitch holes is usually half the total number of signatures
plus one additional hole for an anchor stitch.
The move up, when adding a signature, happens at alternate ends.

PLACE HOLES far enough apart to prevent tearing into each other when working out a
kettle stitch pattern. This is easiest with a thick spine.

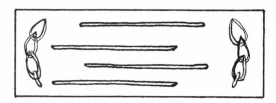 

STAGGER HOLES or place them on a curve to avoid tearing.

LONG STITCH AND
KETTLE STITCH PATTERN
Use eight signatures for this pattern.

MAKE PRACTICE book out of manila file folders to take the mystery out of sewing.
This will be time well spent. Cut up folders for signatures and for a cover. Use a
single leaf as a signature. Sew with planned pattern.

MAKE KETTLE stitch in sequence when moving from right to left. Do not make them
when moving from left to right. A-5, D-5, and G-5 are anchor holes to begin the
kettle stitch. Two signatures share the holes in rows 1 through 4.

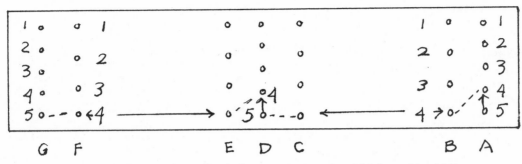

Note rows G, D, A have five holes. Rows F, E, C, and B have four holes.

BEGIN INSIDE last signature at right end of spine with spine edge facing you.
Move out through signature and cover hole at A-5.
Return through spine and signature at A-4 and make anchor stitch. Continue out through signature and spine at B-4.

Tie thread tail around stitch inside signature with double half hitch, p. 226.
Continue along, in through cover and signature at hole C-4 and out through hole D-5 and in signature and cover hole D-4 for another anchor stitch.

Continue along row moving out hole E-4, in hole F-4, and out hole G-5.

Add next signature, move in spine hole G-4, for anchor stitch, and into hole G of new signature. Sew from left to right along row 4 moving in and out of holes in row, skipping hole in row D.

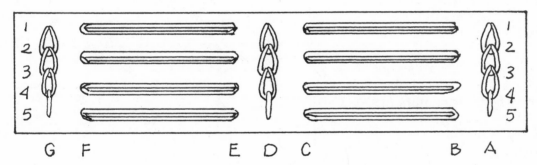

MAKE KETTLE stitch at right end of row 4 by moving out of hole A-3, looping around anchor stitch at hole A-4 and back in at hole A-3. Add new signature and sew into it in row A.

Continue pattern along row 3, from right to left, making a kettle stitch at row D and row G, as before, in stitching first signature.

Pick up a new signature as before in stitching the second signature.
Sew from left to right using holes of row 3 for new signature and skipping over row D.
Continue pattern, adding new signatures, until pattern is complete.

Finish on the inside of the last signature with a double half hitch around the stitch at A and B in row 1.

KETTLE STITCH PATTERN ON A CENTER DIAGONAL

Long stitches are hidden.
The pattern shown uses eight signatures with three holes in each fold. They are placed to match the end holes and diagonal holes in the cover spine.

The spine has a diagonal row of eight holes bordered by a row of five holes at the head and tail.

Anchor stitches are made at holes ABC as first signature is sewn.

The last signature of the book block is sewn in first.

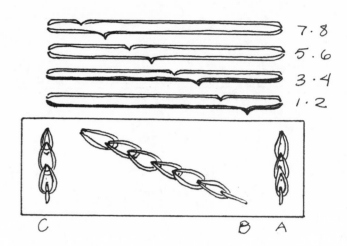

FIVE ROW KETTLE STITCH PATTERN

This style also hides the long stitches and uses eight signatures for the pattern shown.

Every other signature uses three holes. The alternate signatures use four holes to mach the rows of holes in cover spine.

The drawing shows a spine with five rows of five holes each. The last signature of book block is sewn in place first. Anchor stitches are made at each hole, A through E, as first signature is sewn.

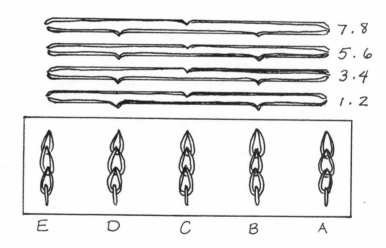

FOLDERS & SOFT WRAPS

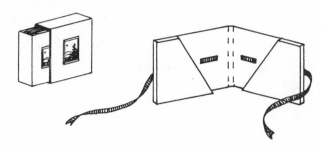

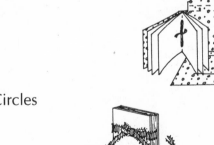

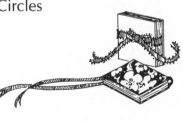

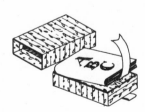

THREE-FLAP FOLDERS

Three-flap folders can serve several purposes. When small like the pattern shown, 2 1/2" by 2", it can be a self enclosed greeting card. With spine thickness added to the three folds, it can be used as a case for a small book. The book format can be a single signature or an accordion fold.

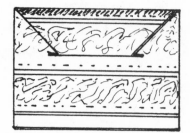

BASIC FOLDER

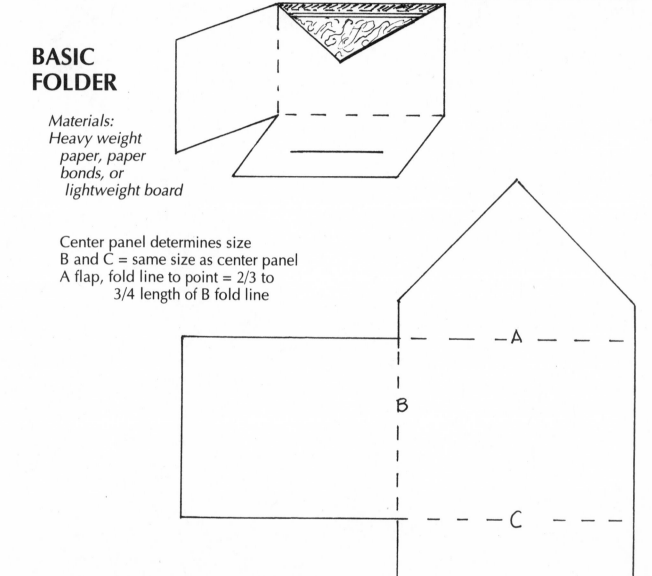

*Materials:
Heavy weight
paper, paper
bonds, or
lightweight board*

Center panel determines size
B and C = same size as center panel
A flap, fold line to point = 2/3 to
3/4 length of B fold line

LAYOUT AND cut out pattern as shown.

SCORE AND make the two horizontal folds, A and C, parallel with the paper grain. Then score and make the cross grain fold, B.

ACCORDION BOOK FORMAT

Materials:
Same as Basic Folder, p. 142
Plus:
Small accordion book
Optional closure ribbon
Adhesive

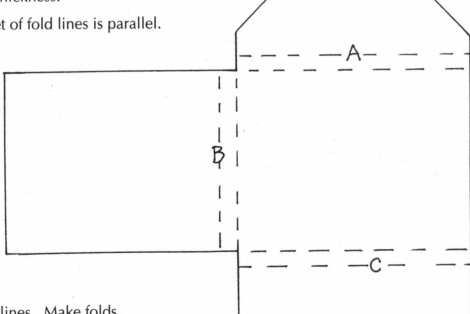

LAYOUT AND cut out folder
   with measurements to fit the book.
   Compress book lightly to measure
   spine thickness, p. 238.

Center panel:
   Height = book height + folding ease
   Width = book width + folding ease

ADD THICKNESS measurement to the flaps,
   forming lines A,B,& C. These become fold
   lines for spine thickness.

Be sure each set of fold lines is parallel.

SCORE ALL fold lines. Make folds.

MOUNT LAST accordion panel to
   the inside center panel of folder,
   centering on panel.
   The accordion illustrated shows
   first and last folds as valley folds.

SINGLE SIGNATURE FORMAT

Materials:
Same as Basic Cover, p. 142
Plus:
Small single signature
  and fly leaves
Thread

Follow directions for *Accordion Book Format,* p. 143, except: stitch and mount as below.

USE B fold space for the spine. Stitch book in place using butterfly stitch, p. 91. Book can be stitched separately; paste back fly leaf to center panel of folder.

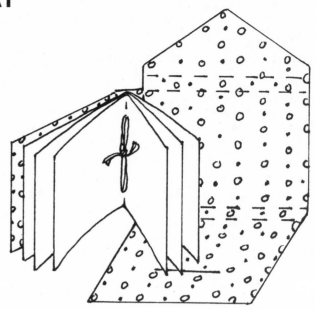

CLOSURE VARIATIONS

Tab flap and two slits.

Ribbon laced through two panels. Flaps can be made narrower than previous project's, as shown here with ribbon closure.
A fourth flap can also be added.

FOUR FLAP FOLDERS

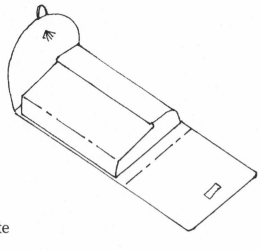

TWO PIECE FORMAT

This folder is sturdier than the previous style. It can be used to house unbound sheets or a single book. The folder is made in two sections which are then pasted together.

Note that one section is vertical, the other horizontal. When patterned papers are used and all folds are parallel to grain, the pattern will run one direction on the inside flaps and the opposite direction on the outside flaps.

Materials:
Heavyweight papers, lightweight board or paper bonds
Closure: button and cord or ribbon, pp. 228, 231
Adhesive

FIGURE MEASUREMENTS on contents size.
   Directions below are for a book.

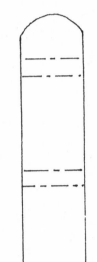

CUT MATERIALS
   Vertical section, cut one
   Height = 2 1/2 times book height
           + 2 times book thickness
           + ease.
   Width = book width

   Horizontal section, cut one
   Height = book height
   Width = 2 1/2 times book width
           + 2 times book thickness
           + ease for folds

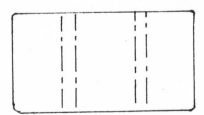

SCORE AND fold all fold lines.
   Folds are best if they run parallel to the grain. If a pattern is to run the same direction on both sections, one section must run across the grain.

MAKE CLOSURE details of choice.
    This can be a slit with tab, ribbon ties or wrap, or a loop and flat button made from
    layers of book cloth or paper, p. 228.

    Cut slits, p. 235.

    Loop for button closure must be long enough for both ends
    to be anchored inside flap. Thread loop through hole in flap,
    unravel slightly, and paste down to inside of flap.

    Sew button in place and unravel thread.
    Finish as with loop.

    For a neat finish, cut small pieces of matching
    paper to paste over thread ends.

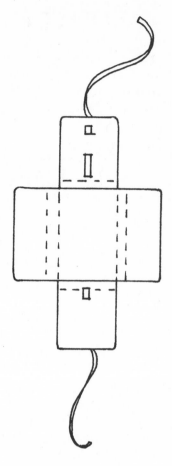

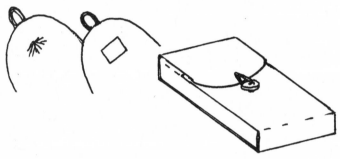

BRUSH ADHESIVE in a cross on
    inside center panel of vertical piece.
    Position horizontal section over it, joining
    both sections. Press until dry.

ONE PIECE FORMAT

This is a lighter weight structure than the Two Piece Folder.
The grain in the two vertical flaps will be opposite the two horizontal flaps.
The pattern will appear sideways on one set of flaps. This will add interest
with some patterns.

Materials:
Same as Two Piece Format, p. 145
Cover paper needs to be
    2 1/2 times content width and
    2 1/2 times content height

BASE MEASUREMENTS on content's size. Directions presented are for a book.

LAYOUT AND cut out folder in one piece.
   Center panel
   Height = book height + folding ease
   Width = Book width + folding ease

   Side Flaps, one on each side of center panel
   Width = 1 spine thickness + folding ease
          + 3/4 book width for each flap

   Head and Tail Flaps, above and below center panel
   Height =1 spine thickness + folding ease
          + 3/4 book height for each flap

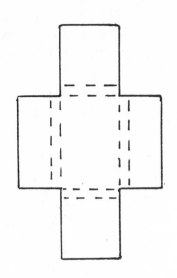

CUT OUTSIDE corners round using a coin for a template.

SCORE AND fold carefully and complete with closure details of choice.

SELF CLOSING FORMAT

This style can hold a heavier, thicker book than either previous four flap folders. It is made in two pieces and held together with adhesive.

Materials:
Lightweight board or paper bonds,
   When all folds are parallel to grain,
   patterns will be at right angles
   to each other when put together.
Adhesive

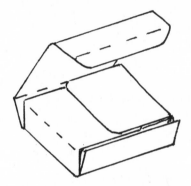

CUT MATERIALS.
   Vertical section, cut one
   Height = 2 1/2 times book height
           + 2 times spine thickness
           + 4 times folding ease
   Width = book width

   Horizontal section, cut one
   Measure with book wrapped in vertical section.
   Height = book height
   Width = 2 times book width
          + 3 times book thickness
          + 2" for flap
          + 5 times folding ease

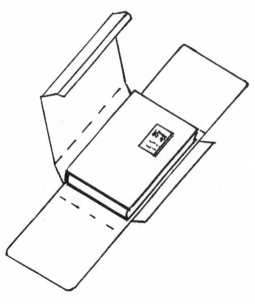

CUT CORNERS of vertical section round using a quarter for a template. Cut a shallow, rounded thumb notch with scissors in center panel as shown.

Place book in center of this piece and score along the head and tail of book. Measure spine thickness from this line and score again as shown.
Fold along score lines.

SET BOOK in place on vertical section. Fold flaps over book.

MAKE FIRST fold in horizontal piece on the right, a little less than one spine thickness from the right edge. Score and fold up.

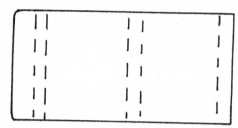

PLACE BOOK wrapped in vertical section against this first fold and score along its left edge. Use the wrapped book as a guide to measure, score, and fold the three remaining fold lines.

APPLY ADHESIVE to a third of the inside surface of the vertical section panel, opposite thumb notch, as shown at left.

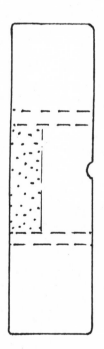

PRESS HORIZONTAL piece in place on top of vertical piece.

WRAP BOOK in waxed paper to protect from moisture and put in folder.

FOLD FLAPS over book in sequence. Flap 5 folds over 3 and tucks in slot at thumb notch.

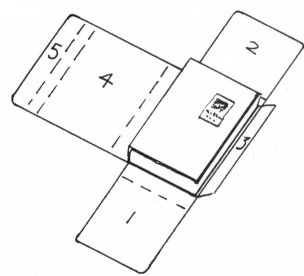

DRY UNDER light pressure with book inside of folder, p. 241.

POCKET FOLDERS

These folders can be used for many things: brochures, post cards, stationery, drawings, etc. Each style is cut from a single sheet. The first has a fold up flap at tail edge; the other styles have flaps on all edges.

STANDARD DOUBLE POCKET

Materials:
Lightweight board or
  paper bonds,
  pp. 239-240
Adhesive
Ribbon ties, optional

Folder needs to be large enough to protect edges of inserts and to move them in and out without forcing.

CUT MATERIAL in one continuous piece
  make grain parallel to spine
  Height = insert height
  + 1/4" to 1/2" extra space
  + desired fold up flap height

Width = 2 times insert width
+1/2" to 1" extra space
+ 1/2" each side for tabs
along fold up flap's edges

If contents are quite thick,
Double Pocket with Closed Edges,
p. 152, is a better choice.

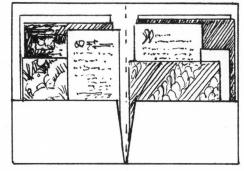

SCORE and make all folds carefully.

CUT NARROW wedge from fold-up flap at spine edge as shown. This prevents binding when in use.

APPLY ADHESIVE to back sides of tabs and press in place.

DRY UNDER light pressure, p. 241.

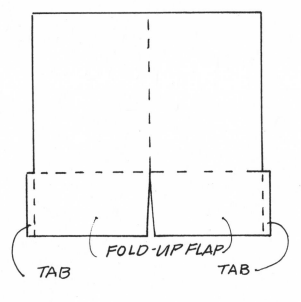

TAB   FOLD-UP FLAP   TAB

SINGLE POCKET WITH CLOSED EDGES

The closed edges keep contents from slipping
out of the folder. When folded,
both sides of flap and pocket
are the same surface. Ribbon
ties can be laced through
panels 2 and 4 if desired.

Materials:
Lightweight board
  or paper bonds
Adhesive
Ribbon, optional

MEASURE CONTENTS.
  Work out dimensions
  on a paper pattern
  first. Have grain
  parallel to panel 3.

Panel 4 size
Height = insert height + 1/8" ease
Width = insert width + 1/8" ease

Panel X size
Height = panel 4 height
Width = thickness of contents
        + 2 cover thicknesses

Panels 1, 2, 4, and 5 are all the same size.
The thickness of this folder is formed by panels 3 and X, Y, Z; all are same thickness.

CUT MATERIALS in one continuous piece
  Height = 4 times panel 4 height
          + 2 times panel X width
          + folding ease
  Width = panel 4 width
          + 2 times panel X width
          + 1 1/4"
          + folding ease

SCORE AND make all folds carefully.

CUT EDGE of panel 5 in a shallow curve or
  V cut along outside edge. This will make it
  easy to remove contents. Use a dish for a template.

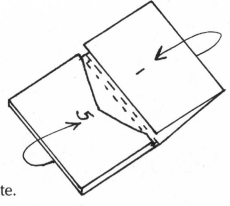

Begin either curve or V cut about 3/8" in from outside corners of panel 5.

V cut: Begin cut at center of V by making small hole with push pin.
Cut V as in Slits For Tapes, Ribbons, p. 235.

TRIM PANEL 1 to end short of fold line at panel 2.

CUT SLITS in panels 2 and 4 for ribbon tie if desired, p. 235.
  Weave ribbon through panels 2 and 4. Keep ribbon outside folder at panel 3.
  Fold panel 1 in place and close flap.
  Adjust ribbon length.

ADD ADHESIVE to panel 1 and press to panel 2.
  Dry under light pressure.

ADD ADHESIVE to the tabs along X and Z and press to inside of panel 4.

WRAP CONTENTS in wax paper, adding extra paper of board to equal thickness
  of flaps X, Y, and Z. Slip inside while drying under light pressure.

DOUBLE POCKET WITH CLOSED EDGES

This style makes a nice travel folder for small sketches, note cards, and envelopes.
Cut drawing and painting paper to size and fill pockets before leaving home.
The extended flaps at head and tail help keep contents from slipping out of place.
The closed edges give more strength to the folder and protect the corners of contents.

This style is recommended
if the spine length is to
be more than 5 1/2".

Head and tail
turn-ins are
narrower than
fore edge turn-ins.

Materials:
Lightweight board
* or paper bonds*
Adhesive

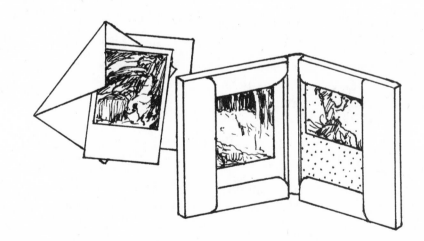

MAKE FOLDER large enough to protect edges of contents and move them in and out
  without forcing. Thickness of A, B, and C need not match X, Y, and Z, but together
  they must add up to match thickness of panel 3.

CUT MATERIAL in one piece.
Front and back panels, 2 and 4
Height = insert height + 1/8" ease
Width = insert width + 1/8" ease

Spine panel, 3
Height = panel 2 and 4 height
Width = total thickness of contents

Thickness for Cover Pockets
B + Y must equal spine thickness, panel 3
Front Cover thickness, B = front cover insert
        thickness (ABC are all same thickness)

Back Cover thickness, Y = back cover insert
        thickness (XYZ are all same thickness)

Head and Tail Turn-ins
Front Cover
A + C thickness + 2 1/2"
one thickness + 1 1/4" is added to both top and bottom as shown
width is the same as panel 2

Back Cover
X + Z thickness + 2 1/2"
divided as front cover

Fore Edge Turn-ins
Front Cover
Height = panel 2 height
Width = 1 B panel thickness
        + 2" for a 2" turn-in

Back Cover
Height = panel 4 height
Width = 1 Y panel thickness
        + 2" for a 2" turn-in

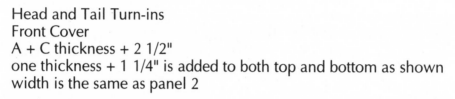

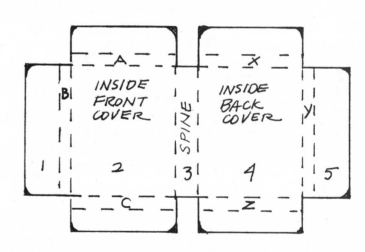

MAKE A practice pattern before cutting into good materials. Paper grain should parallel spine. Draw panels 2, 3, and 4 first. Add all other dimensions to this shape.

COPY PATTERN on good paper. Score and make all folds carefully.
  Cut corners round as shown. Use a coin for a template.

FOLD FORE edge flaps, 1 and 5 in last. Hold flaps in place with adhesive at overlaps. Wrap contents in wax paper, adding extra paper or board to equal panel B and Y thickness. Slip inside pockets while drying under pressure, p. 241.

DIAGONAL SIDE POCKETS

Pockets can be a different thickness; one side can be designed for stationary or note cards, the other for envelopes. If a spine height of more than 5" or 5 1/2" is needed, Double Pocket With Closed Edges, p. 152, is a better choice.

Ribbon can be woven through slits for decoration and closure. Make ribbons long enough to tie. Different weaving patterns can be used for front and back covers. This will distinguish one cover from the other.

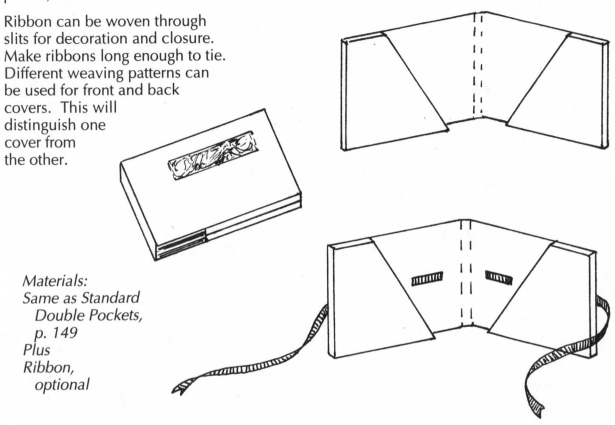

Materials:
Same as Standard
Double Pockets,
p. 149
Plus
Ribbon,
optional

MAKE A practice pattern to work out dimensions
before cutting into good materials. Make folder large enough to protect edges of contents and move them in and out without forcing.

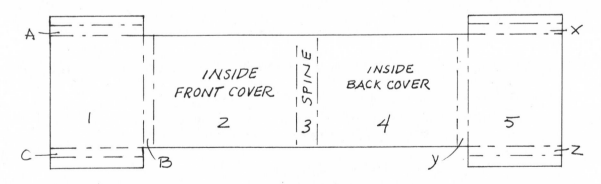

Front and back pockets of unequal thickness:
Adjust thickness of A B C and X Y Z to desired thicknesses.
Total of both B and Y thicknesses must equal thickness of spine, panel 3.

Front, Back Cover and Spine + both pocket thicknesses, (panels 2, 3, 4, + B and Y)
Height = insert height + 1/8" ease
Width = 2 times insert width
       + 1/8" ease + 2 times spine thickness
       (B + Y thickness = spine thickness)

Front Pocket, panel 1
Height = panel 2 height
       + 2 times B width (for A and C space)
       + 1" (for 1/2" tabs adjoining A and C)
Width = 2/3 of panel 2 width

Back Pocket, panel 5
Height = panel 4 height
       + 2 times Y width (for X and Z space)
       + 1" (for 1/2" tabs adjoining X and Z)
Width = 2/3 of panel 4 width

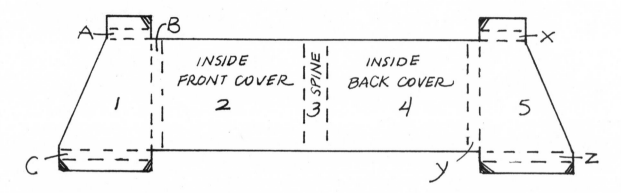

CUT MATERIAL in one piece. Make grain parallel with the spine.

MAKE TABS above and below panels 1 and 5 for the front and back pockets.
  Outside tab edges are parallel to spine.

CUT DIAGONAL edge on panels 1 and 5. Top width = 1/2 of bottom width

TRIM AWAY shaded areas at tab corners as shown. Score and make all folds carefully.

PLAN WEAVING pattern for ribbon ties if desired. Different patterns can be used for
  front and back to help distinguish one cover from the other. Cut slits for ties, p. 235.
  Make ribbons long enough to tie. Weave in place now if slits come near fore edge.

APPLY ADHESIVE to back of tabs on panel 1.
  Press in place along inside head and tail of panel 2.
  Repeat for panel 5 tabs and press in place along inside head and tail of panel 4.

Wrap contents in waxed paper and slip in place while drying folder.
Dry under light pressure, p. 241. When dry, lace ribbon if not already in place.

MATCH BOX FOR SMALL BOOKS

This little box is made in two separate parts. It opens and closes like a match box. Boxes larger than 3 1/2" tend to sag. For larger boxes see p. 169.

Materials:
Small book for insert
Bristol board, 2 ply
Cover paper, optional
Ribbon pull
Ribbon to lift book
Adhesive

Heavily textured papers will not slide smoothly when opening box.

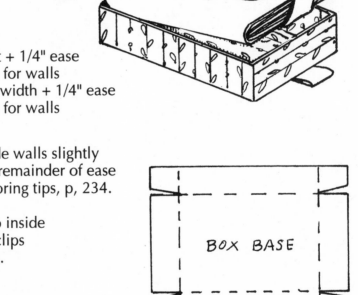

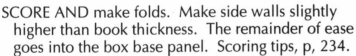

MAKE BASE section first.

BOX BASE, cut one
   Length, head to tail = book height + 1/4" ease
            + 2 times book thickness for walls
   Width, spine to fore edge = book width + 1/4" ease
            + 2 times book thickness for walls

SCORE AND make folds. Make side walls slightly
   higher than book thickness. The remainder of ease
   goes into the box base panel. Scoring tips, p, 234.

TAPER TABS as shown and paste to inside
   walls. Use paper clips or spring clips
   to hold tabs in place while drying.

BASE COVERING
   Outside and Inside Walls, cut one
   Height = 2 times wall height + 3/4"
   Length = 2 times length wall
            + 2 times width wall
            + 1/2" for ease and overlap

Base Lining, cut two
   (one lines inside, the other
   covers outside base)
   Length = box length less 1/8"
   Width = box width less 1/8"

BOX BASE

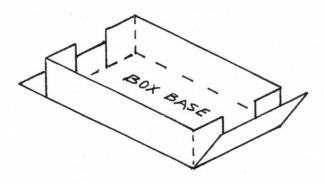

BOX BASE

The following procedure is shown in detail on pp. 171-172.
The Match Box uses narrow margins, 1/4" instead of 1/2".

APPLY ADHESIVE to box base outside walls.
  Place base over covering, begin with overlap
  on back wall. Turn corner, wrap around
  walls, finishing atoverlap where covering
  began. Smooth in place.

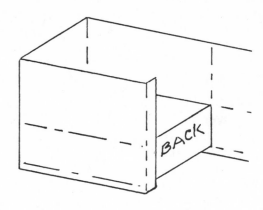

MITER CORNERS on bottom of base. Apply
  adhesive and turn in margins. Do long sides
  first, ends last. Smooth in place.

CUT RIBBON.
  Pull, cut one
  Length = 2 1/2"

  Lift, cut one
  Length = 1 1/3 times book height
          + 1 book thickness.

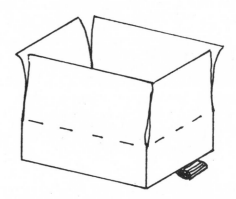

ADD RIBBON pull before turning lining
  inside. Cut a slit for ribbon pull in fold
  at center front width wall.

  Thread ribbon loop through
  slit and paste ends to box
  bottom inside.

CUT TURN-INS to top edge of
  box base at each corner fold.
  Apply adhesive to turn-ins
  and smooth in place.

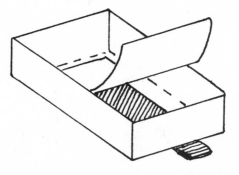

APPLY ADHESIVE to one lining
  piece. Center inside box bottom.
  Smooth in place.

  Repeat process for outside lining piece.

ADD RIBBON lift by pasting end inside box
  base as shown.
  Cut a small piece of lining paper and paste
  over ribbon end to finish if desired.

  Slip a piece of waxed paper between
  ribbon and box base to keep ribbon
  from sticking to box base as everything dries.

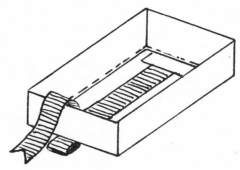

WRAP BOOK in waxed paper and put in base while drying to keep base from warping.

MAKE LID. Lid must be larger
   to fit over base.

Box Lid, cut one
   Length, head to tail = base length
   Width, spine to fore edge =
         2 times base width
         + 3 times base thickness
         + ease for folds and sliding

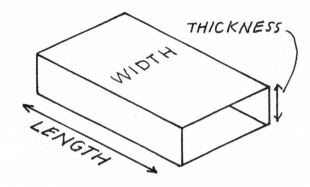

   Panel 5 is narrowed so it will fit neatly
   inside panel 1 when pasted.
   Panels 1 and 3 are same size.
   Panels 2 and 4 are same size.

SCORE AND fold.
   Trim length of panel 5 slightly
   if needed to fit inside panel 1.
   Paste panel 5 inside panel 1.

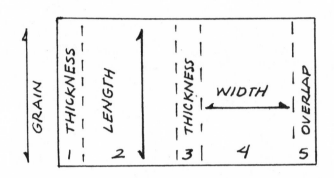

3/8" TURN IN

Lid Covering, cut one
   Length, head to tail = lid length + 3/4"
   Width, spine to fore edge =
         distance around lid
         + 1/2" ease and overlap

APPLY ADHESIVE to outside
   of lid. Place over covering
   paper and carefully wrap
   around lid. Smooth in place.

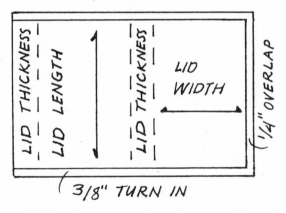

3/8" TURN IN

CUT TURN-IN margins carefully,
   at each corner fold.
   Apply adhesive to turn-ins
   and carefully fold inside.
   Smooth in place.

WRAP BOOK in waxed paper.
   Pad extra space with crumpled waxed paper.
   Wrap base in waxed paper and slide into lid.
   Wrap with an Ace bandage or waxed paper to secure tension while drying.

SMALL SLIP CASE WITH PAPER COVERING

This slip case is designed for small books.
It is ideal for the Wrap-Around Cover
Accordion Book, p. 35.
Use the same cover paper
for the book and slip case.
For larger books, use a box or case
of binder board, p. 169.

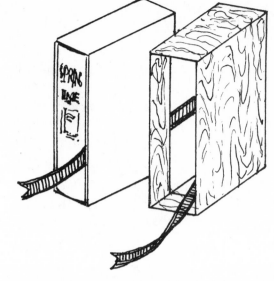

Materials:
Book for insert
Heavyweight paper or Bristol board
Covering paper
Adhesive
Ribbon pull, optional

Case, cut in one piece
   Height, head to tail = book height
   + 2 times spine thickness
   + 3/16" ease
   Width, fore edge to spine =
   2 times book width
   + spine thickness
   + 3/16" ease

Optional Ribbon Pull, cut one
   Length = 2 times book width
              + 2 times spine thickness

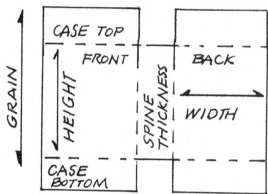

MAKE PRACTICE paper pattern first.
   Ease is needed to allow air to escape
   when closing and reduce friction on
   book cover. Therefore, 1/16" is added
   to both height and width of each
   panel.

PUT CASE together.
   Brush adhesive on one head
   flap. Attach to the other head flap.
   Reverse fold over layers at tail
   of case. Smooth with folder.

ADD RIBBON pull if desired.
Center one end of ribbon pull
along back fore edge, as shown.
Attach with dab of adhesive.
Turn-in will cover it.

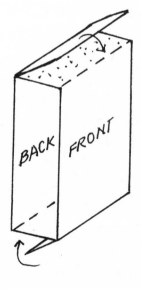

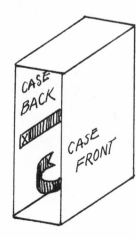

Cover Paper, cut in one piece
  Height, head to tail = book height
                + 2 times spine thickness
                + 1/8" ease
  Width, fore edge to spine =
            2 times book width
            + 1/8" ease
            + 1" turn-in

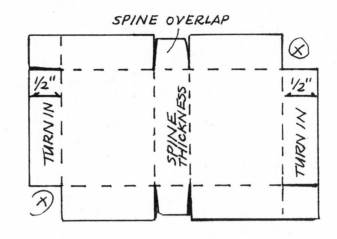

LIGHTLY DRAW all folds on
  inside of covering material to
  help placement when applying
  material to case.

SET CASE in place to test for fit. Make corrections if necessary.

CUT OVERLAP margins to fold line at spine as shown above.
  Clip turn-in margins at fore edge and remove two corners, shown above at X.

WRAP BOOK in waxed paper and put in case.

APPLY ADHESIVE to outside walls of case front, spine, and back.
  Set cover material in place along margin drawn at spine edge.
  Smooth spine piece in place with fingers, then front and back panels.

Follow *PUT CASE together,* p. 158, to apply adhesive to head and tail overlaps.

REMOVE BOOK.

PASTE FORE edge turn-ins and fold to inside.

PRESS EVERYTHING in place with fingers, then smooth with folder.

PLACE WRAPPED book in case and dry under light pressure.

ORIGAMI FOLD

POP OUT BOOKLET

This booklet is formed by folding paper squares into fourths.
It can be a single, folded square or several pasted together.
A one inch square is charming. If made without ribbons,
the Origami Fold Box, p. 162, can house the booklet.

Materials:
Text weight paper
Cover weight paper or lightweight board
Decorative cover paper for boards, optional
Ribbon tie, optional
Adhesive

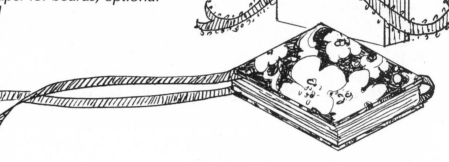

CUT TEXT paper into squares.

FOLD IN half with valley fold on
    inside of square.

Turn 90°, open, and fold in half
again.

Open, turn over, and fold one
diagonal from corner to corner.
This forms a mountain fold inside.

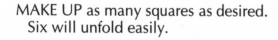

valley   *mountain*

MAKE UP as many squares as desired.
    Six will unfold easily.

PUSH MOUNTAIN fold up and into middle,
    flatten to make smaller square.

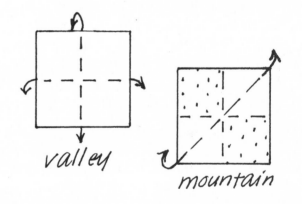

JOIN SQUARES by pasting outside
    sections together, dotted area in drawing.

CUT two cover pieces to fit folded square
    flush or with a small overhang.

PASTE COVER pieces to outside sections of folded squares.

PLACE RIBBON ties between covers and text squares if desired. Ribbon can run across
last folded square and tie around booklet, or it can run diagonally between covers and
text, from corner to corner, across closed point forming a hinge.

MOUNT COVERS.

PRESS OVERNIGHT to crisp folds.

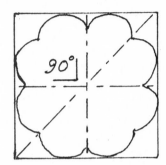

OPTIONAL SHAPES.
Any shape that will adapt
to a right angle will work.
Multiple heart shapes make a
petal-like opening when unfolded.

When cut points and folded points are joined, the format is different.
Experiment with different joining patterns.

SQUARE BOX

This box can be used to house small square books. Try the Pop Out Book, p. 160. It is also fun as a gift box for small things such as earrings.

Materials
Paper, text weight to
medium weight,
gift wrap will work;
since no moisture is
involved, it will not
expand and contract

CUT MATERIALS.
   Base, cut one
   Base square = 2 times diagonal
      measurement of contents
      + ease for removal of contents

   Lid, cut one
   Lid square = 1/4" larger than base
      square

Experimentation with papers will show how much extra needs to be used to make a lid that fits over base easily with a specific paper.

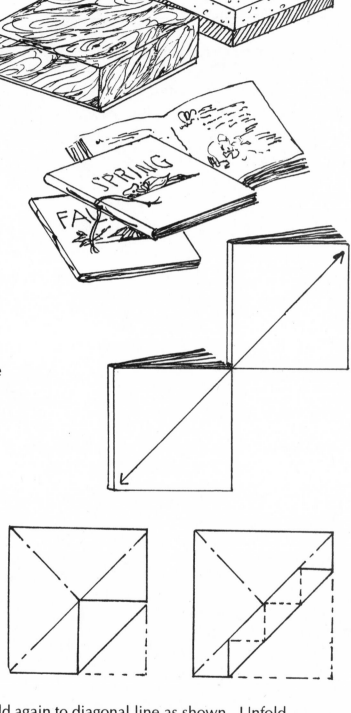

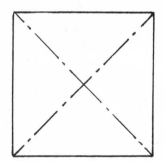

MARK CENTER of square by lightly *drawing* diagonals from corner to corner on inside of square, shown above.

FOLD CORNER to center point. Fold again to diagonal line as shown. Unfold. Repeat folding at each corner. The folds just formed make the side walls of this box.

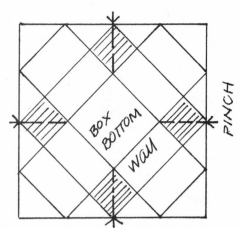

The largest square in the center of the original
square becomes the box bottom.

KEEPING CENTER area smooth, crease the small
shaded squares as shown. These small folds
become part of the box wall corners.

FORM BOX by folding opposite side corners into
the center. Then turn up
along next fold line
forming two
sides.

PULL IN box corners at one end. Fold the rest
of flap inside box. Smooth into position.
Repeat process for remaining side.

FOLD LID from larger square
in the same way as base.

LID VARIATION with lid wall
1/2 base wall height
Fold the same as box base.
Draw a line parallel to paper
edge, passing through the
shaded square points as shown
below.
Trim along these four lines.

REFOLD USING box lid center, lightly
marked in pencil, as guide for first fold .
Edge of center folds, forming square marked
LID TOP, form guide lines for second fold.

BRING AN outside
corner point to inside
center of box LID TOP.
Crease, making a new fold. Bring creased edge
up to refold original lid wall line, the top edge
of large square in center of box. Unfold.
Repeat folding procedure at each corner.

Follow KEEPING CENTER area smooth, above,
and remaining directions to form lid.

ADJUST LID wall to desired depth
by adjusting the trimming margin.
Keeping 1/2 of the arrow length will make the
lid depth = to 1/2 box wall depth.
For a more shallow lid, trim more away.

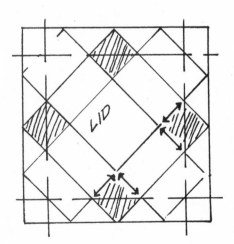

Box wall depth = length of arrows

PINWHEEL WRAP

Use this for a slender book or a gift card. The corners of this wrap are vulnerable and are apt to wear through with much use. To prolong the life of the wrap use long fiber, handmade or bonded paperwith Tyvek or plain Tyvek. If the contents will be thicker than 1/4", the wrap will need to be long enough to allow for the extra thickness.

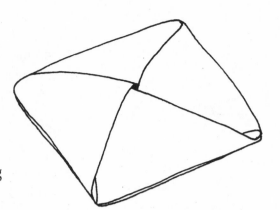

Materials:
Insert of choice
Text weight papers,
A contrast of color or pattern using two papers is interesting. A tissue weight lining square is easy to fold during the original folding. With heavyweight papers it may be easiest to fold one, then put the second with the first and refold.

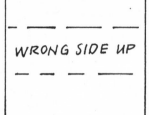

FORM FOLDER from a square slightly more than 3 times the dimensions of the contents.

FOLD SQUARE in thirds horizontally, with wrong side of paper up. Open and fold into thirds vertically. Measuring without math, p. 237.

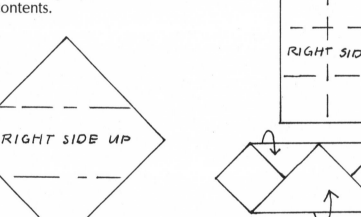

TURN PAPER over, right side up, positioning to form diamond as shown above.

Fold into thirds from top to bottom.

Open paper and fold into thirds from left to right.

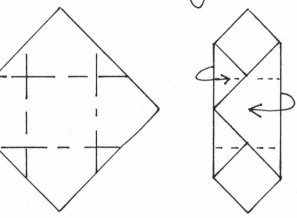

TURN PAPER over, wrong side
up, and fold up lower 1/3.

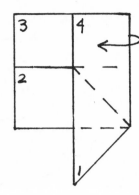

Placing finger at inside top of
lower left square as shown,
gently lift the lower right
square at corner 1 and pull
below fold line. This will
automatically pull the
right vertical panel,
thus folding over the
right 1/3 of large square.
Crease the two diagonal folds just formed.

ROTATE CLOCKWISE 90º with corner 1 pointing to left.

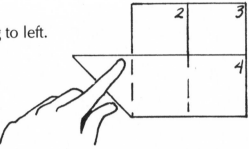

PLACE FINGER at top right point opposite
corner 1. Lift and lower corner 4, gently
pulling corner below fold line. Again the
right 1/3 of large square will pull over.
Crease the two diagonal folds just formed
as shown below.

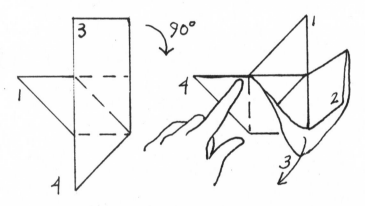

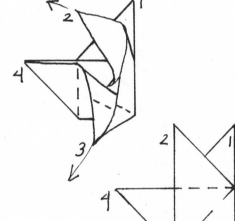

ROTATE CLOCKWISE 90º with corner 4 pointing
to left. Placing left finger at top right point opposite
corner 4, lift and lower corner 3.

Keeping left finger in place, hold corner 3
with left thumb as right hand gently pulls
corner 2 up and left. Crease the
new folds forming shape shown.

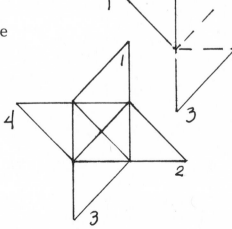

Holding at top left of triangle 3,
lift point 2 up, over, and down forming
last point of pinwheel at right. Crease the
new folds forming the pinwheel as shown.

CLOSE WRAPPER by folding the pinwheel wings over
in a clockwise order, with last
wing tucking
under the
first.

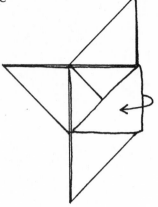 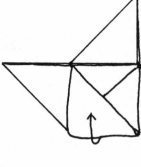 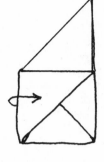 

OPEN WRAP to square,
add the contents, and refold.

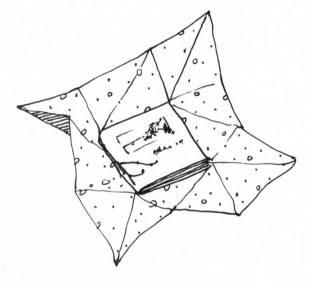

A GIFT card can be added to center
just before pinwheel is closed.

FOLD PINWHEEL wings over card
tucking in last point as shown above,
thus keeping card inside.

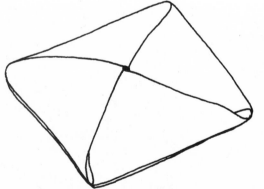

When using two paper layers, place a dab of adhesive in the center to hold the inside
paper in place. A glue stick can be used for this.

SQUARE WRAP FROM CIRCLES

This wrap is made from four individual rounds
of paper. Alternate print and a solid paper
to give a pinwheel effect. Use paper bonds
with a print on outside and a solid inside.
Coordinate with a small booklet.

When made without patterns, use a single
sheet of paper cut in the same outline
as the individual layered circles.

Materials:
Paper, medium to heavyweight,
   paper bonds
   or lightweight board

CUT CIRCLES.
   Circles, cut four
   Circle diameter = 2 times size
                  of enclosure

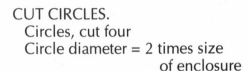

FOLD CIRCLES in half, wrong side
   folded inside. Crease and open.

LAYER CIRCLES with right sides up
                so folds form a square.

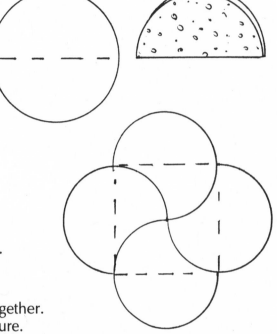

PASTE CIRCLES together.
   Dry under pressure.
      Turn over. Fold circle
      halves in, one over the
      other. Place enclosure inside when 3 sides have been
      folded. Fold last side in, sliding upper part under first
                         circle to close.

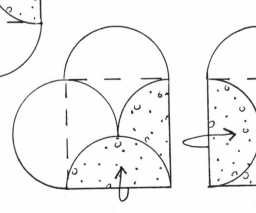

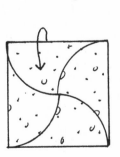

167

BOXES & CASES

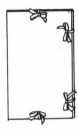

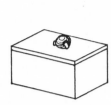

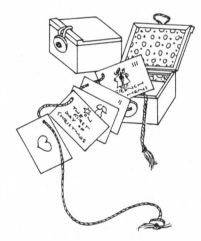

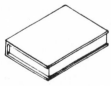

GENERAL PROCEDURES

The following procedures are used many times in this chapter.
Each project will refer to the parts that apply.

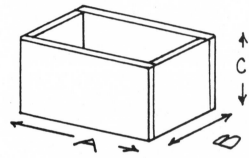

BOX CONSTRUCTION

Shape of contents determines size.
Allow extra space so that contents
can be removed with ease.

DETERMINE GRAIN. Most
materials have a grain direction
which can be determined,
paper, p. 232, board, p. 236.

For almost all construction materials,
grain should run parallel to box spine. Wall boards
are an exception; the grain for both boards and
covering should run parallel to wall length
as shown in first illustration.

Labels in this chapter are:
A = long wall
B = short wall
C = wall height

WRITE NAME of piece on
each section as it is cut out.
This will avoid confusion later.

CONSTRUCT BOXES by brushing
adhesive along wall edges where
they overlap the base board and
each other. These areas are
shown in thick, solid black lines.
Instructions will be given for each
project since the sequence will vary.

PVA sets quickly,
making it a good adhesive choice.

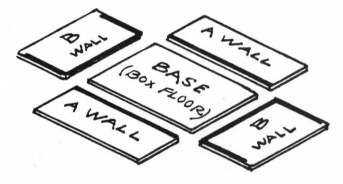

ADD ADHESIVE to one board at a time and set in place. Adjust if necessary to make a
smooth join at outside corner. The outer covering material will not hide a bad join!

Continue around box carefully overlapping the side walls. Masking tape can be
added to outside corners to help hold in place as adhesive sets.

TWO METHODS OF BOX COVERING:

OUTSIDE COVERING AND LINING IN ONE PIECE

Instructions for outside covering different from lining are given on p. 175. Cut covering materials after box is made.

One continuous piece of material wraps both the outside and inside walls of box.

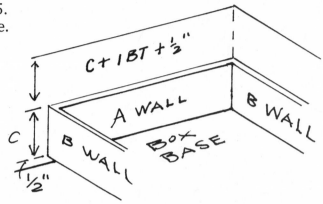

CUT MATERIALS.
   Wall covering,
   cut one continuous piece
   Width = 2 times C
            + 1 board thickness (BT)
            + 1"
   Length = 2 times A
            + 2 times B
            + 4 BT + 1/2"

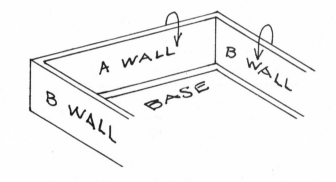

PLACE WRONG side up.
   Draw 1/2" margin down
   left side and along lower
   edge of covering material.

   These lines are used to guide
   placement of box after adhesive
   has been added.

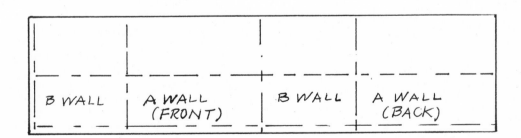

CHECK FIT by lining up box edges along margins and wrap covering around box.
   Make corrections if needed.

   Unless otherwise stated, the last edge should end at box corner.

BRUSH ADHESIVE on exposed box boards rather than covering material.

BRUSH ADHESIVE on one outside
  side wall of box.

Set in place along margin lines
  as shown. With fingers inside box,
  press wall to covering material.

TURN BOX over.
  Placing clean paper
  over covering,
  smooth with folder.

BRUSH 1/2" wide strip
  of adhesive along back wall
  and press margin to box.
  Smooth in place.

BRUSH ADHESIVE
  on one wall at a time.

To avoid air bubbles,
  work the covering
  material around each
  corner by pulling
  it with one hand and
  pressing it to wall
  with the other.

For the last wall, brush
  adhesive on wall board only,
  avoiding covering material
  already glued to box. Lightly
  brush adhesive along under
  edge of covering material
  where it overlaps the beginning,
  shown in shaded area.

Pull covering around corner
  and smooth last wall in place.

MITER BASE outside corners.
  Hold box upside down.
  Pinch excess together.
  Hold scissors parallel to box bottom.
  Keeping enough covering material at corner point to conceal box base board, clip
  excess. Dab adhesive along edge and smooth in place.

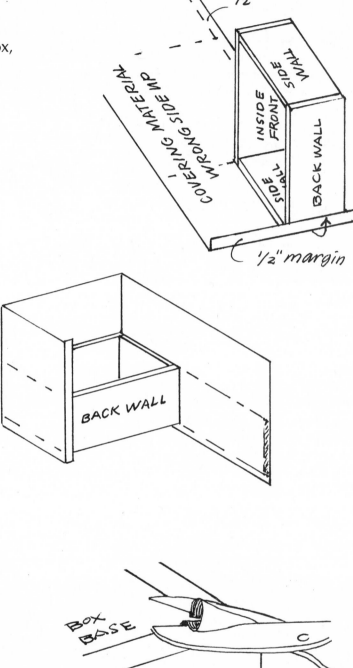

172

WALL CORNERS

Box size determines corner method. For more detailed corner, tools and hands need to fit inside box for measuring and cutting.
Make all cuts before doing any pasting and turning in.

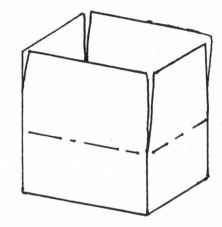

SMALL BOX

TURN BOX right side up. At each corner, cut a *narrow* triangular shape to the box. This wedge should not be wider than 1 board thickness (BT) at top. Cuts will form flaps above the box on all sides.

Follow *FOLD FLAPS inside box* on next page.

LARGE BOX

PLACE BOX on wall A (long wall). Place right angle triangle slightly more than one board thickness (BT) from corner. Using fresh blade, begin cutting 1 BT from wall and continue along triangle to edge of covering material.

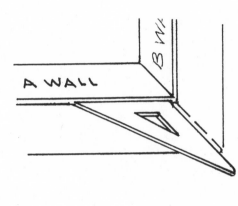

TURN 45° triangle as shown and make a 45° angle cut from outside corner point of box to the beginning of cut already made. *This is a very short distance.*

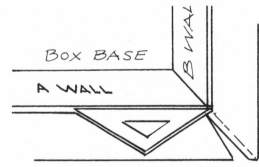

TURN BOX onto adjoining wall B (short wall) to make the next cut.

Draw a line from inside box corner to end of covering material, dotted line in bottom illustration.

Measure wall height (C) +1 BT. Placing knife at this point, cut along dotted line to end of covering material.

Beginning at same point, make a second cut at right angle to the first.

Remove the corner as shown.

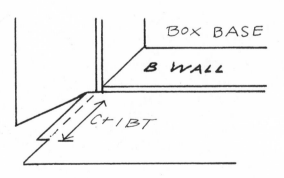

TURN BOX back onto wall A to miter corner on wall A. Measure wall height (C) + 1 BT from wall board and cut corner off at 45° angle.

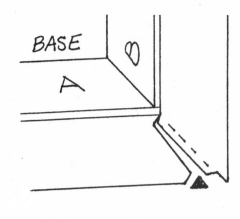

REPEAT AT each A wall corner.

ALWAYS FOLD in B walls first. The covering material's shaped cut fits into box corner, folding over wall B and wrapping around corner to wall A.

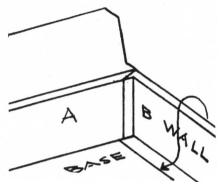

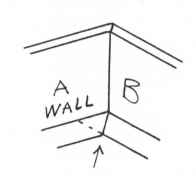

FOLD FLAPS inside box, one at a time, and crease edge along the bottom of the box.

BEGIN PASTING with wall B. Do one side at a time.

Spread adhesive on top edge of box, inside wall, and the narrow adjoining strip of box bottom where lining will overlap.

Pull cloth over top edge of box and carefully press with fingers. Rub with folder. Then pull cloth to inside of box and press onto the inside wall with fingers.

Follow *SMOOTHING SURFACES AFTER PASTING*, p. 240, to smooth out with folder. Be sure to get the corners. Press along the bottom last.

REPEAT PROCESS on second B wall, then A walls.

CUT FILLER piece the same size and shape as exposed board.

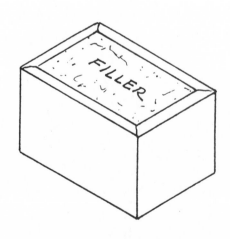

A filler piece is used to raise exposed board space closer to turn-in level. It will not show but is important for a good fit and appearance. A piece of wall covering material or paper of similar thickness can be used for this purpose.

BRUSH ADHESIVE on board. Set filler piece in place and smooth with folder.

OUTSIDE BASE COVERING

Same material as outside wall covering.

> CUT MATERIAL slightly smaller
> than outside box base.
> Apply the same as Inside Base Lining
> described below.

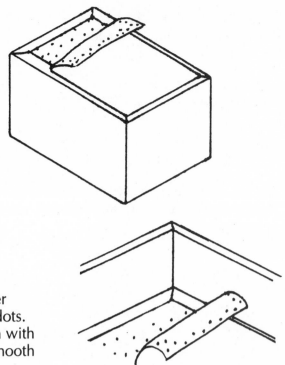

BOX BASE LINING

Same material as inside wall covering.

> CUT MATERIAL slightly smaller than box
> inside. This will allow it to go in easily
> and fit well without getting glue on walls.

> SPREAD ADHESIVE on exposed board or filler
> and along under edges of lining, shown in dots.
> Carefully set lining in place and press down with
> fingers. Cover with protective paper and smooth
> with folder if possible.

OUTSIDE COVERING
DIFFERENT FROM LINING

Instructions for outside covering the same
as lining are given on p. 171.
Cut all covering materials after
the box is made.

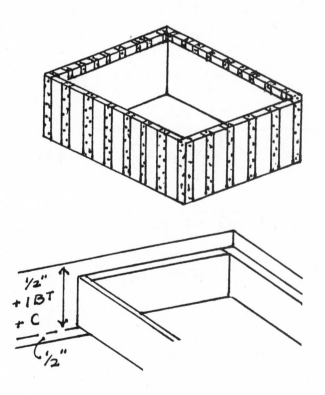

> CUT MATERIALS.
> Outside Walls, cut one
> Width of covering material =
>   C + 1 board thickness (BT) +1"
> Length of covering material =
>   2 times A + 2 times B + 4 BT + 1/2"

> Outside Base, cut one
> Same material as outside walls.
> Cut slightly smaller than
> outside base.

COVER OUTSIDE walls first.

Follow *PLACE WRONG side up,* p. 171.

BOX INTERIOR LINING
This is for book cloth or paper.
For felt lining see next page.

CUT MATERIALS.
Wall Lining, cut one
Width of wall covering material = C + 3/8"
Length of wall covering material = 2 times A + 2 times B + 1/2"

Inside Box Floor Lining, cut one
Cut slightly smaller than inside box floor so it will slip in easily.

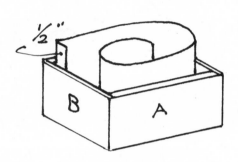

PLACE LINING wrong side up, draw a 1/2" margin along one side and a 1/2" margin along the lower edge as shown below. Fold side margin only. Set inside box, placing fold against back corner of box as shown. The lining will come above box walls.

HOLD WITH one hand and slide the other hand along inside box walls, pressing folds into lining at each corner.
The last edge of lining should end at corner, overlapping the 1/2" margin.
Trim carefully if it is too long.

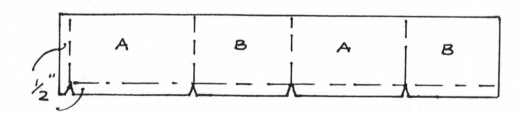

CREASE ALONG lower margin. Cut slits from lower edge to margin line at each corner fold as shown above.

SPREAD ADHESIVE on exposed back wall board, or filler if used on inside walls.
Also spread adhesive on under side of 1/2" side margin.

Beginning with back wall, carefully set lining in place. The top edge should be 1/8" below wall, leaving a visible margin of outside covering material.
Press down with fingers. Press the 1/2" overlap around the corner.

COVER WITH clean paper and using blunt end or side of folder, press smooth.
Be sure to press covering against corner for a finished look.

CONTINUE AROUND box in this fashion until all walls are covered.
  For the last wall, spread a little adhesive along the overlapping
  back edge of covering.

Follow *BOX BASE LINING,* p. 175, to set base lining in place.

FELT LINING

Felt works well on flat surfaces, e. g. inside walls and floors.
To cut felt accurately, it should be backed with paper.
Backing paper should be a color similar to felt.
Apply a thin, even coating of adhesive to the paper rather than the felt. Set felt in place.
Dry under weight, p. 241.

CUT MATERIALS.
  Base, cut one
  Exact size of box floor

  Walls, cut in one continuous piece
  Width = C minus 1/16"
  Length = 2 times A + 2 times B

APPLY ADHESIVE to box floor and carefully set base felt piece in place.
  Press flat with fingers. Smooth with folder and protective paper.

SET WALL piece inside box to check for fit. This piece must wrap the entire inside of
  box, with both ends meeting at a corner.
  A narrow margin of outside box covering will show along the top edge.
  Although the lining is one continuous strip, paste one wall at a time.

BRUSH ADHESIVE on exposed board of one wall only, extending about 1/2" around the
  corner. Brush small amount of adhesive along the back (paper side) of wall lining,
  first wall only.

  Lining up base edge and box corner, set in place.
  Press first wall in place with fingers.

COVER WITH clean paper and press first wall smooth with folder.
  Be sure to press covering against corner for a finished look.
  Continue around box in same fashion until all walls are covered.

BOX WITH REMOVABLE LID

This is a good box to house several
books of varying size.
It also works well as a letter box.

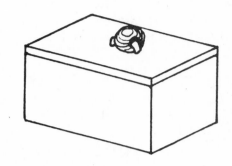

Materials:
Binder board
Cover material, paper or cloth
Lid pull, cloth tie, button, bead, or D ring
Adhesive

CUT BOARDS.
   Box Base and Lid Flange, cut two
(one for base, one for lid flange)
A = length of book, head to tail
      + ease room
      + 2 times covering
        thickness (CT)
B = width of book,
    spine to fore edge
    + ease room
    + 2 times CT

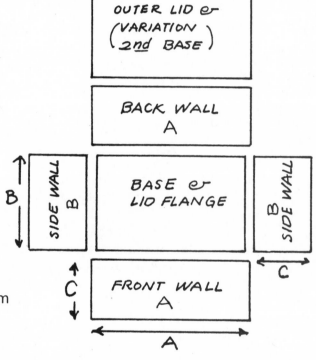

Box Walls:
Front and Back Wall, cut two
A = length of box base given above
    + 2 board thicknesses (BT)
C = thickness of contents + ease room
    + 2 times CT + 1 BT

Side Walls, cut two
B = Box base B
C = Front wall C

Lid, cut one
for variation on p. 179, cut two
(the second is for the outer base)
A = box lid flange A + 2 BT
B = box lid flange B + 2 BT

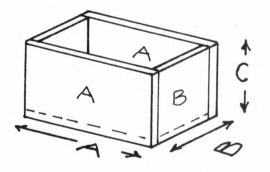

CONSTRUCT BOX.
  Brush adhesive along wall edges
  where they overlap the base
  board and each other,
  shown in solid black lines.

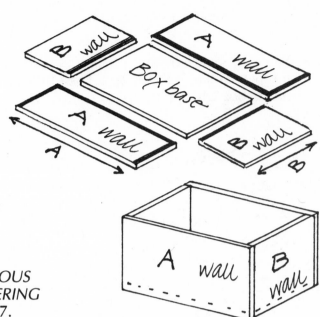

Follow *CONSTRUCT BOXES*,
p. 170, beginning with a B wall.

The inside box base lining and lid
flange can be a contrasting material.

Follow *COVERING IN ONE CONTINUOUS
PIECE*, pp. 171-175, or *OUTSIDE COVERING
DIFFERENT FROM LINING*, pp. 175-177.

CUT LINING.
  Size and mounting instructions are the same
  as given under *BOX BASE LINING*, p. 175.

VARIATION

A second base board is added to box base in place
of outside base covering. The filler is still added to
insure a good bond.

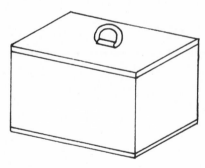

Materials:
Same as Box With Removable Lid,
  p. 178.

Follow *CUT BOARDS*, p. 178.

Follow *CONSTRUCT BOXES*, p. 170, beginning with a B wall.

OMIT OUTSIDE base covering.

FINISH OUTER base. Brush adhesive on each base board. Center it on wrong side of
  covering. Press firmly in place. Turn right side up, smooth with folder.

MITER CORNERS and fold turn-ins in place, p. 245.

ADD FILLER to this board, p.174. Brush
adhesive on filler and adjoining cloth
margin, keeping a 1/8" adhesive free margin
around the outside edge.

Place this board over box base and press
firmly with hand. Turn over. Press firmly
inside box with hand.

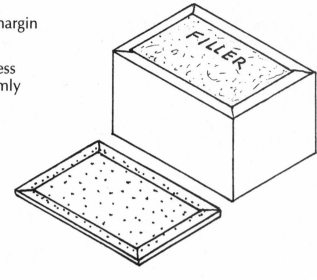

Place weights inside box or place something
heavy over upright box until dry, p. 241.

BOX LID

The outside box walls and lid board are covered with the same material.
The lid flange becomes the lid lining. Since
the lid flange is unseen when box is closed,
it is a nice surprise when different.

CUT COVERING materials.
Lid Covering, cut one
Board size + 1 1/4" both directions

Lid Flange Covering, cut one
Flange board size + 1 1/4" both directions

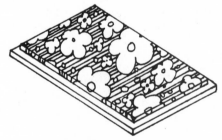

LID PULL VARIATIONS

RIBBON TIE PULL

Generally this pull works best with cloth covering materials. The tie is stitched to the fabric *before* pasting fabric to the board.

Since a knot in the ribbon forms the pull, the ribbon needs to be heavy, like grosgrain.

Ribbon, cut one
    Length = 7 1/2"
    Width = at least 3/4"

FOLD ENDS in half lengthwise. Cut at a diagonal to finish as shown.

Follow *ADD TIE to Covering Material*, p. 182.

CLOTH TIE PULL

Generally this pull works best with cloth covering materials. The tie is stitched to fabric *before* fabric is pasted to board.

CUT CLOTH
    Length = 8"
    Width = 2 1/8"

FOLD CLOTH in half lengthwise with right sides together. Stitch 1/4" seam keeping 3/4" center open.

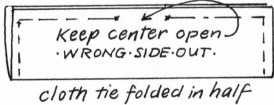

cloth tie folded in half

TRIM POINT off corners leaving a small margin of seam allowance at corner. This eliminates bulk when turned right side out.

TURN RIGHT side out, tuck in seam allowance at open area and press.
    This can be left open since tie will be held in place when tie is stitched to cloth.

ADD TIE to covering material.
  Place covering cloth right side up.
  Center tie over it as shown.
  When tied, tie ends will point
  the same direction as stitching.

  Stitch twice. Tie thread ends in
  a square knot, p. 226, and trim.

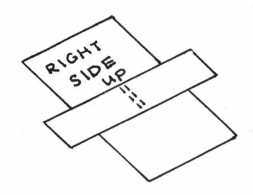

PLACE UPSIDE down.
  Stretch tie out flat.

Follow *FINISH OUTER base,* p. 179, to add cloth to lid board.

SHALLOW SHANK AND SIDE-DRILLED CIRCLE BUTTONS

These can be used on both paper and cloth coverings.

The covering material is pasted to the board first, then the pull and anchor cord are added.

Follow *FINISH OUTER base,* p. 179, to cover outer lid board.

MAKE TEMPLATE for marking pull placement on lid.
  Outline lid board on scrap paper and draw diagonals
  from corner to corner, making an X. Pattern is used
  to position Buttons, Beads, and D Rings.

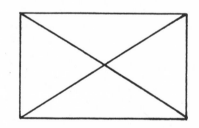

POKE HOLE in center of X on template. Placing
  template over right side of lid, mark hole with
  pencil.

PLACE LID right side up on solid backing,
  such as a block of wood.

DRILL HOLE through lid at pencil mark.
  Be aware that the drill will cut into
  this surface, p. 244.

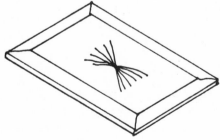

PULL THREAD through button holes and lid
  hole with needle. Set upside down over two
  flat objects of equal height, such as books, allowing
  lid to sit flat with button hanging below lid between the books.

UNTWIST THREAD, fan out around hole. Dot with adhesive and press thread against
  board with finger.
  Cover adhesive area with waxed paper. Rub with folder.

Follow *LID FLANGE,* p. 186, to finish.

DEEP SHANK BUTTONS

This type of button can be used on both paper and cloth coverings.

PASTE COVERING material to board first. Then add pull and
  its anchor cord.

Follow *FINISH OUTER base,* p. 179, to cover outer lid board.

Follow *MAKE TEMPLATE* and *POKE HOLE,* p. 182.

MAKE HOLE through lid at pencil mark with
  a 1/4" chisel. Place lid right side up on solid
  backing, such as a wooden block. Be aware
  the chisel will cut into this surface. Center over
  pencil mark and pound chisel with mallet to make
  hole. See p. 224, *Chisel and Mallet,* for more details.

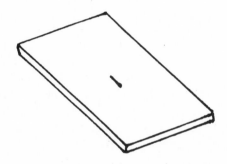

RUN STURDY thread through shank.
  Pull both ends through lid slit. Push shank into lid.

Follow *UNTWIST THREAD,* p. 182.

IF SHANK comes all the way through forming a "bump", a small section of the flange
  board is cut away. This is necessary for the outer lid and flange to rest flat against
  each other.

Mark center of exposed board side of flange. With a sharp knife, cut a small square
  through several layers of board and peel them away. Details are given on p. 246,
  RECESS AREA FOR LABEL.

Follow *LID FLANGE,* p. 186, to finish.

LARGE-HOLE BEADS

A wide anchor band holds the bead in place. For the large hole bead to rest in center of the lid, two holes are needed, one at each end of bead.

Follow *FINISH OUTER base,* p. 179, to add covering to lid board.

Follow *MAKE TEMPLATE,* p. 182. Use template for lid pull placement as shown below.

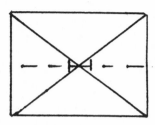 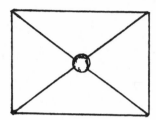

Set bead on paper template, centering over X. Draw a line at each end of bead as shown.

Fold pattern in half length wise.

Open and poke hole where bead end lines cross fold.

Place template over right side of lid and mark each hole.

PLACE LID right side up on solid surface, such as a wooden block. Be aware the chisel will cut into this surface. Carefully center chisel over each pencil dot, placing broad edge of chisel parallel to narrow ends of lid.

Pound hole using chisel and mallet, more details on p. 244. Holes are shown as solid black lines.

CUT ANCHOR for bead.
same material as lid covering, paper or cloth
Finished width = 1/4"
Length = 2 1/2"
Width = 5/8"

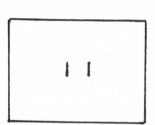

cloth anchor

Cloth Anchor:
Fold into thirds lengthwise. Apply adhesive inside. Refold and weight while drying to prevent curling.

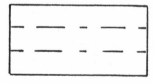

Paper Anchor:
Add a narrow strip of lightweight cloth inside center of anchor strip for strength. Apply adhesive inside, add cloth, refold. Weight while drying to prevent curling.

paper anchor

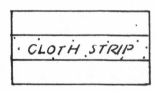

FOLD ANCHOR in half bringing turn-in edges together. Thread anchor through bead. Trim ends at an angle.

Follow *ADD ANCHOR to Lid* to finish, p. 185.

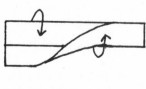

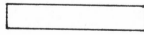

D RING

A wide anchor band holds the D ring in place. In order for it to rest in center of the lid, one hole is needed.

Follow *FINISH OUTER base,* p. 179,
to add covering to lid board.

CUT ANCHOR for D ring from same material as lid covering.
　Length = 2"
　Width = 3 times inside flat measurement of D ring less 1/8"

Follow *Cloth Anchor or Paper Anchor,* p. 184.

THREAD ANCHOR through D ring with turn-in edge
　against ring. Fold in half and trim to point as shown.

POKE HOLE in center of X on paper pattern. Place pattern on right side of lid and mark
　hole. Draw a line centered on dot, parallel with long edge of lid, and slightly less
　than anchor width.

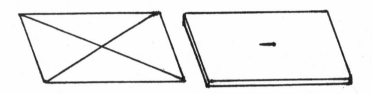

PLACE LID right side up on solid backing, such
　as a wooden block. Be aware chisel will cut
　into this surface. Align chisel with pencil mark,
　being sure it is parallel to long edge of lid, shown
　above.
　Pound hole using chisel and mallet, p. 244.

ADD ANCHOR to lid. Pliers may be
　needed to pull ends to the inside of lid.

FOLD ENDS flat against the lid. Cut around anchor
　edge so that several layers of board can be peeled
　away. This forms a depression for the anchor.
　Since chisel raises hole edges slightly, peel a little
　more off this area so anchor can lie completely flat.

If edges are pushed down with folder instead,
　the board will lump up on outside along anchor edge.
　Pressing lump down from outside tends to make the covering shiny.

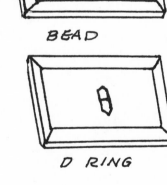

BEAD

D RING

FOLD ANCHOR ends back into depression. Rub along edge with finger. If anchor still "lumps up", peel away a little more board.

SET LID upside down over two books, allowing bead or D ring to hang between them. Dab adhesive into depression and hold anchor ends down. Smooth with folder and protective paper. Avoid denting outside board surface.

LID FLANGE

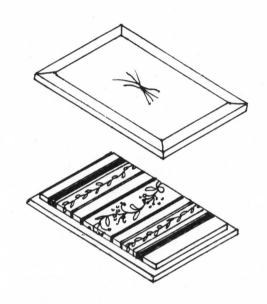

CUT COVERING.
  Height = board height + 1 1/4"
  Width = board width + 1 1/4"

Follow *FINISH OUTER base,* p. 179, and *ADD FILLER to this board,* p. 180.

BRUSH ADHESIVE on exposed flange board and along the inside edge of the turn-in. Keep 1/8" margin around outside edge free of adhesive. This is necessary to avoid adhesive oozing out around the edge.

CENTER FLANGE over outer lid. Keep an even margin of outer lid visible all around flange.

Press around edges with fingers.

Carefully set lid right side up. Cover with paper and press firmly with hand. Weight to dry. Be sure weight is spread evenly across the lid leaving the pull free. Ribbon Pulls are flat, but beads and D rings need to hang out of the way when weighted for drying, p. 241.

HINGED LID BOXS

BUTTON CLOSURE

This book is a modern adaptation of the Eastern palm leaf book. It is strung on cord attached to the box base. The book is never separated from the box. The cord is long enough so that the pages can be strung out and viewed.

A lift cord is added making it easier to lift all the pages from the box.

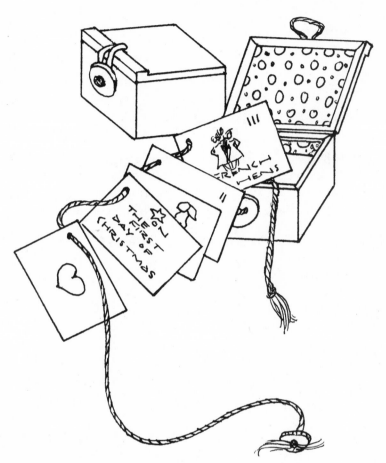

Materials:
Book block,
  heavyweight paper
Binder board
Cover material, book cloth
Adhesive
Button, optional second
  button for end of book cord
Cord, for loop closure,
  book cord and lift
Ribbon lift, optional

Braided embroidery thread can be used.
The lift cord is easier to find if it does not match the book cord.
A different color can be woven into the lift cord or lift cord can be made of ribbon.

PLAN DIMENSIONS and make up book block leaves.
   Making extra leaves now saves time later!

USE A leaf for the box base liner. This liner can be made from a rejected leaf since it will be covered with lining material and will not show. Both book cord and lift will be anchored to the under side of this leaf.

MAKE HOLE in leaves before drafting. Only one hole is used. Work out hole position on a paper pattern. Place pattern on top of stacked leaves and wrap with rubber bands as shown.

DRILL HOLE through stack as marked on pattern, p. 244.

CUT COVER material for liner
 Paper covering = size of leaf + 1/2 " both directions
 Cloth covering = size of leaf + 1/4" both directions

SPREAD ADHESIVE on face side of liner leaf. Center over back side of covering
 material. Press in place.

 Paper covering: miter corners and fold over turn-ins.
 Cloth covering: when adhesive has set, trim off fabric margins.

 Dry under light pressure, see *DRILL: EDGE SEWN BINDING,* p. 244, for tips.

CUT BOARDS. Determine wall height, C dimension.
 Thread text cord through collated leaves leaving at least half behind last leaf. Pile the
 rest on top. Don't try to smash it flat. Loose is better. Measure this pile to determine
 inside box C measurement, adding1/4" to top of text for cord to rest.

Follow *DETERMINE GRAIN* and *WRITE NAME,* p. 170.

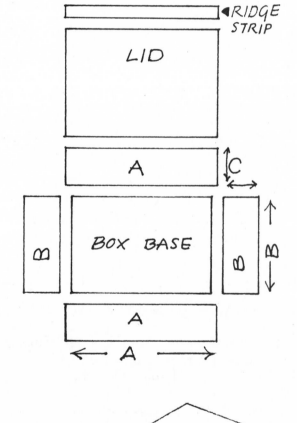

Box Base
A = length of contents
    + 1/8" ease room
    + 2 times CT (covering thickness)
B = width of contents
    + 1/8" ease room
    + 2 times CT

Box Walls
A Walls, cut two
A = base A dimension
    + 2 BT (board thickness)
C = wall height + 1 BT

B Walls, cut two
B = base B dimension
C = same as A walls

Lid, cut one
A = base A dimension + 2 BT
B = base B dimension + 2 BT

Ridge Strip, cut one
A = Lid A dimension
B = 1/4"

CUT ALL box parts listed above at same time.

Follow *WRITE NAME* and *CONSTRUCT BOXES,*
p. 170, starting with a B wall to assemble box base.

ADD COVERING when box walls are stable.

CUT COVERING materials.
  Outside Lid and Back Wall, cut in one piece
  A = lid A + 1 1/4"
  B = lid B + 4 BT + C + 1 1/8"

  Inside Back Wall and
  Hinge Covering, cut 1
  same as outside covering material
  A = 1/8" less than inside width of back wall
  C = back wall C + 1 BT + 1"

  Front and Side Walls, cut in one piece
  Width = 2 times C + 1 BT + 1"
  Length = A + 2 times B + 4 BT + 1"

  Outside Base Covering, cut 1
  Cut slightly smaller than outside base.

COVER BOX front and side walls first.

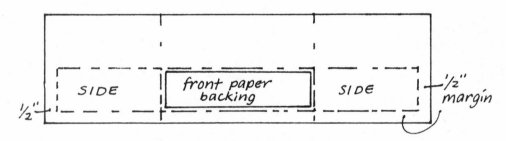

DRAW 1/2" margin along lower edge of covering material on wrong side. Measure box
  height (C) and draw another line parallel to the first.

DRAW SIDE margin line. Center box front wall on strip and trace along its sides.

CUT A manila
  folder to be
  a bit smaller
  than box
  front wall.

  Apply adhesive
  and center over
  front wall section just drawn.

MAKE HOLE with awl for the button cord in center of the panel when dry.

A cord attaches the button to the box. The same cord material can also be used to form the loop closure on box lid. Embroidery thread makes a nice texture. Thickness can be varied. Braid strands of the same or several colors together.

CUT CLOSURE cords.
  Lid closure loop = 2 times distance from button to top wall of box + 1 BT + 1 5/8"
  Button cord = 2"

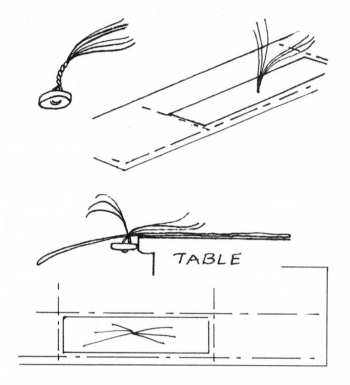

THREAD BUTTON onto cord and unravel both ends. Dampen and twist all ends into one cord on back side of button.
  Use a large-eyed needle to draw thread ends through right side of covering strip, pulling all thread ends to paper side.

LEAVE SLACK in cord on the outside so the button is free of box wall for buttoning.

  Set on edge of table with button hanging over edge.

ADD DAB of adhesive to paper backing near the hole. Spread unraveled cord ends out over it. This will prevent cord from making a visible lump on the outside of box wall when finished.

COVER WITH waxed paper and press down flat with bone folder.

BRUSH ADHESIVE on box outside front and side walls. Center paper backing over front wall and press with fingers.

SLIDE A piece of protective paper under button and rub covering with folder from button to outer edge as shown. Keep paper under folder as pressing moves around button.

PULL COVERING down over the side walls and press with fingers. Turn box on its side and smooth with folder and protective paper. Repeat on other side wall.

Use minimum amount of adhesive
on the two back margins and
smooth in place over back wall.

Follow *MITER BASE outside corners,*
p. 172, and *WALL CORNERS,* p. 173.

Follow *FOLD FLAPS inside box,* p. 174,
to continue with fitting and pasting.
Paste front wall in place last.

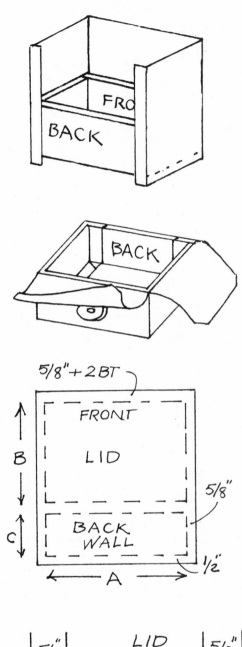

COVER LID.
   Place covering wrong side up and
   draw top margin 5/8" + 2 BT down
   from top edge. This includes fabric
   to cover ridge strip.

SET LID in place over covering.
   Draw line along lid's lower edge
   continuing through the 5/8" side margins.

   Add another line 2 BT below it for cloth
   covering.
   This narrow space becomes the hinge.

   (For Inset Hinged Lid Box with paper
   covering, only 1 BT is needed for hinge.)

CUT DIAGONAL line in margin
   from hinge mark to outer edge
   at lid line, shown below.
   Use a fresh blade.
   To avoid cutting into hinge or
   back wall, see Cutting Slits,
   p. 235.

   The rest of side margin is cut
   away along back wall edge
   as shown.

APPLY ADHESIVE to ridge strip side
   of lid and carefully set in place,
   aligning edges with margin lines
   on covering.

Press hand near center and along
hinge edge of lid.

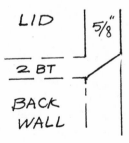

2 BT hinge
Cloth Covering

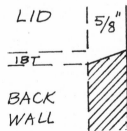

1 BT hinge
Paper Covering

TURN CLOTH side up. Smooth with folder and protective paper.
Slide folder along ridge strip to press covering material into the groove.
Flatten covering material along the top of ridge strip by pressing firmly with folder,
moving from center to each end of ridge strip.
Recheck groove, sliding folder along it again if necessary.

MITER CORNERS, p. 245. Turn ridge strip edge last. Slide folder
around corner to press covering wedge against board thickness.
Put small dab of adhesive on board edge at corner
to hold wedge in place. Repeat at other corner.

BRUSH minimum amount of adhesive along board
edge at hinge. Hold back wall covering firmly on
work surface as lid is turned up and pressed
against table. Be sure outside edge is smooth.

ADD LID closure loop.
Mark center width of box lid at base of
ridge strip with sharp pencil.
Pound awl or use drill to make a small hole.

Thread lid closure loop cord onto needle,
leaving one end longer than the other.
Pull thread through lid from *inside* to *outside*.
Loop over pencil or finger for slack and go back through same hole.

Set lid on box and adjust loop so it is just
long enough to slip over button.
Unravel ends and fan out towards lid center.
Dot threads with adhesive. Smooth with
folder and protective paper, p. 240.

ADD LID to box. Brush adhesive on exposed
board of outside back wall. Wipe almost all
adhesive out of brush, then lightly brush
along inside side edges of back wall
covering as shown in dotted area.

Set lid on top of box, aligning front edge
with outside box front wall. Hold lid in
place. Press covering against back box wall
from top edge to bottom.
Smooth with folder and protective paper.

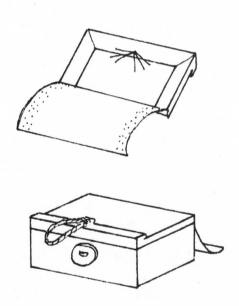

MITER CORNERS of lower margin leaving enough to meet side covering already in
place on base. Brush small amount of adhesive on underside of margin and press in
place.

ADD FILLER to outside box base if needed, p. 174.

Follow *OUTSIDE BASE COVERING*, p. 175, to finish outside box base.
Allow adhesive to set before adding lining.

DRAW 1/2" lower margin on back of back wall lining piece. Crease. Set in place.
 Crease with fingers along top of box wall. If there is a narrow groove between box
 wall board thickness and lid board thickness, press covering in this space as well.
 Be careful not to tear lining.

MARK EXPOSED lid board where wall covering
 ends. This will be about 1/2" from hinge edge.
 Remove covering and draw a straight line
 parallel to hinge at this mark. This line
 becomes the guide for setting lining in place.

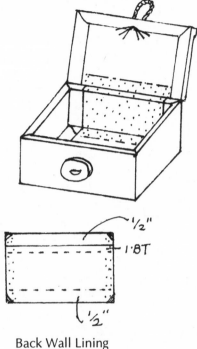

BRUSH ADHESIVE on exposed board of box at
 bottom margin, back wall, top edge of wall,
 and lid margin space, shown in dots.

BRUSH ADHESIVE along side edges of lining
 piece where it will overlap the lining already
 in place along the back wall.

LINE UP ALONG pencil line on lid board and
 lightly press in place with fingers.
 Cover with wax paper and press with folder.

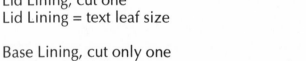

Back Wall Lining

CUT FINISHING materials.
 Lid Lining, cut one
 Lid Lining = text leaf size

 Base Lining, cut only one
 Cloth = slightly larger than text leaf size, edges will be trimmed
                    to match leaf when pasted together
 Paper = text leaf + 1/2" both directions

 Lift Cord, cut one
 Length = 2 times B + C + 1"

 Book Cord, cut one
 Fan pages out as they will be viewed when finished.
 Add 4 extra inches to this length. This can be trimmed later if needed.

ADD FILLER to lid if needed, p. 174.

Follow *BOX BASE LINING*, p. 175, to mount lid lining.

ADD ADHESIVE to top side of extra leaf
for base lining. Mount on base lining piece.

Paper covering: miter corners,
    turn margins, and paste.
Cloth covering: trim edges even with leaf.

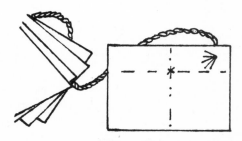

MAKE BOOK cord hole in liner to match
hole placement in text leaves. Pull cord
end through. Finish as cord lift below.

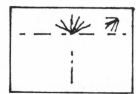

LIFT CORD PLACEMENT

MARK PLACEMENT for lift on back of liner
piece near the center back, shown with X.

Cord Lift: Make small hole and thread cord through hole.
Dot adhesive on backing near hole. Spread unraveled
cord ends over it.

LIFT CORD

Ribbon Lift: Cut a slit the width of ribbon, parallel to box
back wall. Thread ribbon through. Fold toward back.
Dot with adhesive and press flat.

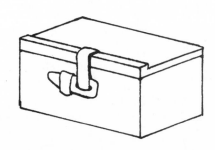

LIFT RIBBON
· LINING PAPER
TURN-INS

BRUSH ADHESIVE on under side of liner, lightly coating
the cord and ribbon ends also. This should not ooze out
at edges when set in place.
Set in place with lift and book cords near back wall.
Press with fingers, then with folder using protective paper.

BONE CLASP CLOSURE VARIATION

This is the *Button Closure* box, p. 187, with closure used
in *Wrap-Around Case*, p. 222.

Follow *MAKE CLASP closure strips,* p. 220.
Only one loop and one anchor are needed.

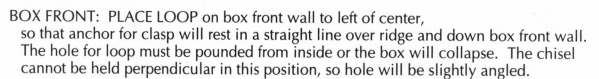

Follow *CHISEL AND MALLET,* p. 244, to
pound holes. Hole placement as follows:

LID: CENTER ANCHOR for bone clasp along
lid's opening edge, against ridge strip.

BOX FRONT: PLACE LOOP on box front wall to left of center,
    so that anchor for clasp will rest in a straight line over ridge and down box front wall.
    The hole for loop must be pounded from inside or the box will collapse. The chisel
    cannot be held perpendicular in this position, so hole will be slightly angled.

Follow *MOUNT LOOPS,* p. 221, and *MOUNT CLASPS,* p. 222, to set in place.

INSET HINGED LID BOX

This is a wonderful box for letters, cards, and stationary. Made like a cardboard cigar or pencil box, it opens with a ribbon tab. The box can be covered with either paper or cloth.

Wall paper is easy to use. Solid colors and small patterns usually look best. When paper is used, a cloth or Tyvek hinge is added to the lid for strength.

Materials:
Binder board
Cover material,
* paper or cloth*
Hinge if paper, cloth
* or Tyvek cover*
Ribbon for lid pull
Adhesive

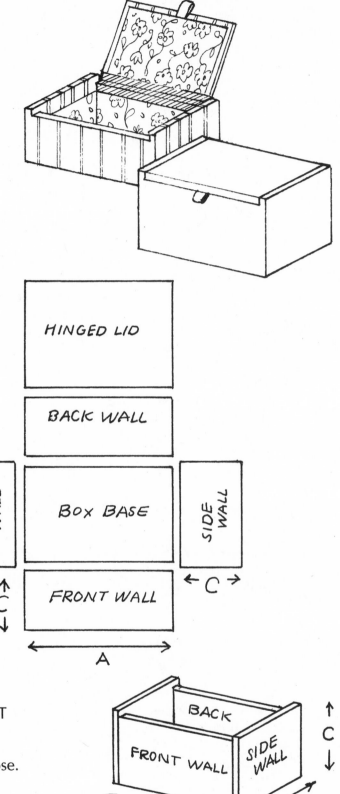

CUT BOARDS.
  Box Base
  A = length of contents
      + ease room
      + 2 times covering
      thickness (CT)
  B = width of contents
      + ease room
      + 2 times CT

Box Walls
A Walls, cut two
A = base A dimension
C = desired inside wall height
      + 1 board thickness (BT)

B Walls, cut two
B = base B dimension + 2 BT
C = desired inside wall height + 2 BT

Lid, cut one
Lid must be smaller than base to close.
A = base A dimension minus 5 CT
B = base B dimension + 2 BT

Ribbon Lift, cut one
Width = 5/8"
Length = 2 1/2"

Follow *CONSTRUCT BOXES,* p. 170, beginning with a B wall to assemble base.
For this project, B walls are 1 BT taller than A walls.

ADD COVERING when walls are stable.

CUT COVERING material.
  In this project, each wall is cut as a separate piece of material.
  The lining can be a contrast in color or pattern.
  Generally the lining looks best if walls and base are the same.

Outside Box Covering
  Cloth
  Lid and Back Wall, cut in one continuous piece
  A = lid A + 1 1/4"
  B = lid B + 2 BT + C + 1 1/8"

  Front Wall, cut one
  A = box A minus 2 BT
    must fit between side walls
  C = box C + 1 1/8" + 1 BT

  Side Walls (B), cut two
  B = box B + 1 1/4"
  C = box C + 1 1/2" + 2 BT

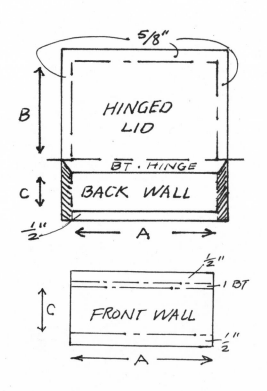

  Paper
  Lid and Back Wall,
  cut in one continuous piece
  B = lid B + 1 BT + C + 1 1/8"

All other dimensions are the
same as Cloth Covering.

DRAW MARGINS on back of
  both side pieces.
  Top margin = 1" + 1 BT
  Side margins = 5/8"
  Bottom margin = 1/2" + 1 BT

COVER B walls first.
   Turn box up on side wall and place over side covering to make sure it fits.

BRUSH ADHESIVE on one outside B wall of box. Set in place along margin lines. If covering has a pattern, be sure it faces desired direction.

   With fingers inside of box, press wall down on covering material. Turn box over.
   Smooth with folder and protective paper, p. 240.

MAKE CUTS for corner turn-ins of top wall. Set box on B wall with top edge facing you. Place right angle triangle against this edge, one wall thickness from wall corner as shown.

   Use a very sharp knife. Begin cut one wall thickness from box top edge and continue at right angle to the edge of covering material.

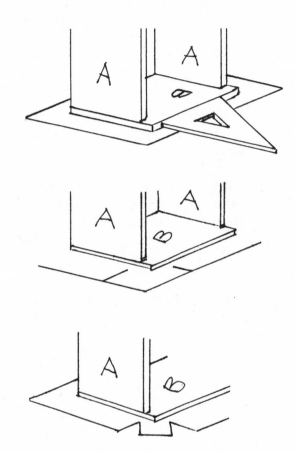

MOVE TRIANGLE around corner. Place against side edge and align with top of A wall. Begin second cut one wall thickness from box top edge and continue at right angle to the edge of covering material.

   Cut tongue long enough and wide enough to cover the corner comfortably.

REPEAT PROCESS at other corner.

PUT ADHESIVE on tongue and pull over corner, keeping tongue centered. Press in edge along top and front wall to form pleats.

ADD ADHESIVE to 3/8" strip along front wall at side edge. Brush a little adhesive along flap edge and fold flap in place. Smooth with folder.

REPEAT PROCESS with back wall at side edge.

Follow *MITER BASE outside corners,* p. 172.

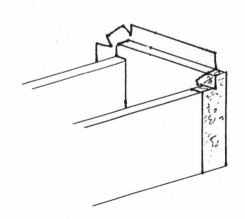

SPREAD ADHESIVE along top edge of box
and along 7/8" margin inside, shown in
dots. Brush a little adhesive along flap
edge. Pull covering over edge of box
and carefully press in place with fingers.
Smooth with folder.

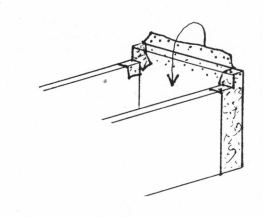

REPEAT FOR other B wall.

DRAW MARGINS on wrong side
of box front covering.

ADD ADHESIVE to the exposed board of
box front. Brush a thin coat of adhesive
along the edges of covering where it
overlaps the side flaps. Set in place
being careful to keep covering centered.

Fold in the top and bottom flaps and
carefully press in place with fingers.
Smooth with folder, p. 240.

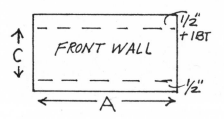

ADD OUTSIDE box lid covering.
Cloth
ADD CLOTH outside covering to lid before lid is mounted on box.
The lid and outside back wall covering form the hinge.

Follow *COVER LID* and continuing directions, p. 191-192, to mount outside covering
on box lid and back wall. Note top margin is different since this box has no ridge strip
along lid front edge.
Top edge margin = 5/8"
Hinge space = 2 BT

Follow *OUTSIDE BASE COVERING*, p. 175, to finish base. Then follow *ADD RIBBON
lift,* p. 199, and remaining directions to finish project.

Paper
ADD PAPER outside covering to lid after lid is mounted on box.
The lid is held in place by a cloth hinge mounted inside.
It will not show in finished box.

CUT HINGE strip.
Torn cloth gives a softer edge which
is less visible than if cut with scissors.
Width = 1 1/2"
Length = same length as lid's A
       dimension

MOUNT HINGE.

Set box back wall on a board scrap. Line up edges of wall and scrap as shown. Place lid on working surface against scrap. The box edge will form a ledge above the lid.

Brush adhesive along the top of inside back wall, board thickness and lower edge of lid, shown as "cloth hinge". Press cloth in place over adhesive. Smooth with folder and let adhesive set, p. 240.

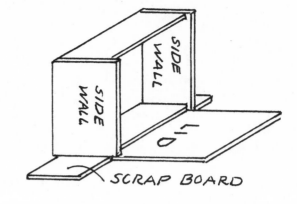

SCRAP BOARD

Follow *COVER LID* and continuing directions, p. 191-192, to mount outside covering on box lid and back wall. Note top margin is different since this box has no ridge strip along lid front edge.
    Top edge margin = 5/8"
    Hinge space = 1 BT

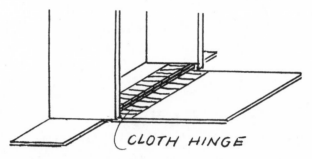

CLOTH HINGE

Follow *OUTSIDE BASE COVERING*, p. 175, to finish outside base.

ADD RIBBON lift.

Use 1/2" wide ribbon for small boxes and 3/4" for large boxes.
To decide overhang length, fold ribbon in half, place at center front edge inside box, and close lid. Slide ribbon in and out a little to decide what length looks best.

Follow *RECESS AREA IN BOARD*, p. 246, to inset if ribbon. Make cut just wide enough for ribbon. The 1/16" extra margin is not desired in this case. Thick ribbons look better with this step. Recessing is not necessary if ribbon is thin. Cut along edge of turn-in on exposed board rather than flange. Dab adhesive in this area and between ribbon ends. Set ribbon in place. Press in place.

CUT LINING material.

Side and Front Walls, cut in one piece
Width of wall covering material = front wall C + 3/8"
Length of wall covering material = A + 2 times B + 1

Back Wall and Hinge Covering, cut in one piece
Width, paper covering = C + 1 BT + 1"
cloth covering = C + 2 BT + 1"
Length = slightly less than inside A dimension so that it can slip between side walls

Base Lining and Lid Lining , cut same size.

Follow *BOX BASE LINING*, p. 175, for size and mounting.

ADD LINING to side and
   front walls first.

Follow *PLACE LINING,*
p. 176, to draw margins
and test for fit.
Lining begins and ends
with a 1/2" margin against
back wall.

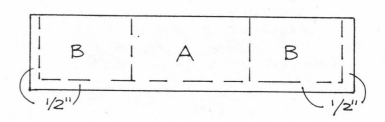

Follow *CREASE ALONG* lower margin, p. 176, to finish mounting to side and front
walls.

Follow *BOX BASE LINING,* p. 175, to finish inside box base, using filler if needed, p.
174. Mount lid lining in the same way.

CLAM SHELL BOX

This is similar to the Lipped Clamshell Box, p. 203. It is faster to make but not as accurate
a fit. After making several, it goes together quickly. It lacks the tailored quality of the
Lipped Clamshell but is still a very nice container.
In this style both base and lid are three sided.
They are joined together as lid closes
over the base.

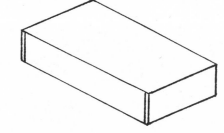

Materials:
Binder board
Cover material,
   cloth outside, paper inside
Adhesive

Building this box differs
from other boxes.
Boards are not joined
to each other as in other
boxes previously described.

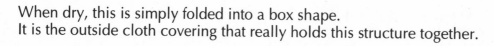

Boards are cut and
mounted on an uncut
paper lining piece. Lining
paper is then turned over and mounted
on an outside covering, with boards sandwiched between.

When dry, this is simply folded into a box shape.
It is the outside cloth covering that really holds this structure together.

CUT BOARDS.

Base Shell Base, cut one
A = book A + 6 CT (covering thickness) of lining material (allows 4 CT clearance)
B = book B + 3 CT of lining material (allows 2 CT clearance)

Base Walls
B Walls, cut two
B = base B
C = thickness of book + 1 BT

A Wall, cut one
A = base A
C = thickness of book + 1 BT

Lid Shell Base, cut one
A = base A + 2 BT + 6 CT
    (allows 2 CT for clearance)
B = base B + 1 BT + 4 CT
    (allows 2 CT for clearance)

Lid Walls
B Walls, cut two
B = lid B
C = base wall C + 1 1/2 BT

A walls, cut two
The second becomes the spine
A = lid A
C = base wall C + 1 1/2 BT

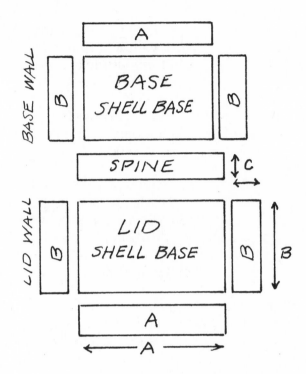

LAY OUT all board pieces on
   underside of lining paper.

Use L square or straight edge and
triangle to draw a square corner
in lower left corner of lining paper.
From corner draw 1/2" margin line
along lower edge and up one side.

With straight edge on margin line,
use triangle to draw all placement
lines on underside of lining paper.

Leave a 1/2" margin all around.
Leave 1 1/2 BT on each side of spine.
Leave 1 BT between other boards.

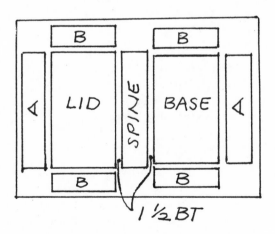

Lining paper lay out

ADHERE ALL parts to lining paper. *Do not press paper into the grooves or case sides will not fold up.* Press with hand. Turn over and smooth with folder and protective paper.

When adhesive is set, trim lining paper flush on dotted lines as shown, top of A and B walls and spine of B walls. Do not trim outside corners of B walls where flap remains.

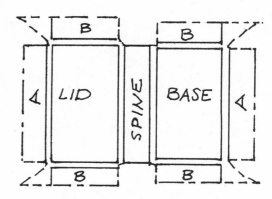

Paper Lining trimming pattern

BRUSH ADHESIVE on exposed boards except the outside corners of B walls, shown in dots.

PICK UP and carefully place bonded unit onto underside of cover cloth. *Do not press cloth into the grooves.* Press all parts firmly in place with hand. Turn over. Smooth with folder and protective paper, p. 240.

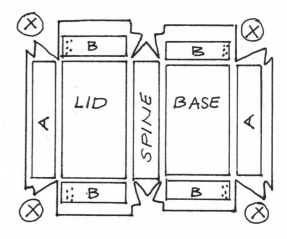

Cover Cloth trimming pattern

TURN LINING paper side up. Trim cloth side as shown. *Do not cut off lining paper flaps that extend beyond cloth on B walls at each X corner.* Leave at least 1 BT of cloth along wall edges at X corners to cover BT when cloth is folded to inside.

FOLD UP box walls when adhesive has set. Paper will go down into joints at wall base.

FOLD POINTS of B wall and spine to inside. Brush thin coat of adhesive to underside and press in place.

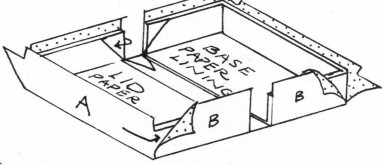

FOLD A wall points around corner on to B walls. If cloth has adhered to board at corner of B wall, peel just enough away from wall board so that the wedge of cloth can tuck inside. If a layer or two of board peels off, it won't matter.

TRIM TOP edge so all walls have a 1/4" margin overlap to be folded onto inside walls.

BRUSH SMALL amount of adhesive on undersides of A point and exposed board at B
corner, shown on previous page. Smooth point in place on B wall with fingers.
Press B wall covering over wedge, shown here.
Hold in place while adhesive sets.
Repeat process at each corner.

FINISH ONE shell at a time.
Brush adhesive along
an A wall edge and
cloth margin above
it, including the
corner point tops.
Fold in place and
press with fingers,
then press with folder.
Do adjoining B walls next.

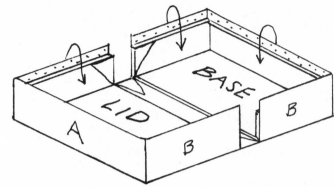

REPEAT PROCESS on other shell.

LIPPED CLAM SHELL BOX

This box is frequently used by libraries to
house special or rare books. Its attractive
style also forms an accurate fit.

Box lining for rare books is chosen with
care; felt, handmade paper, or alkaline-
buffered paper are used most often.

The box is not hard to make, but it takes
time to make the first one. It is a good
idea to make several other projects
in this chapter before this one.

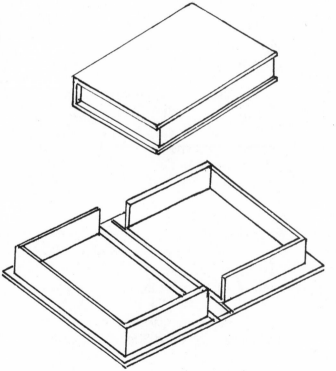

Materials:
Binder board
Book cloth
Lining: paper, felt,
  or same book cloth
   as outside
Adhesive
Weights

DETERMINE GRAIN, p. 170, before cutting board.

Follow *LARGE BOOKS*, p. 209, to alleviate sagging along the spine if opening edge of shells is 8" or more.

MAKE MEASUREMENTS.
Attention given to measurements insures the box will close well and the book will not slide around inside. All information needed for a good fit is given.
Follow measurements carefully.
Measurements that fall above a given mark on ruler should be raised to the next 1/16".

CUT BOARDS.
Base Shell Base, cut one
A = length of book from head to tail + 6 CT (covering thicknesses)
(allows 4 CT for clearance.)
B = width of book from spine to fore edge
+ 3 CT (allows 2 CT for clearance)

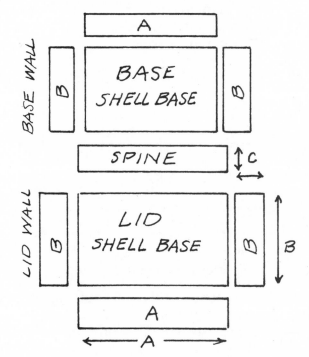

Base Shell Walls
A Wall, cut one
A = box base A + 2 BT
C = spine thickness + 1 BT + 3 CT
(allows 2 CT for clearance)

B Walls, cut two
B = box base B dimension
C = same as base A wall C
dimension

Follow *CONSTRUCT BOXES,* p. 170, to assemble base shell, beginning with a B wall. These directions apply to both base and lid shells.
Make the base shell first.

CUT COVERINGS.
Wall Covering Cloth
Base Shell wall dimensions, cut one
Entire outside circumference of all three walls + all BTs + margins at shell's open edge
Width of covering material = 2 times C + 1 BT + 1 1/2"
Length of covering material = A + 2 times B + 4 BT + 1 1/2"

Lid Shell wall dimensions, cut one
Same formula as Base Shell Wall Covering Cloth given above

Shell Lining, cut two
A = book length from head to tail minus 1/16"
B = book width from spine to fore edge + 1/2" + 1 BT

Follow *PLACE WRONG side up*, p. 171, to mount cloth to outside shell walls.

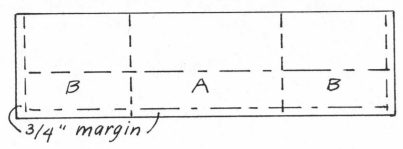

3/4" margin

MOUNT B wall first as shown at right.
  There will be a 3/4" margin at open edge
  of both B walls. This margin is not adhered yet.

Follow *MITER BASE outside corners*, p. 172, to miter
under-side corners of A wall and paste in place.

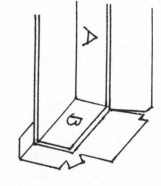

3/4"

Follow *LARGE BOX*,
  p. 173, to cut top corners
  at shell fore edge turn-ins.

CUT BOTH corners where shell
  base meets B wall at spine turn in.
  Do not fold
  inside yet.

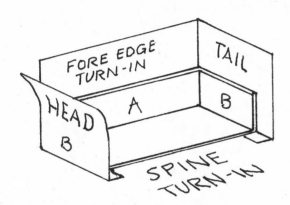

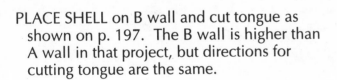

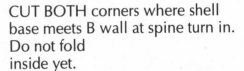

PLACE SHELL on B wall and cut tongue as
  shown on p. 197. The B wall is higher than
  A wall in that project, but directions for
  cutting tongue are the same.

DO ALL cutting before pasting
  down and turning in.

Follow *PUT ADHESIVE on tongue*,
  p. 197, to mount tongue, 1, in place.

Follow *ALWAYS FOLD B walls first*,
  p. 174, to fit and paste down
  remaining flaps in numerical order.

ADD FILLER to shell base if needed, p. 174.

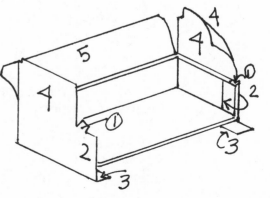

Follow *BOX BASE LINING*, p. 175, to mount
shell base lining. It is easiest to align along
A wall when setting in place. Lining will
extend past shell's open edge. Adhere to
underside of shell, being careful to pull
tight over shell's open edge.

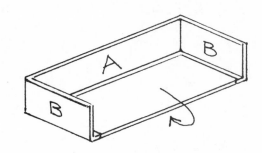

SMOOTH IN place.

MAKE LID Base Shell.
    Lid Shell Base, cut one
    A = finished base shell A + 6 CT (allows 2 CT for clearance)
    B = finished base shell B + 4 CT (allows 2 CT for clearance)

    Lid Shell Walls
    A Wall, cut one
    A = finished base shell A + 2 BT + 6 CT (allows 2 CT clearance)
    C = finished base shell wall C + 1 BT + 2 CT (no clearance is needed)

    B Walls, cut two
    B = lid base B
    C = same as lid shell A wall C dimension

MAKE AS base shell, p. 204.

CASE DIMENSIONS' measurements have
a 1/16" lip at head, tail, and fore edge.
Flush head and tail variation is given on p. 209.

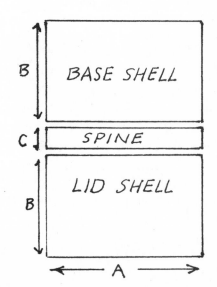

MAKE CASE.
    Case Boards, cut two
    Board grain can run parallel to B dimension
    for added strength.
    A = finished lid shell A + 2/16"
    B = finished lid shell B + 1/16"

    Case Spine, cut one
    Board grain runs parallel to A dimension
    A = same as case board A dimension
    C = lid shell wall C dimension

    Spacer Board, cut one, see p. 5
    3 x 6", using 7 layers of covering material
    Joint width is difficult to determine accurately. Place gauge between boards as
    placement lines are drawn and as boards are mounted on cloth.

Outside Case Covering, cut one
A = case board A dimension + 2 BT + 1 1/2"
B = 2 times case board B dimension + case spine C + 2 BT + 1 13/16"
(allows 5/16" for the 2 joints; each joint width = 1 BT + 7 CT)
Spine Lining, cut one
A = outside length of lid shell wall A
C = spine board C + 5/16" (for the 2 joints) + 4 BT + 1"

TURN CASE covering material underside
up. Use L square or straight edge and
triangle to draw a 3/4" turn-in line down
left side and along lower edge.

With straight edge along lower margin
line, set case board along these lines.
Mark spine side of this board.

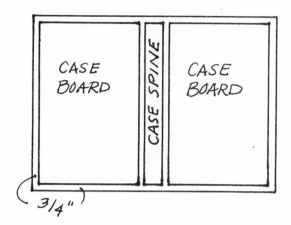

PLACE SPACER against each board to
mark placement line. Use triangle and
straight edge to draw all placement lines.

PLACE STRAIGHT edge along bottom turn-in
line. Brush adhesive on one case board and carefully set in place along straight edge.
Press hand firmly in center of board, avoid sliding hand. Press firmly near each
corner.

Spread adhesive on spine board and set in place. Press hand firmly in center.
Slip spacer between the two boards at head and tail to be sure gap is even.
Be sure lower edges are against the straight edge. Repeat for last board.

TURN CLOTH side up. Smooth with folder and protective paper, p. 240.

Follow STANDARD MITER, p. 245,
to finish turn-ins. Keep 2 BT covering
material at corners.

SPINE COVERING should be the
same length as outside lid base shell,
the larger of the two shells.

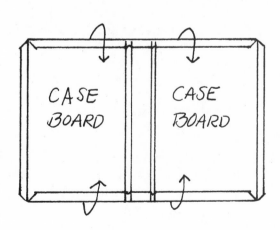

BRUSH ADHESIVE on exposed board of case spine, also along under-edge of spine lining adjoining lid case board, shown in dots.

Center lining piece over spine. Press in place and into groove along spine using folder and protective paper. Press the glued edge of spine lining onto case board.

CENTER BASE shell along case board edge at spine. Mark where shell ends at outside B wall on spine lining piece. Remove shell to cut point off diagonally from spine edge groove to mark, shown as shaded area along base shell at spine edge.

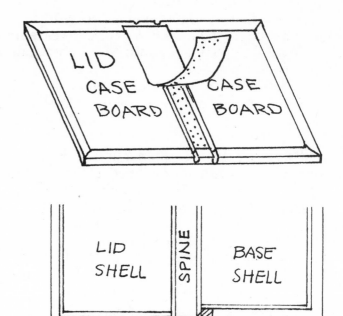

ADHERE BASE side of lining to case. Press cloth into groove using folder and protective paper. Press remaining edge onto case base board.

PLACE WEIGHTS inside each shell when mounting to base, to insure corners are firmly attached. Have weights ready before continuing, pp. 5, 241. A book does not have enough weight for this purpose.

ADD FILLER to underside of both shells and to exposed case board where shells will be attached, p. 174.

BRUSH ADHESIVE on underside of lid shell's filler and adjoining cloth turn-in, keeping a 1/8" adhesive-free margin around shell's outside edge.

Use a thin coat of adhesive. A thick coating will ooze out and stain covering material as shell is pressed to the case. A thick coating can also cause the shell to slip out of position.

Distribute adhesive evenly before positioning shells.

ALIGN LID SHELL over case board. Center head and tail. Place open edge flush with case board at joint.

Firmly press hand down in center of shell, then press near each corner.

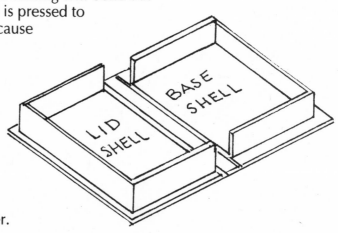

FLUSH HEAD AND TAIL VARIATION

This is good for a box with a thick spine or heavy contents to be stored vertically.

Follow LIPPED CLAM SHELL BOX directions, except:
for a 1/16" lip at fore edge and flush head and tail,
subtract 2/16" from case board A dimension given on p. 206.

PLACE WEIGHTS inside shells while adhesive sets, p. 241.

LARGE BOOKS

Lipped clam shell boxes made for large books tend to sag along spine if under pressure. When closed, the spine is the only part of the case with a single board thickness. This problem can be corrected by adding a double thickness of covered board to inside spine when finishing the case. Allowance must be added when cutting Base Shell base board B dimensions.

CHANGE MEASUREMENT in Base Shell Base.
  B = measurement given + 2 BT + 2 CT

ADD REINFORCEMENT Spine Boards to mount inside case, cut two
  Length = book spine length, head to tail
  Width = base shell wall C dimension minus 1 BT minus 1 CT
        (same as finished wall C measurement *inside* covered base shell)

Reinforcement Spine Board Covering, cut one
  A = reinforcement spine board A + 4 BT + 1"
  B = reinforcement spine board B + 4 BT + 1"

ADHERE REINFORCEMENT spine boards together, press firmly with hand in center and
  then at each end.

APPLY ADHESIVE to one side of board and center on underside of cloth covering.

Follow *STANDARD MITER,* p. 245 to finish turn-ins. Keep 3 BT at corners.

ALIGN REINFORCEMENT piece with base shell.
  Mount in place over inside of case spine. Place weights over area until dry, p. 241.

PORTFOLIO WITH TIES

With one base board and four flaps, this portfolio is somewhat awkward to open and close. It is better suited for things that aren't handled often. It does provide excellent protection for its contents.

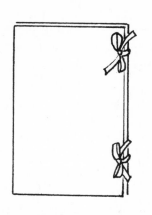

The portfolio boards are covered with a single piece of cloth. Ties form the closure. For small sizes, one tie at fore edge is enough. As size increases, more ties are needed.

Flap 1, shown on next page, must be folded in first to provide uniform pressure and keep the contents smooth.
As a folding reminder, flap 1 and the base are lined with a contrasting material of paper or cloth. All other flaps are lined with the outside covering material.

> *Materials:*
> *Board, must all be same thickness*
> *Covering material, book cloth*
> *Lining material, book cloth plus paper or felt*
> *Ribbon*
> *Adhesive*
> *Sandpaper*

CUT BOARDS.
Base and Flap boards, cut four
A = Length of book from head to tail, + 1/8" + 2 LT (lining thickness)
B = Width of book from spine to fore edge 1/8" + 2 LT

Trim two boards to make flaps.
Flap 1, make A = base board length minus 2 BT
          make B = base board width minus 2 BT

Flap 2, make A = baseboard length minus 1/8"
          make B = base board width minus 1 BT (board thickness)

Spacer Board, cut one, see p. 5
3 x 6", using 5 layers of covering material
Joint width is difficult to determine accurately. Place gauge between boards as placement lines are drawn and as boards are mounted on cloth.

Divide length of Flap 2 board in half to make two boards. Taper spine and fore edge sides by trimming just under 1/8" from the outer corners, tapering to nothing at inner corners as shown.

Flap 3 remains the same size as base board. It will become the top of portfolio when closed.

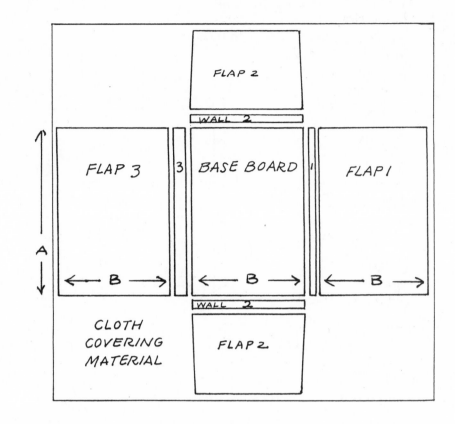

Wall Boards
Wall 1, cut one
adjoins Flap 1
A = flap 1 A dimension
C = height of material to be housed inside + 2 LT + 3 CT

Wall 2, cut two
adjoins Flap 2
A = flap 2 B dimension at widest edge minus 1 BT
C = wall 1 C dimension + 1 BT + 2 CT

Wall 3, cut one
adjoins Flap 3
A = base board A
C = wall 1 C dimension + 2 BT + 4 CT

LIGHTLY SAND the two outside corners of all flaps to soften corner points.

CUT COVERING material for outside in one piece.
Length = 2 times base board A dimension + 2 times wall 2 C dimension
    + 4 joint widths (use spacer to determine this dimension) + 3"
Width = 3 times base board B dimension + walls 1 and 3 C dimensions
    + 4 joint widths (use spacer to determine this dimension) + 3"

TURN CASE covering material underside up. Lay all boards on underside of cloth with base board in center as shown. Use L square or straight edge and triangle when aligning boards.

Use the spacer between boards and draw placement of all wall and flap boards.

Align walls 1 and 3, plus flaps, with base board.

Align walls 2, plus flaps, with base board.

BRUSH ADHESIVE on boards and mount boards one at a time.

Turn over and smooth with folder and protective paper. Do not press material into the grooves.

DRY UNDER weight, p. 241.

TRIM TURN-INS to 1 1/2" when dry.

CUT DIAGONALLY into each of the four corners to base board as shown.

MAKE CORNER pieces of covering material to hide the thickness of the four corner tips and base board.

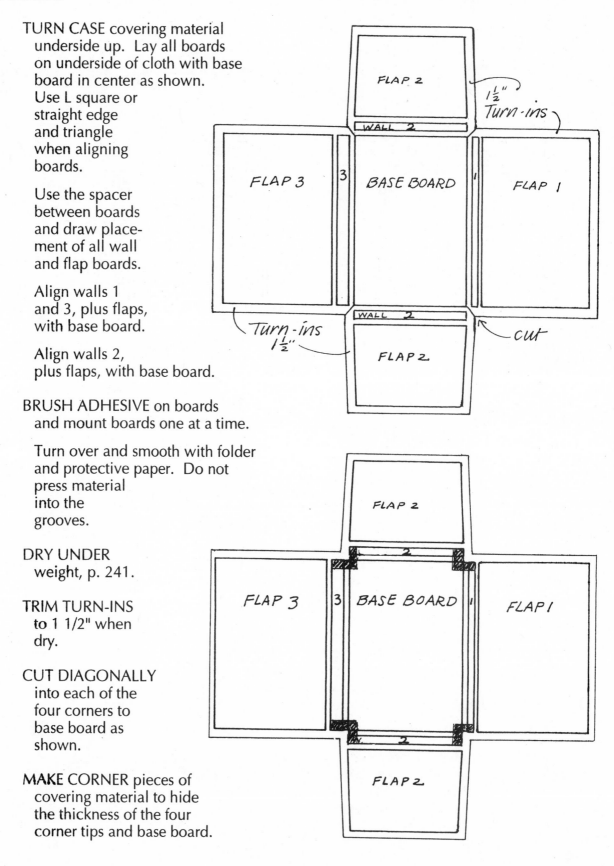

BEGIN PATTERN with a 1 1/2" square.
To form the L shaped shaded areas in the illustrations:
    Cut one mirror image set for wall 1
    add 2 BT + 1 joint thickness + adjoining wall 1 C dimension to one side of square
    add 2 BT + 1 joint thickness + adjoining wall 2 C dimension to and adjoining side

    Cut one mirror image set for wall 3
    add 2 BT + 1 joint thickness + adjoining wall 3 C dimension to one side of square
    add 2 BT + 1 joint thickness + adjoining wall 2 C dimension to and adjoining side

BRUSH ADHESIVE on boards and attach corner pieces. Be sure to cover the
thickness at base board corner point. Hold base board portion in place, as corner
piece is pressed into joint and onto adjoining wall board.

MITER OUTSIDE corners of flaps, p. 245. Finish all turn-ins except flap 3.
    These turn-ins are finished after ties are added.

CUT RIBBON for ties.
    Each pair uses 18" of ribbon, cut in two 9" pieces
    Ties are added to base board and flap 3.

MAKE TEMPLATE the length of needed
  edge (X, Y, Z) for ribbon slit placement.

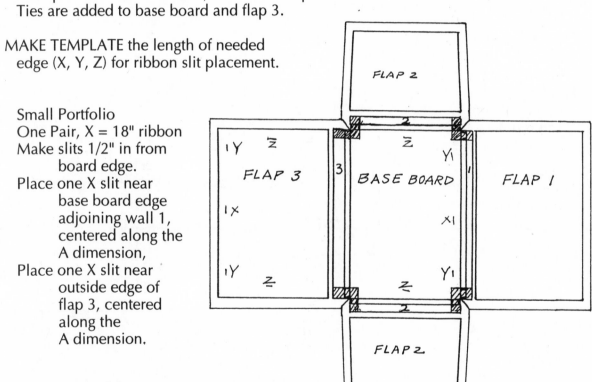

Small Portfolio
One Pair, X = 18" ribbon
Make slits 1/2" in from
    board edge.
Place one X slit near
    base board edge
    adjoining wall 1,
    centered along the
    A dimension,
Place one X slit near
    outside edge of
    flap 3, centered
    along the
    A dimension.

Medium Portfolio
Two Pair, Y = 36" ribbon
Make slits 1/2" in from board edge.
Place two Y slits near base board edge adjoining wall 1,
    a quarter of the A dimension, or less, in from each end.
Place two Y slits near outside edge of flap 3
    along the A dimension, the same distance from flap end as base board Y slits.

Large Portfolio
  Four Pair, Y and Z = 72" ribbon
  Make slits 1/2" in from board edge.
  Place two Y slits near base board edge adjoining wall 1, a quarter of the A dimension,
        or less, in from each end + 1 Z slit near base board edge adjoining both walls 2.
  Place two Y slits near outside edge of flap 3 along the A dimension,
        same distance from end as base board slits,
        Y + 1 Z slit centered along both B dimensions of flap 3.

Follow *MAKE HOLE through lid,* p. 183,
to pound slits from the outside with a chisel.
Careful placement is necessary.
Slits must be slightly longer than ribbon width.

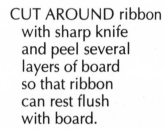

WRAP END of ribbon with thin paper or tape to
  help ribbon through slits without unraveling.

PULL RIBBON through boards from outside
  to inside bringing 1/2" to 5/8" to inside.
  Lay back towards center of board.

CUT AROUND ribbon
  with sharp knife
  and peel several
  layers of board
  so that ribbon
  can rest flush
  with board.

  Dab adhesive
  under ribbon
  and press
  in place.

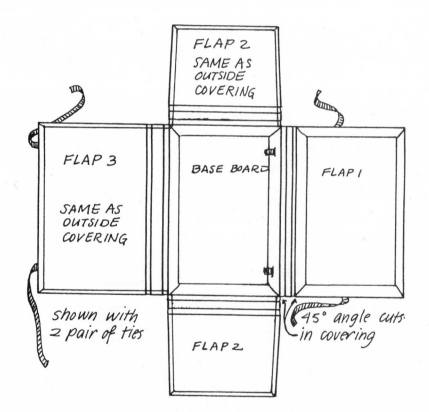

FLAP 2
SAME AS
OUTSIDE
COVERING

FLAP 3

SAME AS
OUTSIDE
COVERING

BASE BOARD

FLAP 1

shown with
2 pair of ties

FLAP 2

45° angle cuts
in covering

CUT LINING.
  Wall 1, cut one
  Same fabric as outside
  A = wall 1 A dimension minus 1/8"
  C = wall 1 C + 2 joints + 3"

Wall and flaps 2, cut two
Same fabric as outside
A = flap from outside edge to wall + wall 2 C dimension + 2 joints + 1 1/2"
B = wall 2 B minus 1/8"

Wall and flap 3, cut one
Same fabric as outside
A = wall 3 A dimension minus 1/8"
B = flap 3 B dimension + wall 3 C dimension + 2 joints + 1 1/2"
Base and flap 1, cut two using a contrasting material
A = base A minus 1/8"
B = base B minus 1/8"

MOUNT LININGS for both of flaps 3.
　　Place 1/16" in from outside edge.
　　Trim to size if too large.

Flap 3 lining will
cover the ribbon
ends attached
to board.
Part of ribbon
ends on base
will still be
exposed.

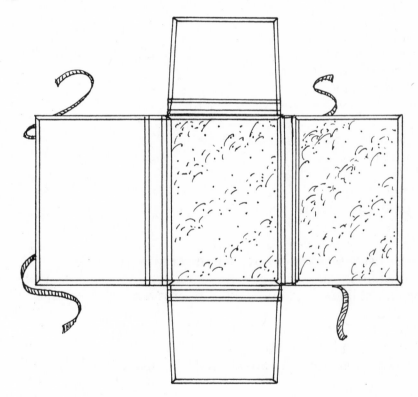

Follow *OUTSIDE BASE COVERING,*
p. 175, to mount lining over flaps and base. Center each lining piece over its board.

PRESS UNDER weights until dry, p. 241.

THREE PANEL PHOTOGRAPH CASE

Both outside covering and lining are the same book cloth.
Ribbon can be same or contrasting color.

Materials:
Binder board
Book cloth
Tape or ribbon
Adhesive

DECIDE DIMENSIONS. The panels must be large enough to show a margin on all four
   sides of the photograph. Margin needs to be wide enough to conceal the ribbon at
   corners. Directions are given for a 1/2" margin. This works well, but it is a personal
   choice. If wider or narrower margins are needed, simply change the number given for
   the margins.

CUT BOARDS.
   Panel boards, cut three
   all three panels are the same size
   To minimize warping ,make board
   grain direction run perpendicular to
   base edge of the case as it will be
   displayed.

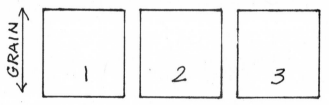

Height, head to tail = picture height + 1" for margins
Width = picture width + 1" for margins

Spacer Board, cut one, see p. 5
3 x 6", using 6 layers of covering material
Joint width is difficult to determine accurately. Place gauge between boards as
placement lines are drawn and as boards are mounted on cloth.

OUTSIDE COVERING material, cut in one piece
   Height, head to tail = board height + 1 1/2"
   Width = total width of all 3 boards + 7 spacer thicknesses + 1 1/2"

Follow *DRAW TURN-IN margins,* p. 219, to mark placement of panels. If panels are to
fold closed, three spacer thicknesses are needed between panels 1 and 2. Four spacer
thicknesses are needed between panels 2 and 3. All four turn-in margins will be 3/4". If
panels are not to fold closed, two spacer thicknesses between each panel is fine.

Follow *USE A straight edge,* p. 219, to mount panels in place. Be sure gap between
panels is even and lower edges are against the straight edge.

CUT LINING material.
  same material as outside covering
  Joint Lining, cut two
  to go between panels 1 and 2, and 2 and 3
  Height, head to tail = panel height minus 1/4"
  Width = panel width minus 1/8"

LINE JOINTS first.
  Lightly brush adhesive along under edge of one joint lining piece.
  Center over joint and press in place.

COVER WITH protective paper. Slide folder along joint.
  Press edges in place along the board thickness on each side of joint.
  Be sure lining stays pressed into joint as well.

ANGLE TAPE or ribbon across corners to hold
  photographs in place. Make slits in lining to
  slip tape through, p. 235.

  Paste tape ends in place on back of lining
  material before lining is mounted in place.

REPEAT FOR second joint

Follow *BRUSH ADHESIVE on exposed board,*
p. 223, to mount panel lining.

DRY UNDER light pressure.

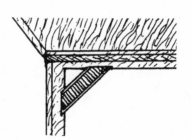

TWO PANEL CERTIFICATE CASE

Follow *THREE PANEL* directions, p. 216,
using only panels 1 and 2. Panel 1 becomes
the case cover when closed and the back
support when open. The lining piece for
panel 1 is the same material as outside
covering.

Note board grain runs perpendicular to base
edge of the case as it will be displayed.

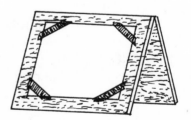

WRAP-AROUND CASE

The bone clasp closures give this case an Oriental feeling.
Its dimensions are determined by measuring
the book or books to be housed inside.
Be accurate in measuring.
Books can be damaged if
case is too large or too small.

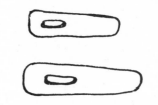

Materials:
Board
Book cloth
Lining, book cloth, paper, or felt
Bone clasps
  For contents under 3/4" thick:
      #8 (about 1" long)
  For contents over 3/4" thick:
      #10 clasps (about 1 1/4" long)
Adhesive

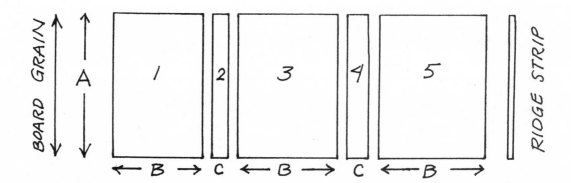

BOARD GRAIN

A

1 2 3 4 5

RIDGE STRIP

←— B —→ C ←— B —→ C ←— B —→

DETERMINE DIMENSIONS.
  A dimensions are the same for all pieces.
  A = book height from head to tail + 2 BT
  Each B dimension is different.

LABEL EACH piece by number as it is cut.

CUT BOARDS.
  Panel 1, inner lid, cut one
  B = book width

  Panel 2, fore edge wall, cut one
  C = thickness of book at fore edge

  Panel 3, case base, cut one
  B = width of book from spine to fore edge + 1 BT

Panel 4, spine wall, cut one
B = Board 2 B dimension + 1 BT

Panel 5, outer lid, cut one
B = Board 1 B dimension + 2 BT

Ridge Strip = 1/4"

MAKE A spacer using 5 layers of cover material, p. 5.

OUTSIDE COVERING material, cut in one piece
A = board A dimension + 1 1/2"
B = B dimensions of all 5 boards + 4 spacer thicknesses + 2 BT + 1 1/2"

MOUNT RIDGE strip to board 5 aligning with board edge.
This will be the outside of case outer lid.

DRAW TURN-IN margins down left side and along lower edge of under-side of
covering material. Use a 3/4" margin. Set board 1 along these lines and mark its
other side along joint. Place the spacer against board 1 to mark placement of board 2.
Mark placement of all boards in this fashion.

The turn-in
along
panel 5
will be 2 BT
wider than
the other
turn-ins.
The extra
covers the
ridge strip.

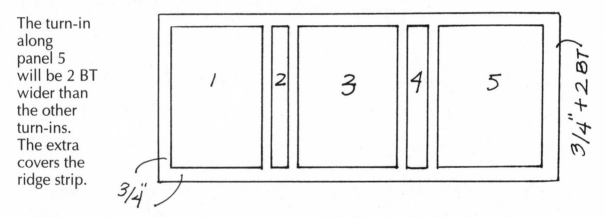

USE A straight edge along the bottom turn-in line as a guide in accurately placing
boards. Brush adhesive on board 1 and carefully set in place.
Press hand firmly on board at center, top, and bottom. Do not slide hand.
Slip spacer between boards at head and tail to insure boards are parallel as each new
board is added.

ADD ADHESIVE to ridge strip side of panel 5. Place with ridge strip along turn-in edge.
Press hand near center of board and along joint edge.

TURN OVER. With cloth side up, smooth all boards, except ridge strip area, with folder
and protective paper, p. 240.

TURN BOARD side up on clean paper.
Wipe up any adhesive that may have come out around boards.

TURN CLOTH side up on clean paper and slide folder along ridge strip.
Press covering material against edge.
Flatten covering material along the top of ridge strip by pressing firmly with folder,
moving from center to each end of ridge strip.
Recheck groove, slide folder along it again if necessary.

MITER CORNERS, p. 245:
Panel 5: keep 3 BT of covering material at points by ridge strip.
Panel 1: keep 2 BT of covering material at points on corners.

ADHERE B dimension, head and tail, turn-ins first. Be sure the material is attached to
the board at corners before turning in A dimension, fore edge, of boards 1 and 5.

MAKE CLASP closure loop and anchor from outside covering material.

Closure Loop,
cut one
1" x 3 1/8"

Clasp Anchor,
cut one
3/4" x 7 7/8"

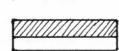

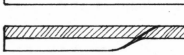

closure loop   clasp anchor

APPLY ADHESIVE
to back and fold
into thirds lengthwise.

PLACE STRIPS under weight so they will dry flat. When dry, cut the length of each piece
in half on a diagonal. Trim ends on diagonal as shown.

FOLD LONGEST two pieces in half with raw edge to the
inside. Thread through clasps to form clasp anchors.
Flat side of clasp is to the back. Clasps will point
towards each other. Set aside.

Clasps are placed 1 1/8" in from each end of case.
This allows case to close flat.

MAKE TEMPLATE on paper, for placing anchor
and loop strips. Use X to mark outside
case corner as shown.

Measure 1 1/8" from X corner and draw a line,
1/4" long, to mark clasp anchor placement
shown as #5.

Leave a 1/16" space.
Then draw a second line, 3/8" long,
to mark closure loop placement shown as #2.

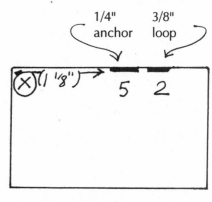

Template

TURN CASE cloth side up.
Place paper gauge against ridge strip with X at outside corner. Mark each end of #5 hole with pencil. Reverse card to mark other end of ridge strip.

Follow *MAKE HOLE,* to make the holes, using chisel and mallet, p. 183.

MARK LOOP placement on board 2. When thickness is less than 3/4", use one hole to mount each loop. When thickness is more than 3/4", use two holes to mount each loop.

One Hole:
With case cloth side up, place template with X along case's outside edge of panel 2.
Center pattern along panel width.
Mark each end of #2 hole position.
Reverse card to mark other end of panel 2. Make holes with chisel.

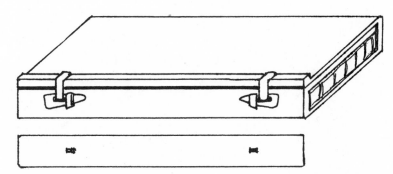

Two holes:
With case cloth side up, place template with X along case's outside edge of panel 2.
Center pattern along panel width.
Place flat side of clasp against case, so it points to center of panel 2.

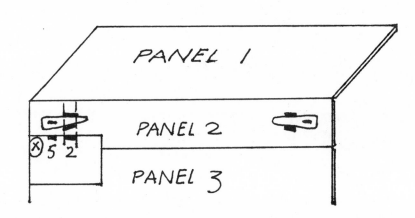

Mark loop placement along the top and lower edge of clasp as shown. Note the line under clasp angles upward.

MAKE HOLES using chisel and mallet.

MOUNT LOOPS in panel 2.
Fold the two short closure strips in half with raw edge inside.
Position loop with raw edge pointing toward center of panel 2.
Thread through holes. Pliers may be needed to pull ends to the inside of case.

Insert the two clasps
and pull loops tight
from inside of case.
Spread loop ends
flat against inside
of case.
Add adhesive
and press in place.
Slip clasps out of holders,
lay case flat, inside up,
and pound loop ends several times with mallet to make them lie flat.

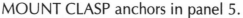

OUTSIDE #2

INSIDE

MOUNT CLASP anchors in panel 5.
Place clasps pointing to center of panel 5, flat side toward ridge strip.
This will allow flat side to rest against case when closed.

PULL CLASP anchor through holes far enough to make bone clasp line up with closure
loop. Fold case closed to check needed length.
Do not slip clasp in closure loop.
Clasp anchor must be taut when lined up with holders on board 2.
If loose, finished case will not close flat.

CUT LINING material.
Panels 2 and 4, cut one each
Use same material as outside covering
A = board A dimension minus 1/4"
B = board B dimension + 1 3/16"

Panels 1, 3, and 5, cut one each
Lining material
Looks best if different from outside covering material and lining on panels 2 and 4
(in illustration on p. 223, this is patterned paper)
A = board A dimension minus 1/4"
B = board B dimension minus 1/4"

LINE PANELS 2 and 4 first.
Brush adhesive on exposed board of panel 2, keeping it off the cloth turn-ins.
Lightly brush along under edge of panel 2 lining cloth.
Center over panel 2 and press in place.

COVER WITH protective paper. Slide folder along joint.
Press edges in place along panels 1 and 3. Be sure lining stays pressed into joint.

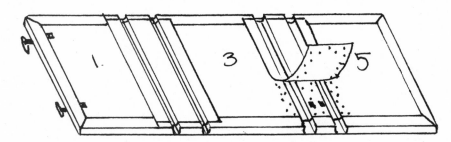

REPEAT
   for panel 4.

BRUSH ADHESIVE on exposed board of panel 1
   and under edges of panel 1 lining paper. Keep cloth turn-ins free of adhesive.

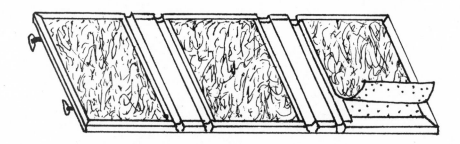

Center lining
over panel and
press in place.

REPEAT FOR remaining panels.
   Use a board scrap under panel 5 against the ridge strip to support it.
   Cover with clean paper and pound lining down well over pasted ends of clasp cords.
   This will help them to lie flat.

THE BOOK or books to be housed
   inside can be wrapped in waxed
   paper and closed in case.

*Do not slide clasps in holders until
clasp anchors are completely dry!*

Cut or fold paper to fit area
between the holders. Wrap paper tightly around case. Secure with tape.

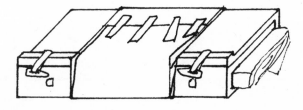

PRESS WHILE drying, p. 241.

ATTACH A paper title strip when case is dry if desired.

BINDER'S TOOL CHEST

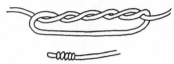

DOUBLE HALF HITCH KNOT, to tie off an end.

LOOP KNOTTING end around
anchor end and pull to tighten
before making a second loop
next to first loop.
Pull second loop tight.
Overhand knot with single
half hitch is shown on p. 76.

SQUARE KNOT, to join 2 ends together.

CROSS LEFT end over right end,
bring ends back and cross
right end over left end.
Pull it tight.

A surgeon's trick keeps
first loop from slipping
before knot is finished.
Make 2 turns with right end
around left end.
Complete knot as above,
L over R, R over L.

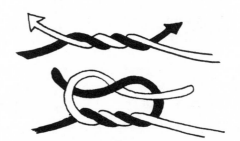

WEAVER'S KNOT, to add new length to thread.

FORM LOOP in old length end. Place short
end of loop on bottom. Hold this in left
hand. Make loop in new length, placing
short end of loop on bottom and hold new
loop in right hand.
Pass left-hand loop underneath,
into right hand loop.
Hold in place with left thumb.

Pass short end of right-hand loop under and
through left-hand loop.
Pull short end of left-hand loop and both
ends of right-hand loop away from each
other until knot is tight. Trim ends.
Make knot inside signature, close to spine.

CHINESE BUTTERFLY KNOT, to join 2 strands for 4 ends.

FOLD EACH thread length in half forming
2 loops. Put one loop through the other.
Bring tail ends of strand through its loop.
Pull tight.

Use this knot to
hang ends from
a fixed strand
for a fringe.

COIL KNOT, decorative ending or stopper.

MAKE LOOP in strand.
Wind free end
over top of loop
several times.
Pull on end to tighten
loops into coils.

MATTHEW WALKER KNOT, decorative ending for 3 strands.

START WITH strands parallel and extending straight out from the braid. Loop them in a
parallel curve so they lie across the braid in the order shown. Follow arrows to form
the knot and gently pull each strand into place.

This will work with
multiple strands
gathered into
3 groups.

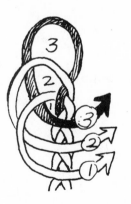

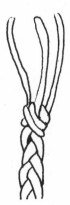

OVERHAND KNOT, decorative ending or stopper.

USE ON one strand or several strands
gathered together as one. Make a loop
over the strand with the short end.
Pass the end around under the strand,
then back through the loop, down
through it, and out. Pull tight.

Use it close to the end
or a distance away and
fray strand ends.

Overhand knot with
single half hitch finish for flat cord, p. 76.

WHIPPING CORD ENDS, decorative ending or to prevent raveling

LAY SEPARATE piece of lightweight thread,
formed in a loop, along cord to be whipped.
Wrap thread tightly and neatly over
loop and around cord. Wind up
along cord away from cord end.
When wrap is desired length
and loop end still visible,
thread winding end through loop.
Pull opposite end to draw loop
out of sight.
Trim ends and dot with PVA.

FLAT BUTTONS, to match or complement bindings.

MAKE FROM book cloth or paper.
Bond layers of book cloth or paper
until thick enough to make
buttons. Let dry before
cutting out desired
shapes. Make holes
with a drill or
pointed tool.

ROLLED BUTTONS AND BEADS

MAKE BUTTONS from long strips of paper cut parallel with paper grain.
 Paste strip on underside for about an inch at each end to anchor strip together.

Roll strips tightly around a fine knitting needle. Make several on one needle.
Wax needle or wrap with waxed paper held on
with tape for easy removal when dry.
Leave in place until dry.

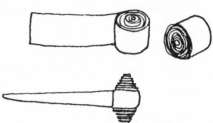

A continuous width makes a cylinder bead.
A long tapered cut makes a tapered bead.
Strips with torn edges give an unusual effect.

Experiment with colors and patterns.

CLAY BEADS

MAKE BUTTONS from polymer clay, see notes under CLAY COVERS on p. 17.
 These beads can be quite decorative. After baking they can be painted with acrylic
 paints. There are a number of books on the use of this clay. Check library, book
 store, or craft store.

CHINESE BALL BUTTONS

MAKE FROM lengths of braid, homemade cord, or buy ready made.
 For buttons matching book cloth bindings, cut a book cloth strip 7/8" 14" long.
 Fold in thirds to about 1/4" width and hold together with adhesive.

Loop strip around as arrows indicate in drawings to form ball.
Ease it all together after loops are formed. Trim ends to desired length.
Use another strip for a loop to slip button through.
See Mount Loops, p. 221, to mount in board.

MONKEY'S FIST KNOT, a ball on the end of a line.

Sailors use it to weight a line thrown aloft. Finished size depends on cord size, inside
 bead size, and the number of winds used in making it.
 A cord about 1/16" in diameter and a bead of 1/4" make a ball 1/2" to 5/8" in diameter
 using winds as shown. It takes about 2 feet of cord.

Try cutting a bead from a vinyl pencil eraser. It does not need to be perfect.

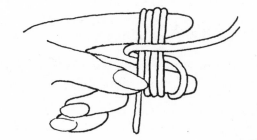

BEGIN WITH
   4 vertical winds
   around two fingers.

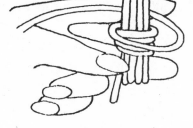

MAKE SECOND set of winds around vertical winds,
   stacking winds from bottom to top.
   Bring last wind through top loops, as shown.

REMOVE FINGERS
   and tuck bead
   down in center
   of both winds.

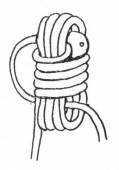

MAKE ANOTHER
   set of winds inside first
   set and over second
   set enclosing
   bead.

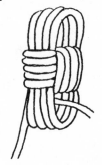

FINISH KNOT
   by gently pulling cords
   one at a time to tighten
   them around bead.
   Trim end.

BRAIDED CORD
   CHOOSE FROM ribbon, embroidery floss, perlé cotton, yarn, raffia, etc. to match or
   complement a binding for a special personal touch. Choose one or a variety of colors
   and braid them together for one cord.

MACRAMÉ CORD
   USE DOUBLE Half Hitch and Square Knots to make unique cords.
   Depending on materials, macramé can be homespun or sophisticated.
   Beads can easily be added to macramé.

TWISTED CORD

USE REGULAR sewing thread to twist colorful cords on a sewing machine.
Mix several colors together. Metallic thread adds sparkle although metallic coverings tend to separate from thread with abrasion.

Expect to use 5 times needed finished length to make a cord.

CUT 3 to 6 strands of thread.
Align threads together
and fold in half.

PLACE FOLD on center of
machine wheel as shown.
Gather all thread ends
together and hold out
from wheel and fasten
length with tape as
shown in second
illustration.

Run machine to twist
thread together.
Make fairly tight twist.

With cord still attached
to wheel, double cord by
bringing ends up to
where cord is attached.

KEEPING ALL ends together,
remove cord from wheel
and allow it to twist on
itself.

Remove tape.
Tie an overhand knot in the end
that was fastened to machine
leaving a little tail end.

Cut tail end loop for a fringe.

Use opposite end for sewing.

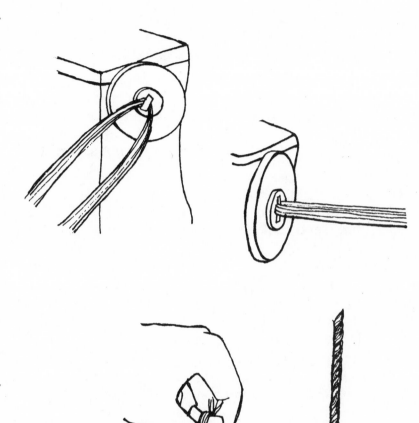

WORKING TIPS

PAPER TIPS

CHOOSING PAPERS
Choice depends on use, availability and personal preference.
Choices include handmade papers, mold-made papers which resemble handmade papers, and machine-made papers.

Knowing paper weight helps direct paper use. More information is given in Materials section, p. 258, and with the Paper Chart, pp. 261-264.
Most papers have a side carefully prepared for its intended use.
Watermarks often indicate the best side of a sheet, as the watermark is read correctly when held up to the light, but this is not a hard and fast rule.

Grain matters. This is the direction in which the individual fibers have been aligned during manufacture. Both paper and board have grain direction.
Handmade paper usually has no distinct grain direction.
Fabric and book cloth have grain direction parallel with selvage edges.
The term *long grain* refers to grain direction running the long dimension of a sheet of paper while *short grain* refers to grain direction running the short dimension of a sheet of paper.
Grain direction will influence how materials can be cut for use.

FOR A BOOK TO OPEN PROPERLY,
AND PAGES TO LIE QUIETLY FLAT WHEN OPEN,
GRAIN OF ALL MATERIALS IN A BINDING MUST RUN PARALLEL WITH THE SPINE.
Materials expand and contract with moisture from adhesives.
Materials with conflicting grain direction move in opposing directions causing boards to buckle, papers to cockle, crease, or split, and covers to gape.

PAPER GRAIN DIRECTION TESTS
Carefully curl a sheet over in on direction and lightly press on the resistance. Curl it the other direction and compare resistance. The curl with the least resistance is parallel with the grain.

Paper tears smoothly with the grain and roughly across the grain.

Dampen one side of a small strip of paper. It will curl across the grain.

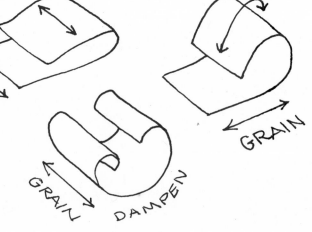

BOARD GRAIN DIRECTION, p. 236.

HANDLING PAPER
Keep hands clean to avoid surface damage from soil and body oils.
Lift a sheet of paper with two hands to avoid unwanted creases. Use one hand near the top and one hand near the bottom on opposite edges of the sheet.

FOLDING PAPER
Paper folds easily parallel with the grain. Folding across the grain is harder.
Difficulty increases in proportion with paper weight.

Fold sheet with a folder to keep it clean and make folds crisp.
Small weights can hold corners in place to free hands.

Depress fold with one hand. With other hand, place folder flat in middle of fold.
Press down lightly and move folder to one end of fold, then to opposite.

FOLDING LARGE SHEETS INTO SMALLER DIVISIONS
Folding into halves, quarters, eighths etc. is the easiest way to divide without waste.
Finished size depends on parent sheet size.

With heavyweight papers, fewer leaves are better; even 1 leaf can be a signature.
With medium weight papers, fewer leaves than the traditional 8 will probably work best.

With very lightweight papers, more leaves can be used.
Octavo fold is often used, forming 8 leaves or 32 pages for a signature.

The names quarto, octavo, etc., do not indicate a specific size of paper. They are only given to the corresponding subdivisions of any size of parent sheet.

| folio | quarto | octavo | sextodecimo |

Fold once, into halves, making a folio.
Fold again into quarters, making a quarto or *4to.*
Fold again, into eighths, making an octavo, or *8vo.*
Fold again into sixteenths, making a sextodecimo or *16mo.*

It is easiest to slit each fold as it is made.
Fold each leaf in half and insert inside each other to form a signature.

SCORING PAPER

Scoring along fold lines bends the fibers and solves most folding problems.
Run a dull pointed tool, e.g. a folder, dull table knife, knitting needle, etc. along a straight edge aligned with the fold.

Allow for width of scoring tool along side of straight edge.
Use medium pressure and move tool like a pencil.

After scoring, it often helps to fold paper up along the edge of a straight edge.
It is best to score on the outside of a fold but not always practical.

Heavyweight papers and lightweight boards may need more than scoring for a neat fold. Use a sharp knife to lightly break or scratch surface along fold line before folding.

TEARING FOLDS

Fold paper. Place folder in fold and hold at an angle. Move along the fold with a series of short even strokes. Keep one hand flat on surface of the sheet to keep it from sliding around. Keep tension steady and move holding hand to keep it opposite the folder.

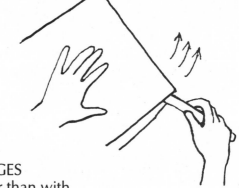

TEARING PAPER TO CREATE A VARIETY OF EDGES

A tear across the grain makes a more ragged tear than with the grain. A tear along a soft fold is more ragged than along a crisply creased fold. A tear along a metal straight edge gives a neater tear than tearing along a fold. It is best if the straight edge is long enough to span the whole tear.

Tear on the back side of the paper to avoid a dent along the edge of the tear.
Dents can often be smoothed away with folder or thumb nail.

How close to the straight edge a tear will happen depends on paper weight.
Experiment to learn what will happen.
Use one hand to press firmly on straight edge; the other hand lifts the paper to tear.
Move pressure hand as tear happens to keep hands working opposite each other.
Tear with steady, even pressure and rhythm.

Needle nose pliers or tweezers help with strips too narrow for fingers to hold.

TEARING A WET FOLD OR EDGE

A tear along a wet folded edge gives a controlled, soft edge tear.
Tear varies with width of water line and type of paper.

Use a clean brush in clean water to wet crease with narrow to wide line. Give water time to penetrate paper before tearing. *Pull paper apart* with a hand on each side of the wet line and steady even pressure. Experiment to see what can happen.

Oriental papers with long fibers are often hard to tear; use wet line technique.

Use wet lines to tear free forms. Experiment to find papers that tear well.
Draw shape on paper with water. Allow to penetrate. Slowly pull paper apart.

SIMULATING NATURAL DECKLES

Shave and tease away a torn edge to match an original deckled edge.
Use any tool that works. Try knives, razor blades, or scalpels.
Work slowly and shave edge little by little.

CUTTING PAPER WITH A KNIFE

Use a sharp blade to avoid dragging and tearing the paper.

Paper and board dull blades quickly. Replace or sharpen blades often.
It is best to cut against a steel edge. Knives can cut into aluminum or plastic.

Plastic is a good cutting surface and will not dull blades as quickly as cardboard.

Avoid corrugated cardboard or plywood since density variations cause a blade to veer
off course. Avoid cross hatching the cutting surface for the same reason.

Align straight edge for cutting the same way as for tearing.
Test how far from the straight edge the blade width will cut, and adjust for it.

Hold blade straight and at a constant angle with the cutting surface.
Move steadily with even pressure.

Use a hand to press down on the straight edge to keep it steady and move the pressure
hand so it is always opposite the knife.

A clamp can be used to hold one end of the straight edge to the table.
Cut through board with a series of light cuts rather than one hard cut.

Try to make all cuts on waste side of paper.
If knife veers away from blade, it will cut into waste paper instead of part to be used.
Turn sheet as cuts are made so blade is always on waste side of straight edge.

CUTTING SLITS FOR TAPES, RIBBONS, ETC.

Using a push pin or similar tool, punch a
small hole at each end of line marking area
to be cut. Use a blade to cut from one end
hole toward center, then turn piece and cut
from opposite end hole to center.

Keep little finger of cutting hand on paper
and pull knife into hand. This prevents over
cutting line length.

Since the knife blade tends to roll the
edges, it's best if cuts are made from the
side that will be the most visible.

INSIDE COVER

TRIMMING A FORE EDGE

Temporarily sew signature or use clips to keep pages from moving while trimming. Use L square or triangle to be sure cut will be at right angle with top edge and parallel with spine edge. Clamp or firmly hold straight edge along cut.
Make a series of light strokes until cut is completely through all pages.

CUTTING WITH SCISSORS

Move paper into the scissors rather than scissors into the paper.
Use steady pressure to pull paper into blades as they open.
Cut will be smooth rather than jagged.

REMOVING WRINKLES FROM PAPER

With time and patience most wrinkles can be removed from good quality white papers. Colored papers may cause problems and bleed.
Use two pieces of glass larger than the damaged paper. Plexiglas will work but it is not as heavy.

Place large sheets of white blotting paper between damaged paper and glass, one on top and one on bottom. Use a spray bottle filled with water to mist blotting papers on sides away from damaged piece.

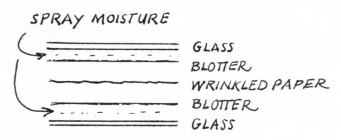

When working on damaged paper with original art on it, spray water on the blotter at the back side of the art but leave the other one dry.

Test a section to see if medium will bleed. Weight glass evenly when using extra weight. Leave it for 24 hours before checking to see if wrinkles are gone. If damage is fixed, replace damp blotters with dry ones and press for another 24 hours. Repeat dry blotter sequence several times. Otherwise, repeat misting sequence until damage is gone.

BOARD TIPS

BOARD GRAIN DIRECTION TEST

Most of the time grain runs parallel to short length of a new board. Bend in middle both ways. It is easier to bend parallel to grain. Mark grain in corner with pencil.
It is a good idea to continue to mark grain on scraps with pencil as board is cut.

To determine grain direction on smaller pieces, carefully bend a corner of the board to feel for resistance along edge 1. Compare with resistance along edge 2. The grain runs parallel to the line of least resistance and perpendicular to the "softer" edge.

236

SQUARING BINDER BOARD CORNERS

Binder board corners are not square. Cut or drawn a square corner and measure from this edge.

CUTTING BOARD

Use a utility knife comfortable to the hand rather than an Exacto knife.
A sharp blade is important for good results.
Use a straight edge long enough to span the whole cut if possible.
Clamp or use steady hand pressure to keep the straight edge from moving.
Keep hand pressure opposite cutting hand as it moves along the straight edge.
Make a series of light cuts until all the way through the board.
See *Cutting Paper with a knife,* p. 235.

MEASURING TIPS

MEASURING ACCURATELY

A scrap of paper rather is usually a quicker and more accurate measuring tool than a ruler. Place strip of paper on or next to what is to be measured. Mark size on strip. Transfer measurements from strip to needed area.

Wooden pencil leads can vary in width. Automatic pencils with hard lead will have the least lead width variation. To be more accurate, mark position by indenting the surface with a fingernail or a blunt tool rather than with pencil, used on p. 110.

MEASURING WITHOUT MATH

Here are several methods to consider:
Divide and fold a paper scrap the length needed into divisions needed.

To be more accurate, use a ruler positioned diagonally across surface to be divided and mark divisions from ruler to indicate where divisions fall. Place 0 on one edge and number divisible by needed parts at other edge. Make a mark at each division needed. Use straight edge and triangle to draw division lines.

Sample shows four equal parts using 0, 3, 6, 9 and 12.

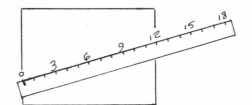 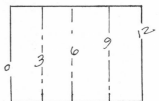

To duplicate a part, accurately draw around original part with a thin leaded pencil line. Cut new part out along the inside edge of the pencil line.

To figure folding ease measurement accurately, fold a paper strip (same weight as paper to be used in final project) around the item to be measured. Transfer measurements to project.

MEASURING SPINE THICKNESS BEFORE SEWING
Place hand on stack and compress as flat as possible; let hand rise slightly and measure thickness.

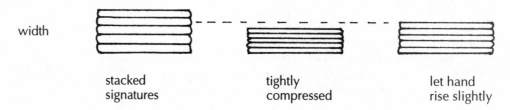

width

| stacked signatures | tightly compressed | let hand rise slightly |

When signatures are not compressed enough, they twist and slide inside the cover. When too tightly compressed, the book will not close well, gapping at the fore edge and pinching at the spine.

Measure spine thickness for a single signature case binding as shown on p. 110.

MEASUREMENT FORMULAS
When planning dimensions for a binding or box, write out a formula before cutting. The letters given below can be used for this purpose.

Measure twice and cut once.

Books:
H = height,
    from head to tail
W = width,
    from spine edge
    to fore edge
BT = board thickness
E = ease,
    the extra space
    used in folding,
    extra space needed
    around a book in a
    box etc.
J = space needed for joints
    or hinges
T = turn-ins or overlap
ST = spine thickness, from front
    to back of book

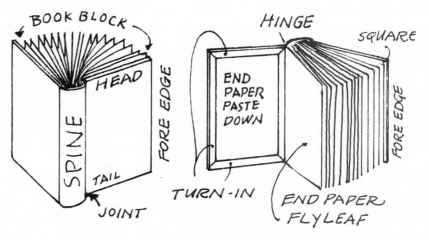

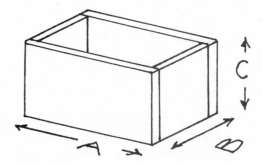

Boxes and Cases:
A = longest wall   CT = covering thickness
B = shortest wall   LT = Lining thickness
C = height of wall   WT = wall thickness

PASTING TIPS

PASTING AND BONDING OR LAMINATING

These are activities where everything happens and everything is needed at the same time. Have materials organized and easy to locate before you begin.

Adhesives set up faster than expected.
Hands must be wiped constantly to avoid staining materials.
Have a damp sponge or rag ready to use. Set on dish or discarded plastic lid.

Have plenty of waste paper available for protecting work area and materials; use shelf paper, butcher paper, used computer paper, Kraft paper bags, news print, or waxed paper, etc. Waxed paper is resistant to moisture and is easier to remove from fabrics and porous papers when adhesive is dry.
Discard waste paper as it is used to avoid accidentally spreading adhesives.

Papers expand with adhesive moisture and contract as they dry.
Read section on adhesives, p. 249, and choose the best adhesive for the project at hand. There are many choices and no simple answers.

PASTING TOOLS

BRUSHES need to be stiff enough to move adhesive easily.
A brush about 2" wide and a narrower brush about 1" are useful sizes.
Use small one for spaces narrower than 2".
Use synthetic bristles for PVA and natural bristles for vegetable adhesives.
Keep brushes in water when not in adhesive.
Wipe water from brushes before returning to adhesive container to avoid diluting mixture.
Avoid contaminating and diluting adhesive supply by working from a small amount poured into another container. Wipe excess adhesive from brush onto one side of container edge only. This leaves a clean area for handle to rest.
Short handles help to avoid tipping over jars.
Clean brushes well using soap and water when finished.

CREDIT CARDS spread adhesives efficiently. Cut card across narrow width giving square corners to one end. Leave the other end's corners round.

STIFF PAPER SCRAPS can push adhesive into a narrow or tiny opening.

SPREADING ADHESIVE

Beginning in the middle of the piece, move brush toward the outer edges.

WASTE PAPER

A thin even coat works best.
Bonds are not stronger with more adhesive. More adhesive slows drying time, allowing moisture to seep into other parts.
As surface is smoothed with folder, extra adhesive squeezes out to stain edges.

The right degree of tack is important. There is an adhesive consistency for every job.
Too wet can seep through and stain while too dry will not bond properly and too
thick will be lumpy.

A consistency like thick cream will do for light materials and fabrics.
A heavier mixture is better for medium to heavyweight materials.
The best results come with practice and experience with materials and procedures.
See *Adhesives*, pp. 249-254, for more information.

SMOOTHING SURFACES AFTER PASTING

This removes any air bubbles, wrinkles and uneven deposits of adhesive.
Use a clean sheet of waste paper between surface and folder to keep surface clean
and prevent shiny spots from forming.

Working through waxed paper will provide some visibility but can transfer a little of
the wax.
Test to see if it changes surface.

USING MOISTURE BARRIERS

After pasting, separate dry part from wet parts with waxed paper or plastic wrap until
wet parts are dry to prevent damage to dry parts.

PASTING IN A LIMITED AREA, e.g. along

the edge of a page, lay waste paper up to
exposed area to be pasted and cover the
rest of the page. Move brush, *in one
direction only*, from waste paper over
area to be pasted.

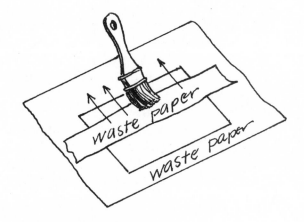

This helps keep mixture from creeping
under edge of waste paper. Remove
waste paper carefully to avoid smearing.

EXPANSION OF MATERIALS

Handmade paper tends to expand equally in all directions while
papers and boards with grain will expand more in cross grain direction.

BONDING
STAINED EDGES ARE HARD TO AVOID WHEN BONDING.

Join larger pieces than needed. When dry, trim to size, removing stained edges.

JOINING 2 PIECES OF UNEQUAL WEIGHT

Lighter piece may shrink more than the heavier. Make lighter piece a little larger and
trim to size when dry. Spread adhesive on heaviest piece and place the lighter piece
on it. Smooth with folder. Dry under weight.

JOINING VERY LARGE PIECES

When using straight PVA over a large area, the PVA will begin to dry before it has all been spread.

To compensate, spread PVA in 3" to 4" wide strips across the narrow width of heaviest piece. Lay material to be joined on wet adhesive, leaving 1/2" to 1" strip of wet adhesive exposed.

Quickly smooth pieces together. Lay another 3" to 4" strip of adhesive and blend with exposed strip.

Proceed in this manner until it is all joined. Dry under a weighted board. Adhesive mixtures will dry more slowly; see *Adhesives*, p. 249, for details.

ADDING PASTE DOWNS

Spread adhesive on exposed cover surface and edges of paste down.

Place paste down in place and smooth with folder. Add waxed paper moisture barrier and dry under weight, see below.

PRESSING WHILE DRYING

Materials tend to curl as they contract after expanding with adhesive moisture. Pressing inhibits curling. Heavy pressure is not necessary.

Place pieces to be dried between layers of stiff cardboard before covering with pressing board and weights.

USING WEIGHTS

Wrapped bricks, chunks of marble, heavy books, containers of rocks, sand, or lead shot placed on top of boards spreads weight evenly.

Use a zip lock bag as a container to fill surface inside a box evenly.

Uneven surfaces will need padding to make a level surface for pressing boards. Use strips of binder board to even surface.

Use waxed paper barriers between pasted parts and board strips.

Thick pads of newspaper on top and under pieces help distribute pressure.

Ace bandages can be used to wrap an object while drying. Fill the object with something solid so the shape will not collapse.

CURLING BOARDS

Sometimes, because material bonded on one side exerts a stronger pull, boards will curl even after careful drying under pressure.

Materials need to be similar in weight and absorbency to avoid curling.

Often, a sheet of bond paper added to the other side helps equalize tension.

FILLERS

In case binding or box making, fill exposed board area between turn-ins to make a better surface for paste downs and covering materials. Use board, paper, or covering material to minimize height differences, pp. 112, 176.

SEWING TIPS

NEEDLES
English binding needles have eyes that are polished to avoid cutting the thread. Darning, tapestry or crewel needles may be substituted.

THREAD
Unbleached linen thread, waxed with beeswax to prevent tangling, has been traditionally the thread of choice. It is strong, comes in several weights, and is archival. Thread of cotton, silk, wool, etc. will work. Explore embroidery threads for exciting colors and yarns for interesting textures. The dyes in colored threads are not archival.
Cotton carpet thread is a strong sturdy weight to work with.

Weight
Thread too heavy will swell signatures along spine edge as they are sewn. Thread too thin tends to cut the folds. In edge sewn bindings, thread is a visual part of the total design. Its dimension is a factor because thread must pass through holes more than once.

Length
Measure length needed by adding the number of times thread travels up and down the spine, times the spine length, plus enough extra for knots. Long lengths may be awkward when sewing signatures together. Shorten thread to a manageable length.

Join lengths together with a weaver's or square knot, p. 226.
Knotting is usually done inside signatures to avoid lumps under cover material along the spine.

Waxing
Waxing helps prevent stretching and tangles. It reduces friction as thread moves through the holes. Friction gradually wears thread thin.
Pull thread across a block of beeswax to wax it. Beeswax can be purchased in fabric stores and from bindery suppliers. Paraffin may be substituted, but it is not archival.

BUTTERFLY STITCH, p. 91.

CLAMP
Hold signature in place while stitching with simple clamps, p. 134.

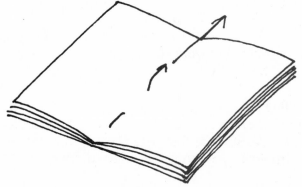

ELIMINATING SLACK IN THREAD
Pull thread *parallel with* signature folds. When thread is pulled out at right angles to fold, it usually tears the paper at the hole.

MAKING THE HOLES

THE TEMPLATES
SINGLE AND MULTIPLE SIGNATURE TEMPLATES
These are quickly made and easy to use.
Use durable paper or light board.

THREE hole template
Use a 3" wide strip of paper same height as
signature. Fold in half across width. Fold
again about 1/2" to 5/8" in from each open
end. Open and fold in half lengthwise.
Poke holes where folds meet.
Cut a notch in one side of top edge, making it
easy to always position template in the same
direction.

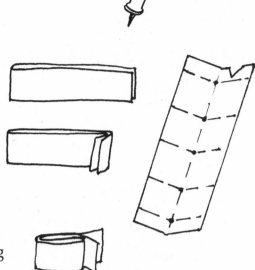

FIVE Hole template
Follow *THREE Hole* above except divide space
between middle fold and end folds in half, bring
middle fold over to meet end folds.

SEVEN Hole template
Follow *THREE Hole* above except divide space
between middle fold and end folds into thirds.

EDGE SEWN BINDING TEMPLATES
Use durable paper or light board.
Make inner binding holes first, p. 64.
Mark sewing pattern hole positions along
edge. Place template along stitching line to mark hole positions.
Follow *EDGE SEWN BINDING HOLES,* p. 244, to make holes.

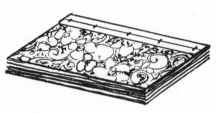

THE HOLES
All tools used in making holes (sharp pointed tool, drill, chisel) will make holes in the
desired object and the surface under it. Work over something that can be destroyed.

SHARP POINTED TOOL: SINGLE AND MULTIPLE SIGNATURES
Use any sharp pointed tool, awl, ice pick, compass point,
push pin, etc., p. 1. Liquid soap on end of tool will
make it go through paper more easily.
Choose a work surface kind to tool tip, e.g. plastic,
wood, cardboard, or a pad of paper.

Open each signature, one at a time, to make holes.
Place template in fold of open signature with v cut aligned
at head. Clamp or firmly hold template in place to keep pages
aligned while making holes. Hold punching tool vertically so holes will align.
Drive tool in a turning motion far enough to pierce lowest leaf, then withdraw.

Burrs on hole edges help keep sheets aligned after holes are made.
Check frequently to be sure holes are all being made in the folds as planned.

DRILL: EDGE SEWN BINDING HOLES
Secure with inner binding first, before adding cover, p. 64. Inner binding hole placement can be marked directly on top page since the cover will hide the marks, holes, and stitching.

Score regular stitching line on top cover.
Place template along line and mark hole placement.

BE AWARE: DRILL WILL MAKE HOLES IN SURFACE UNDER THE BOOK.
DRILL INTO SOMETHING THAT CAN BE DESTROYED.
A board, larger than project, reserved for this purpose, works well.

Clamp everything to table edge and drill holes.
Quick Grip mini bar clamps, p. 1, or the substitute illustrated below can be used.
Place book block on working surface. Place a piece of masonite, several layers of binder board, or 1/8" or 1/4" plywood, longer than spine length, over book block. This will keep clamps from denting book block. It will also help pages stay more compact as drill is withdrawn.

Make holes with either hand or electric drill and bit.
Position bit over mark and drill. Be sure bit enters book straight up and down so holes will be the same distance from spine edge all the way through.

To remove drill, continue to turn drill in same direction while pulling bit up and out.
Paper from hole comes out with bit.

Substitute strips of wood held tight with rubber bands for mini bar clamps.
Build up area around book with strips of wood so everything balances securely without rocking.

Slender Book Block holes can be made with any punching tool, following *MAKING THE HOLES* suggestions, p. 243.

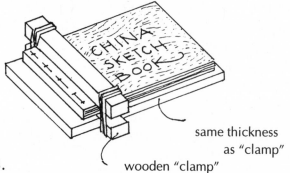

same thickness
as "clamp"

wooden "clamp"

CHISEL AND MALLET
Place object right side up on solid backing,
such as a wooden board. Be aware the chisel will cut into this surface.
Pound hole in scrap board first to get the feel before cutting into project.
Center chisel over pencil placement mark, aligning along beveled edge of chisel.
Pound chisel with mallet to make hole.

PAPER PUNCHES
Use a punch to make holes when practical. They come in several sizes.

MITERING TIPS

Mitering corners removes bulk and accurately joins cover material edges turned in over boards. The success of a miter depends on knowing what to expect from materials. Experiment with scraps of materials being used.

STANDARD MITER:
  Make miter after cover material has been pasted to boards, before turn-ins are folded in. Miter corners at a 45° angle, keeping extra covering material at point.
  Be sure to make clean cuts and neat turn-ins.
  The tips of case board corners will still be visible after the project is finished.

Keep 2 BT (board thicknesses) to cover 1 board thickness
Keep 3 BT to cover 2 BT

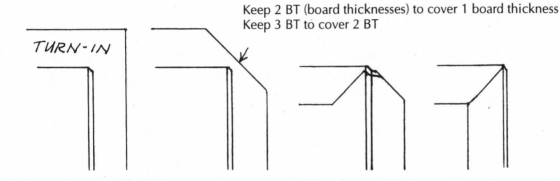

Adhere head and tail turn-ins first.
Apply adhesive to head turn-in and adjoining board thickness.
Lift turn-in on waste paper to fold over edge of board to inside.

Smooth on board edge and inside of board with folder. An extra bit of turn-in will extend beyond corner. Fold this around corner at fore edge and smooth against board edge with folder, (nick in).

Be sure the material is attached to the top and sides of the board at corners before turning in the fore edge. The fore edge is always turned in last.
Use plenty of waste paper.

Repeat at all four corners.

MODIFIED MITER:
  Remove section of
  cover material
  from each corner,
  as shown.

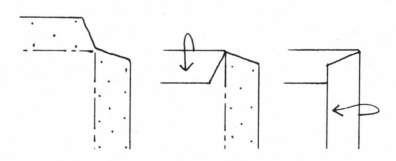

LIBRARY CORNER MITER:

Usually these are used for bindings that receive heavy use. However this method is also good with fragile cover materials or fabrics that fray easily.

Fold cover material over head corner on the diagonal. Paste it down, fitting and smoothing against board edges on both sides of corner.

Put adhesive across head board thickness and surface where turn-ins lap up and over. Lift turn-in over edge and smooth with folder.
Turn fore edges last.
When all 4 corners are finished,
squeeze gently to remove any extra bulk.

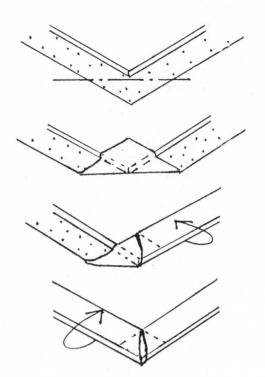

COVER LABEL TIPS

Labels are practical solutions to indicate which way
to hold and open a book. Labels can be pasted directly on covers.
This works well for soft bindings although label may eventually be damaged by friction. A recessed spot cut in a binder board cover protects label from friction.

Some suggestions for accenting the front of a book are: a hand lettered title on a strip of paper, a decorative strip of paper, a favorite post card, postage stamps, embroidery, painted design, buttons and other decorative objects.

RECESS AREA IN BOARD
FOR LABEL, outline area with pencil. Leave 1/16" extra space on all sides of recess area to allow for cover material bulk. With a sharp knife cut down into board along penciled outline. Lift an edge of the board inside label area and peel a layer of board away. Continue to lift and peel until area is recessed enough for label. It does not need to be deep or smooth.
With book cloth covering, small imperfections will not show.
With paper covering, surface may need to be smoother.
If design is embroidery, use a thin layer of padding between board and cover material.
This will soften thread patterns between embroidery patterns. Plan for padding depth.

Apply cover material as usual. Gently work material into recessed area.
Avoid poking holes or tearing material while pressing it into corners and against edges. Paste label in place on finished cover before drying.

FOR RIBBON ties and lifts, follow *For Label* above. Often the 1/16" extra margin is not needed and cut only needs to be wide enough for the ribbon. Before cutting into project, cut on scrap of same board. Use same covering and ribbon to test fit.
A thin ribbon thin ribbon does not need to be recessed.

PROTECTING PAPER SURFACES TIPS

Coatings can be applied to papers to protect them from soil, moisture, and abrasion.
Any coating should be tested first to find out how it reacts with chosen surface.

PARAFFIN WAX
  Rub gently over paper surfaces.
  This is a petroleum distillate and should not be considered archival.

SPRAY FIXATIVES
  These are usually an acrylic resin base and they will penetrate paper some.
  Read labels carefully to avoid trouble.

METHYL CELLULOSE
  Often used as a sizing, methyl cellulose can be painted on paper with a brush.
  Described on p. 252.

JOHNSON PASTE WAX for wood surfaces, from super markets, works well.
  It has a vegetable base of carnuba wax. It adds strength to folded edges and makes
  paper somewhat resistant to soil and moisture. Papers are slightly changed. Some
  become darker and some take on a golden glow.

TO APPLY, gently rub wax on right side of cover
material with a soft cloth. Hold piece firmly with
one hand and rub out, away from holding hand.
Back and forth rubbing usually
makes wrinkles.
Surface will look dull
and feel sticky.

Let dry for
7 to 10
minutes.

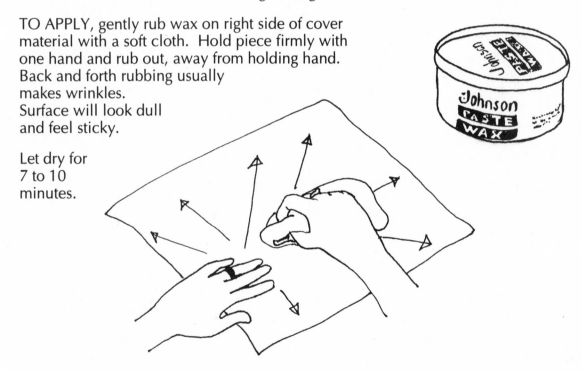

Buff gently
with clean soft cloth by rubbing away from the holding hand again. Paper will feel
smooth and take on a soft shine. Cover papers can be waxed before or after binding.

HAND DECORATED PAPER IDEAS

It is beyond the scope of this book to give detailed information on decorating paper. This page is offered to stimulate ideas of your own. Good books on paper decoration can be found in libraries and book stores.

Paper can be decorated with a variety of unique designs using any of the techniques listed. This is an opportunity to coordinate an entire book. Patterns made for a binding might also be used as design elements in the book block and the box or wrap. For total control over papers used in bindings, decorate your own.

Air Brush
Batik, Fabric, or Paper
Collage
Crumpled or Creased Paper
Embossing
Eraser, Linoleum or Potato Prints, hand cut
Fold and Dye Papers
Gocco Printing
Impressed Patterns
Marbling and Suminagashi
Monoprints
Paste or Starch Papers
Photo-light Exposed Photo Prints
Pierced Papers
Resists, Crayon, Ink, Acrylic, etc.
Rubber Stamps, commercial
Rubbings
Silk-screen Prints
Sponge, Spatter, and Spray Papers
Torn Edge Papers
Stencil Prints
Watercolor Techniques involve a wide variety of finishes made
    by using brush strokes, salt, plastic film, blotting, splattering, etc.

Several books we like are listed in the Bibliography:
  Bookcrafts for Juniors, A.F. Collins.
  Creative Bookbinding, Paulien Johnson.
  North Light Illustrated Book of Painting Techniques, Elizabeth Tate.
  Paper Pleasures, Faith Shannon.

ADHESIVES

Adhesives are used to hold things together. Some adhesives are called pastes, and some are called glues. Usually, vegetable products are called pastes and animal products are called glues. This book does not include animal glues.

Pastes are made from grain starches or flours mixed with water and heated, usually, to make a soft, flexible adhesive. Some adhesives come premixed. Others need to be mixed from a dry powder.

Cold resinous adhesives such as polyvinyl acetate, (PVA), are translucent, white, somewhat flexible, thermoplastic liquids.

Each adhesive listed below is discussed in more detail on the following pages.

QUICK REFERENCE ADHESIVE CHART	SETTING TIME	STRETCH PAPER	SHELF LIFE	HOLD POWER	USES
PVA	fast	some	good	good	read label
Wheat Starch Paste	slow	much if thinned	poor	good	all
Corn or Rice Starch Pastes	slow	much if thinned	poor	good	all
Flour Paste	slow	much if thinned	poor	good	all
Methyl Cellulose	slow	some	good	light	light bonds and to size paper
Adhesive Mixtures PVA & Methyl Cellulose	medium	some	good	good	all
PVA & Wheat Starch Paste	medium	some	poor	good	all
Wheat Starch Paste & Methyl Cellulose	medium	some	poor	good	all
Yes Paste	medium	much if thinned	good	good	not archival

PVA

This resinous adhesive is often called white glue. It is found under a number of registered trade names: Elvace, Jade 403, Promatco, Magic Mend, Elmer's Glue All, Sobo, and Tacky Glue to list a few. It is easily applied and readily diluted with water. It contains no flammable solvents and needs no preservatives or fungicides. Buy PVA's from binding suppliers, craft stores, art stores, etc.

SETTING TIME is fast but will vary with the brand.
    When mixed with a paste or methyl cellulose, setting time is slowed.

FLEXIBILITY is good although it varies from brand to brand.

REVERSIBILITY for PVA alone is usually not possible. When mixed with flour, starch paste, or methyl cellulose, it is sometimes reversible in water.

STRETCHES PAPER slightly when used undiluted.
    It stretches more when diluted with water.

PREPARE it by pouring a usable amount out into a small container to avoid contaminating basic supply.
    Use straight or thin with water to desired consistency.

SHELF LIFE is good, 1 to 2 years, depending on brand.
    It may thicken over a long period.
    Do not let it freeze.

USE for a flexible fast-drying adhesive where reversibility is not important.

OTHER CHARACTERISTICS: PVA stains range from hard to impossible to remove when dry. Setting times vary with formulas. Read labels for details.

WHEAT STARCH PASTE

Buy starch in powder form from binding suppliers.

SETTING TIME is slow.

FLEXIBILITY is good.
    It is more flexible than flour paste.
    Add a little PVA for more flexibility.

REVERSIBILITY is good with water.

STRETCHES PAPER more than with PVA, especially when thinned with water.

PREPARE paste by mixing 7 tablespoons cold water and 1 tablespoon wheat starch together. Cook in double boiler, stirring constantly until mixture thickens to a stiff paste. Continue to cook and stir for 2 to 3 more minutes after thickening.
It will change from milky white to nearly translucent. Thin with additional water to desired consistency. This makes a little more than 1/2 cup.

SHELF LIFE is short. It will sour in 2 to 3 days.

USE for all binding procedures where a slow drying adhesive is needed, including bonding papers or fabrics and tipping in.
Mix with PVA for quicker drying.

OTHER CHARACTERISTICS: Of all the starches, wheat is superior because of the way its molecules are arranged. When wheat is changed from flour to starch, the glutens are removed, making it unattractive to insects.

CORN STARCH OR RICE PASTE

Buy from grocery or health food stores.

PREPARE RICE OR CORN STARCH paste by sprinkling about 1 TBS starch into 10 TBS water. Boil gently for about 5 minutes stirring constantly until translucent. Strain through cheesecloth or nylon stocking to eliminate lumps.

SHELF LIFE is short. It sours quickly after 2 or 3 days.
Do not refrigerate.
To retard mold growth, store in a container sprayed with Lysol Disinfectant.
Then it will last 1 to 2 weeks.

CHARACTERISTICS are similar to wheat starch paste. All three make an extremely smooth paste that has been safely used for centuries.

FLOUR PASTE

Use regular wheat flour from a grocery store or buy pre-cooked wheat flour paste in powder form from binding suppliers or wallpaper stores.

SETTING TIME is slow. Mix with PVA to speed up setting time.

FLEXIBILITY is good when thinly applied. Thick applications are not as flexible.
Methyl cellulose can be added to increase flexibility.

REVERSIBILITY is good with water.

STRETCHES PAPERS substantially, especially when thinned down with water.

PREPARE PRE-COOKED FLOUR PASTE by sprinkling powder into water, while beating until it is the needed consistency. Strain if needed, it is often gritty.

PREPARE FLOUR PASTE in a heavy stainless steel pan. Combine 2 1/2 tablespoons unbleached flour with enough cold water to make a mixture like nonfat milk. Part may be corn starch, rice or potato flour.

Use a sturdy wire whisk to stir constantly, as mixture is heated over medium setting; heat until it is thick and transparent. Lower heat a little and continue to cook and stir vigorously for at least 15 minutes. Add a little boiling water if it becomes too thick.

Remove pan from heat and place in larger pan of iced water. Continue to beat until it is cool. Transfer to another bowl or jar. Beat again before using. Store uncovered in refrigerator.

SHELF LIFE is short, about 3 to 4 days. It molds quickly.

USE for all bookbinding projects where a slow drying adhesive is needed. Mix with PVA for quicker drying.

OTHER CHARACTERISTICS: Flour paste has a long history of use for bookbinding. It can usually be wiped off with a damp rag.

METHYL CELLULOSE

A granular powder produced by treating cellulose, from wood or cotton, with an alkali, such as sodium hydroxide, followed by methyl chloride.
Buy from binding suppliers and some art supply stores.

SETTING TIME by itself is slow.

FLEXIBILITY is good. Add it to other adhesives to increase flexibility.

REVERSIBLE with water. It is soluble in cold but not in hot water.

STRETCHES PAPER moderately, more than PVA and less than pastes.

PREPARE by stirring 2 teaspoons into 1 cup of cold water; let stand for 1 hour, stir occasionally. Use water to thin further if desired.

SHELF LIFE is good after mixing, keeping several months at room temperature.

USE to size paper, clean spines, remove labels and adhere paper collage. Add to other adhesives to increase strength, flexibility, and adhesion.

OTHER CHARACTERISTICS: it does not attract insects. It is very good for making paper bonds.

ADHESIVE MIXTURES

The three mixtures given below are commonly used in binding. For some tasks, a mixture might have advantages over using just one of its components.

PVA & METHYL CELLULOSE
PVA & WHEAT STARCH PASTE
METHYL CELLULOSE & WHEAT STARCH PASTE

SETTING TIME for PVA is slowed considerably when mixed with methyl cellulose or wheat starch paste, allowing more time to adjust placement of materials if necessary. A mix of methyl cellulose and paste is slow to set.

FLEXIBILITY of a mixture is greater than paste alone.

REVERSIBILITY of a PVA mixture is sometimes possible, although it depends on the kind of PVA. Methyl cellulose and paste mixtures are reversible with water.

STRETCHES PAPER moderately.
   PVA alone stretches paper less than methyl cellulose or paste mixtures alone.

TWO MIXTURES: 2 parts PVA to 1 part methyl cellulose
                   3 parts PVA to 2 parts wheat starch paste

Put through cheese cloth or nylon stocking to work out lumps.
Thin with water if necessary. Proportions can vary to suit working pace and use.

SHELF LIFE is good if mix is made with methyl cellulose.
   PVA does not improve shelf life of paste mixtures.

OTHER CHARACTERISTICS: Generally, mixes make excellent all around adhesives.
   Wheat starch mixed with PVA combines the best of all characteristics.

YES PASTE

A commercially prepared vegetable paste made from corn dextrin, corn syrup, water, and a small amount of preservative.
Buy it from art supply stores and some binding suppliers.

SETTING TIME is moderate, not as fast as PVA or as slow as pastes.

FLEXIBILITY is good.

REVERSIBILITY is good with water.

STRETCHES PAPER and can cause it to cockle when diluted with water.
   Manufacturer claims it will not stretch papers when used straight from the jar.

NO PREPARATION is needed. It may be thinned with water if desired. Whisk or beat with hand mixer and strain if lumpy when thinned; keep in covered jar in refrigerator.

SHELF LIFE is excellent.

USE when there are no archival considerations to deal with.

OTHER CHARACTERISTICS:
It tends to yellow photo chemicals when used to mount photographs.
Insects are attracted to it, and its other archival properties are unknown.

SPRAY ADHESIVES
Read labels for adhesives in aerosol cans carefully to avoid trouble.
They are not recommended for extensive use in bookbinding but more as a temporary adhesive for quick projects.

BLAIR SPRAY-STICK is a mounting spray for binding paper to paper.

KRYLON SPRAY ADHESIVE comes in a non-clog aerosol can.
It is non-staining and will not bleed through lightweight surfaces.
Use it as a temporary bond for papers, fabrics, films, or foils.

GLUE STICKS
Of some value as a non-permanent adhesive. They are easy for children to use, non-toxic, and clean up with water. A solid is preferable to a liquid since paper stretches with more moisture. There are several registered trade names. Read the label. They do not all work well with photographs.

INSTANT BOND GLUE
Useful for attaching beads or other decorative objects that cannot be tied on. There are several registered trade names. Read labels carefully.

MATERIALS

BOARDS

Buy board from binding suppliers, art stores, and other paper outlets.

BINDER BOARD: a generic name for dense board available in several weights and thicknesses. Machine-made boards are generally available in several qualities. *Davey* board is an American product of single ply binder board made from wood pulp. It is solid board, made to full thickness in one operation, not a laminate. It is gray in color like a tablet back.

BRISTOL BOARD: available in several ply, 1 through 4. It comes with plate or vellum finishes. Lightest weights fall in heavyweight paper range.

CHIPBOARD OR PASTEBOARD: a laminated board made from wood pulp. It is similar in appearance to binder board but not as strong.

ILLUSTRATION BOARD: a white art board with a durable surface. It comes in hot or cold press finish and 2 weights.

MANILA FILE FOLDERS: weight is similar to 1 ply Bristol board. The name comes from a plant in the Philippines whose fibers went into rope and paper products.

MAT BOARD: board used for mounting prints, matting, etc. It comes in several qualities. Conservation, museum or rag boards have high dimensional stability and permanence. Solid core board is the same color all the way through. Most mat board is a single thickness while museum board comes in 2 to 4 ply.

PRESSBOARD: a tough, dense, highly glazed and polished rag or wood pulp board used where strength and stiffness are needed in a relatively thin sheet. It comes in several colors with a mottled surface. It is frequently used as covers for notebooks and pamphlets in libraries.

WOOD VENEERS: usually plywood with a veneer of hard wood on the outside. They come in different weights or thicknesses, the thinnest being 1/64", and a variety of woods. Buy these from a hobby shop.

BOOK CLOTH

Buy book cloth from bookbinding suppliers or back your own fabric.

BOOK CLOTH is a generic term for woven fabrics used in covering books. The cloth is backed with tissue and easy to work with. It is available in linen, cotton, and rayon weaves. Rayon spots easily but comes in a wide range of colors. Linen is the most forgiving.

CLOSURES

Use anything that works: handmade buttons, treasures from the beach,
garage sales discoveries, commercial clasps or fasteners.

BEADS may be purchased at craft and fabric stores and jewelry suppliers, or handmade
from rolled paper or polymer clay, p. 229.

BUTTONS may be found at garage sales, in antique or fabric stores, or handmade from
polymer clay, paper, cord, or book cloth, as shown on p. 228.

CLASPS OF BONE are handmade in Japan and may be bought through Aiko's Art
Materials or Colophon Book Arts supply, p. 274.

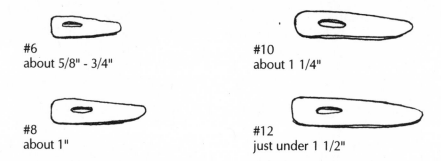

#6
about 5/8" - 3/4"

#10
about 1 1/4"

#8
about 1"

#12
just under 1 1/2"

HINGES

Traditionally, hinges were made from super or mull, a heavily sized fabric resembling
cheese cloth.

SUBSTITUTE unbleached muslin or fine linen. When starch is used to stiffen fabric,
eventually bugs may enjoy it. Stiffen fabric by ironing between pieces of waxed
paper. Protect board and iron with Kraft paper bags. Use low heat, no steam to melt
wax into fabric. Tear edges rather than cut for a softer edge.

BOOK CLOTH: when cut hinge width; endpaper paste downs are needed to cover
remaining exposed board. When cut same size as signature, the cloth becomes the
paste down. Stitch with fabric side toward signature.

TYVEK works well. Use PVA for the adhesive.

PAPER can work, experiment. Shave the edges to avoid lumps under paste downs, see
SIMULATING NATURAL DECKLES, p. 235.

THREAD

Thread is used for both functional and decorative roles.
Buy from binding supplier, fabric store, etc.

LINEN THREAD is the traditional binding fiber because of inherent strength and neutrality. It is archival, a neutral color, and available in several weights.

Most suppliers will send a sample card on request.
It can be used decoratively as well as functionally.

EMBROIDERY FLOSS is a multi-strand thread of cotton. It may be divided into smaller strands. Braid or twist several of the many colors together for a multicolored strand. The dyes make it non-archival.

PERLÉ COTTON comes in several weights. The higher the number, from 8 to 3, the finer the strand. It is a lustrous cotton and comes in many colors.
The dyes makes it non-archival.

COTTON, SISAL, AND HEMP TWINES provide interesting textures. They come in various weights. A macramé band using double half hitches and square knots might be perfect for a book closure instead of ribbon.

RAFFIA, from craft stores, comes in natural and various colors. Twist or braid into multicolored strands, macramé into cords, or used for sewing.

TAPE can be purchased at binding suppliers, import stores, and fabric stores.

LINEN BOOKBINDING TAPES are neutral, tan or gray, some with white edges. They are handsome in appearance and archival.

VARIOUS OTHER TAPES OR CORDS MAY BE SUBSTITUTED. Choose from silk, sisal, ribbons, shoe laces, yardage store tapes, and other trimmings with woven edges. Flat woven Japanese tape and cording also work well.

PAPERS

Paper falls into three categories: working, artist, and decorative.
Buy from art supply stores and find at home.

WORKING PAPERS are used during the binding process and then discarded. They are not part of finished product.

WASTE PAPER is used when pasting to keep work area clean. Kraft paper bags, wrapping paper, plain newsprint, shelf paper, butcher paper, and computer printout paper will keep surfaces clean with little cost.

WAXED PAPER is versatile during pasting and construction. Place it between the papers being bonded and the pressing boards while drying. Use it between a book block and binding as a moisture barrier or around a book, placed in a case while the case is drying.

Use as waste paper when pasting and lifting turn-ins up over board edge. It can be used between the surface and folder when smoothing turn-ins in place.

ARTIST PAPERS tend to be more forgiving and respond better in hand bookbinding than commercial papers finished for printing.

There are differences in composition and performance between artist papers, (whether handmade, mold-made or machine-made), and papers made for commercial printing or office use. Often, commercial papers are easily damaged by moisture and not as strong as artist papers which have been designed to accept art materials.

Commercial papers are sometimes available from printing firms as off cuts or larger pieces. Experimentation will show if these are an economy or headache.

Archival qualities, e.g., pH and acidity, need to be carefully explored if this is an important consideration in a binding. Rag versus vegetable fibers is often a question in the life expectancy of a paper.

HANDMADE PAPERS have been made the same way for centuries. They are usually made from cotton and linen rags which are boiled, shredded, and beaten to separate the fibers. This makes a smooth flowing pulp which is run over a fine screen and shaken by hand into a thin, even layer. Each sheet is dried and pressed. The screen molds create a deckle on all 4 sides. There is no distinct grain direction because the fibers settle in many directions.

MOLD-MADE PAPERS usually have a deckle edge on 2 sides only and look much like handmade papers. They have a grain direction because the cylindrical mold revolving a vat of paper pulp settles the fibers in one direction.

MACHINE-MADE PAPERS have 4 cut edges and a definite grain direction created by the forward motion of the machine.

PAPER DIMENSIONS were originally determined by the size sheet which could be printed, folded, and trimmed with the greatest economy. This varies with paper type, p. 234.

PAPERWEIGHT is based on the weight of a ream, usually 500 sheets, in its standard or parent size.
There is great variety in paper weights, and the distinction between paper and board is vague.
Generally, board is heavier, thicker, and stiffer than paper.

Paper weight is expressed in grams per square meter, gm/m^2, or in pounds.
When the weight is known, it is easier to know how to use a paper and what to expect from it.

When comparing weights: 100 gm/m^2 is similar to 50#.
130 - 150 gm/m^2 is similar to 60 to 75#.
185 gm/m^2 is like 90#.

Lightweight papers usually serve as text papers and vary in weight,
95 gm/m^2 for Ingres Antique to 120 gm/m^2 for Frankfurt.

Medium weight papers such as Canson Mi Teintes, 160 gm/m^2, has a weight between lightweight and heavyweight. It is used as both text and cover paper.

Heavyweight papers are sometimes called by the generic term *cover stock*. A wide range is placed in this category: 185 gm/m^2 (Arches 90# watercolor paper); 250 gm/m^2 (Arches Cover); 300 gm/m^2 (Arches 140# watercolor paper). Heavyweight papers are used for folders, soft bindings, and book wraps. A signature can be single leaf of heavyweight paper instead of several lightweight paper leaves inserted inside each other.

DECORATIVE, TEXTURED PAPERS
GIFT WRAP is tempting to use in binding. Some papers work well while others expand too much with moisture from adhesives. The resulting wrinkles are difficult to remove. Experiment to see how a chosen paper will function.

MARBLED PAPER is made by transferring floating inks or paints onto paper. It comes in beautiful colors and patterns. Suminagashi is an ancient Japanese style of marbling. Persian marbling dates from the 15th century.

Watercolors are generally used. Watercolor marbling can rub and transfer its color onto the sheet next to it in a binding. Seal it in order to minimize this, p. 247.

Oil colors are also used, although they do not allow the fine control or produce the clean sharp lines of watercolor marbling.

ORIENTAL PAPERS are made from vegetable fibers; gampi and kozo, and have long fibers in comparison with Western papers, giving strength to light weight papers. They bond well with Western papers. They come in unusual textures and many colors. Look for patterned silk screened papers, *Chiyogami*, for colorful bindings. Colors are not always light fast. Most are handmade.

TYVEK is a thin white plastic product originaly an air and moisture barrier in construction. It is now available by the sheet with soft patterned swirls on both sides. There is also a Tyvek for clothing that is crinkly. Tyvek bonds well using PVA. It is acid free and does not give off fumes which might harm adjacent papers. It is very tough. Because of its strength and resistance to tears, it has become a popular material for mailing envelopes.

WALLPAPER is made to be used with adhesives and usually performs well for binding and box making. Sample books are often available from wallpaper stores; the pieces are limited in dimensions so plan accordingly.

PAPER SURFACES vary in texture depending on finishing and sizing.
Handmade paper surfaces depend on type of screen used.
Mold-made and machine-made papers have surfaces simulated during manufacture.

PAPER SURFACE TERMS
COLD PRESS is usually used to describe watercolor paper.
It is a mildly textured surface midway between rough and hot press surfaces.

DUO PAPER is a laminate of two colors, often two textures.

HOT PRESS is a term usually used to describe watercolor paper.
Its smooth, glazed surface is formed as paper is pressed between hot rollers or plates.

LAID is a term used to describe a sheet with a prominent pattern of ribbed lines.
Handmade papers use a screen closely set with parallel horizontal wires crossed at
right angles by vertical wires spaced further apart. Mold-made and machine-made
papers have the pattern embossed into the wet paper by a *dandy roll.*

MACHINE-MADE paper is produced on a rapidly moving machine which forms,
dries, sizes and smooths the sheet in one continuous process. Uniformity of both size
and surface texture are traits of machine-made papers. Finishes will vary from matte
to high gloss, depending on the type of paper.

MOLDMADE paper, made in a slowly rotating machine called a cylinder-mold, looks
like handmade paper.

PLATE FINISH is a smooth finish.

ROUGH is used to describe watercolor papers. It is a heavily textured surface.

VELLUM FINISH has a slightly rough, toothy surface.

WOVE paper has a uniform unlined surface and smooth finish.

Many of the textures embossed on machine-made surfaces are described in fabric
terms: linen, homespun, buckram, corduroy, burlap, etc.

PAPER CHART

The Daniel Smith Inc. Reference Catalog, printed each fall, provides far more detailed information about papers than the scope of this book allows. It also includes colored photographs of sheet corners, very helpful when choosing and ordering papers, p. 275.

Weight is usually in grams per square meter, gm/m^2, unless noted otherwise with a # sign for weight in pounds. Grams per square meter is a European measure of paper weight; the other is American.

pH is a measure of the acidity or alkalinity of a substance expressed on a scale of 0 to 14. A pH value of 7 is neutral. Lower numbers are progressively acidic, higher numbers are progressively alkaline. Acid free papers can be made with any kind of pulp, and have a pH measurement of 6.5 or higher. Paper with a pH value of 7 is considered desirable for artwork meant to have a long life.

CHART CODE:	H	handmade	HS	heavy size	WL	water leaf
	MO	moldmade	MS	medium size		
	MA	machine-made	LS	light size		

ARTISTS PAPERS	HOW MADE	DECKLE EDGES	SIZING	NEUTRAL PH	WEIGHT
Arches 88	MO	4	WL	x	300
Arches Cover, black	MO	3-4	MS	x	250
Arches Cover, buff or white	MO	4	MS	x	250
Arches HP, 90#	MO	4	HS	x	185
Arches HP, 140#	MO	4	HS	x	300
Arches Text Wove	MO	4	MS	x	120
Archival Parchment	MA	0		x	60#
Art Print, heavyweight	MA	0	MS	x	245
Art Print, Rising Paper Mills	MA	0	MS	x	190
Bristol , Strathmore Series 500	MA	0	MS	x	2 to 5 ply
Canson, Ingres	MA	0		x	100
Canson, Mi Teintes, many colors, black is not acid free	MA	0	MS	x	160

ARTISTS PAPERS	HOW MADE	DECKLE EDGES	SIZING	NEUTRAL PH	WEIGHT
Coventry Rag	MA	0	MS	x	235 & 290
Folio	MO	2	HS	x	250
Frankfurt, white or cream	MO	4	LS	x	120
Gutenberg Laid	MO	4	MS	x	130
Ingres Antique, many colors	MO	4	LS	x	95
Ingres, Fabriano, Heavyweight, many colors	MO	2	MS	x	160
Lana Laid	MO	2	MS	x	100
Larroque Pastel, many colors	H	4	MS	x	250
Nideggen, white, cream, pale blue	MO	4	MS	x	120
Pentalic Meridian Drawing	MA	0	MS	x	90
Rising Gallery 100	MA	0	MS	x	245
Rising Stonehenge, soft colors, white	MA	2	MS	x	245
Rives BFK, white	MO	3 to 4	MS	x	250
Rives Lightweight	MO	3 to 4	MS	x	115
Roma, Fabriano, many colors, white	H	4	MS	x	130
Strathmore 400 Alexis Drawing	MA	2	MS	x	100#
Superfine	MA	0	MS	x	120
Twinrocker Calligraphy cream, two sided, CP/HP	H	4	MS	x	125
Twinrocker Simons's Green	H	4	MS	x	125
Twinrocker White Cotton Rag, CP, laid and wove	H	4	MS	x	125
Twinrocker White Feather	H	4	LS	x	350
Umbria (Fabriano)	H	4	LS	x	150
Watercolor Papers	not listed with exception of 2 Arches HP papers				

ORIENTAL PAPERS, PLAIN	HOW MADE	DECKLE EDGES	SIZING	NEUTRAL PH	WEIGHT
Gampi	H	4	WL	x	95
Goyu	H	4	WL	x	50
Hosho Professional	H	4	WL	x	80
Inomachi Nacre	H	4	LS	x	180
Iyo Glazed	H	4	LS	x	95
Kitakata	H	4	LS	x	30
Kizukishi	H	4	MS	x	14
Kochi	H	4	WL	x	109
Kozo Graphic	H	4	LS	x	120
Kozo Lightweight	H	4	LS	x	55
Masa	MA	0	LS	x	70
Mulberry	H	4	LS	x	45
Okawara	MA	2	LS	x	60
Sekishu	H	4	LS	x	30
Suzuki	H	4	MS	x	60
Torinoko	H	0	LS	x	125

DECORATIVE PAPERS	HOW MADE	DECKLE EDGES	SIZING	NEUTRAL PH	WEIGHT
Banana Paper	H	4	WL	x	1 to 2 ply
Chiri	H	4	LS	x	36
Cogon Grass Paper	H	4	WL	x	1 to 3 ply
Fantasy Papers	H	4	LS		30
French Marbled Papers	MA	0	MS		170

DECORATIVE PAPERS	HOW MADE	DECKLE EDGES	SIZING	NEUTRAL PH	WEIGHT
Indian Handmade Papers; Wool, Tea, Straw, Sea and Bagasse	H	4	MS	x	250
Japanese Tea Chest Papers; gold and silver	H	0	MS		45
Kasiri	H	4	LS	x	40
Kasugami	H	4	LS	x	30
Kinwashi	MA	2	MS	x	30
Kyoto, (Echizen Washi)	MA	0			
Lace Papers	H	4	LS	x	8
Larroque Fleurs	H	4	MS	x	
Larroque Mouchette, many colors	H	4	MS	x	250
Mexican Bark Papers	H	4	WL		
Mitzutama Black, open lace with silver and gold flecks	H	4	LS	x	8
Moriki, Yatsuo, many colors	H	4	LS		40
Ogura	H	4	LS	x	108
Sugikawashi	H	4	MS	x	80 to 130
T Unryu, pastel shades	H	2	MS	x	40
Tableau	MA	0	LS	x	45
Thai Reversible Unryu, many colors	H	4	WL	x	50
Thai Unryu, many colors	MA	4	WL	x	25
Twinrocker White Feather Rounds; 5" and 12"	H	yes	MS	x	140

GLOSSARY

ACCORDION FOLD: A strip of paper folded back and forth along parallel lines forming "pleats", so that it opens and closes like a concertina. Also called zigzag fold.

ADHESIVE: A general term for any of several substances capable of bonding materials to each other.

AWL: A pointed tool used for piercing holes in papers and other materials.

BINDER BOARD: A generic term used to designate a dense board used in making a hard cover book or box. It comes in several thicknesses.

BINDING MARGIN: The area along the fold between two facing pages. Also called Inner Margin or Gutter. On side sewn pages this margin is on the side to be bound.

BOARDS: Various board-like materials used in bindings.
Hard covers in a case binding.
See also pressing boards, p. 4.

BOARD SHEET: The part of an endpaper which is pasted to the inside of the board in a case binding, see Endpapers.

BOARD THICKNESS: The thick dimension of board. Often referred to when measuring cover materials.

BOND: Joining two surfaces together with adhesive to form a single unit or laminate.

BOOK BLOCK: The collated and assembled leaves of a book either before or after binding.

BOOK CLOTH: A generic term for a bookbinding material of woven fabric backed with tissue.

BRISTOL BOARD: A lightweight board of rag content paper originally made in Bristol, England. It comes in several weights and is not necessarily of rag content now.

BRUSHES: Several styles are used to apply adhesives, p. 239.

BUTTERFLY STITCH: A sewing procedure for single signature books using an odd number of holes, p. 91. Also called Figure Eight Stitch.

CASE: A box or binding made to hold a book block. Also cover boards ready to be attached to a book block.

CASING-IN: Attaching a book block to the boards of a binding case.

CHAP BOOK: A style of soft cover binding for a single signature, p. 96.

COCKLE: A wrinkled or puckered condition in a sheet of paper or board. Usually caused by moisture and non-uniform drying and shrinking.

COLLATE: To arrange the pages of a book in the correct order for binding.

COLOPHON: An inscription, usually at the end of a handwritten manuscript, giving facts about production; originally details about the scribe and the manuscript. This information is more often omitted or found in the front of books in type.

CONCERTINA: An accordion or zigzag folded strip of paper.

DECKLE EDGE: The feathered edges on a sheet of handmade paper formed by the mold. Deckles are simulated in mold-made and machine-made papers.

DRUMMING: A technique for applying cover material leaving the material loose from the board on the outside and secured on the inside.

EASE: The amount of additional space taken for materials to fold or wrap around an edge.

EDGE SEWN BINDINGS: A binding method using holes along an edge of a book block to sew through rather than sewing in the gutter or a fold of a book block.

ENDPAPERS: The blank leaves at the beginning and end of a book or pamphlet. Those which adhere to the inside of the cover boards concealing the raw edges, are known as paste downs or board sheets. Those which are free are called fly leaves.

FILLER: A piece of paper or outside covering material cut the shape of bare board inside of covered boards. This is done to prevent warping from outside tension or to provide a level surface for endpapers.

FLUSH: A binding is called flush when the cover is the same size as the book block without any square or overhang.

FLY LEAVES: One or more of the outermost leaves at the beginning and the end of a book block. A transitional step, with no structural purpose, often a design accent. Also called blank leaves.

FOLDER: A bookbinding tool, usually of bone, used for folding and slitting paper and smoothing materials after pasting.

FOLDING GAUGE: A wooden device used for accurately folding accordion pages, p. 3.

FOLIO: Originally a book size resulting from folding a sheet of paper in half. Size is no longer absolute, it may be an individual leaf of any size.

FORE EDGE: The edge of a binding, book block, or leaf opposite the spine. Also called front edge.

FORMAT: Shape, size and general make-up of a book or box.

FRENCH FOLD: A horizontal and vertical fold dividing a sheet of paper into fourths. Only the outside surfaces are used, leaving the insides blank.

GATHERING: The group of leaves formed by folding and combining the sheets which make up a signature (section). The process of arranging, in proper order, the sheets or signatures for binding.

GLUE: In bookbinding, glue is an adhesive made from animal materials such as hides and bones.

GRAIN: The direction in which the majority of the fibers are oriented in mold-made and machine-made papers and boards. Papers and boards will change dimension more in cross grain direction. Handmade papers do not have grain direction. Fabric grain parallels the selvage edge.

GUTTER: The blank inner margins of facing pages of a book. See binding margin.

HEAD: The top edge of a book, binding, leaf, or page.

HINGE: A strip of fabric or paper used to provide additional strength at a point of flex in a binding.

JOINT: The exterior junction of the spine and cover in a case bound book.

KNOCK UP: The process of squaring a book block by tapping it at the spine and head to align all the pages.

KNOTS: In this book, knots are used to join threads together, to finish cords, and decorate. Useful bookbinding knots are described on pp. 226-230.

KRAFT PAPER: Brown paper bags from the grocery store are made of Kraft paper. This paper can be used in making patterns. It also makes good waste paper when pasting to keep work area clean.

LAMINATE: A bonding together of papers and/or fabrics with adhesive.

LANDSCAPE: A format that is wider than it is tall.

LEAF: A piece of paper folded in half, forming one unit of a signature; four pages, two on each side. The front side is called recto, the back side is called verso. In an open book, the recto is on the right; verso is on the left. See also, French Fold.

LIMP BINDING: A binding with a soft cover, usually of vellum.

LONG STITCH BINDING: A binding style for multiple signature book blocks with a visible sewing pattern along the spine joining book block and cover.

MULL: See Super.

NEEDLES: A long, slender, round steel instrument pointed at one end with an eyelet at the other for thread to pass through. Used to sew a book during binding.

NICK IN: On a corner miter, extra material beyond the board's corner is folded around corner and smoothed along the fore edge making a small tuck. It is "nicked in."

NON-ADHESIVE BINDING: A cover, (binding), designed to hold a book block without the use of adhesives or sewing.

OCTAVO: A book size resulting from folding a sheet of paper with 3 right angle folds. This makes a leaf one-eighth the size of the sheet and forms a 16-page section or signature, p. 233.

OVERHANG: See Square.

OVERLAP: The extra length and width cut at the head, tail, and fore edges of cover material. It is turned over the edges of cover boards and pasted to the inside board surface. Also called turn-in.

PAGE: One of four sides in a leaf. The right hand side is called a recto page, and the left hand side is called a verso page.

PASTE: The process of applying adhesive.
A general term for vegetable-based adhesives.
Glue is generally considered separately from paste because it is animal in origin.

PASTE DOWN: The part of an endpaper which is pasted to the inside of the board in a case binding, see Endpapers.

pH: A measure of the acidity or alkalinity of a substance expressed on a scale of 0 to 14. A pH value of 7 is neutral. Lower numbers are progressively acidic, higher numbers are progressively alkaline. Acid free papers can be made with any kind of pulp, and have a pH measurement of 6.5 or higher. Paper with a pH value of 7 is considered desirable for artwork meant to have a long life.

PLEAT BINDING: A binding method holding pages in a pleat or series of pleats.

PLY: A single web (full width as it comes from the machine) of paper used by itself or laminated with one or more additional webs as it is run through the paper making machine.

POCKET OR POUCH: A sheet of paper folded in half, bound along the open edge, fold at the fore edge, is said to be a pocket or pouch page.

PORTRAIT: A format that is taller than it is wide.

PRESSING: To prevent warping, a book is placed between pressing boards or weighted while drying. Also papers and/or fabrics being bonded need to be pressed while drying.

PVA: An abbreviation for polyvinyl acetate. PVA is a clear, water-white thermoplastic resin.

QUARTO: A book or page size made by folding a sheet of paper twice with the second fold at right angles to the first, p. 233.

QUIRE: Folded sheets fitting one within another. A set of all leaves required for a book.

RECTO: The right-hand page of an open book. It usually carries odd numbers.

SCORE: To make a linear indentation or crease, bending the fibers in a sheet of paper or board to make it easier to fold.

SECTION: See signature.

SIGNATURE: A group of folded leaves inserted one inside the next for binding. When heavyweight paper is used, a single leaf may constitute a signature. Also called a gathering, a section, or a quire.

SINGLE SIGNATURE BINDINGS: A variety of bindings suitable for single signatures as opposed to bindings for multiple signature, accordion book blocks, or edge sewn bindings.

SIZING: Process of adding materials to a paper to provide resistance to liquid penetration. Sizing may occur during manufacture or after.

SOFT COVERS: Bindings usually made of flexible cloth or papers without stiff boards, see Limp Binding.

SPACER: A device for measuring space between boards in case and box making shown on page 5.

SPINE: The back of a book.

SPINE EDGE: The edge of the book block or cover where binding takes place, opposite the fore edge,

SQUARE: The difference in margin between a book block edge and binding edge. Also called overhang, see Flush. Also at right angles, not oblique.

SQUARE CARD: A device for measuring shown on page 5.

SUPER: A thin, stiffened fabric resembling cheese cloth. Used to attach the book block to the case.

TAPE: The word "tape" is used here to mean linen tape (binding supply), twill tape (fabric store), Japanese flat cord (binding supply or oriental art supply), or similar material. It is used for closures, holding signatures together, holding book block to cover, etc.

TAIL: The lower or bottom edge of a binding, leaf, or page.

TEMPLATE: A pattern or gauge used as a guide in accurate placement of holes for stitching, mounting anchors for closures, etc.

TEXT BLOCK: The area of writing or printing on a page.

TIPPING IN: The process of pasting the edges of a page to an adjacent page. Endpapers are sometimes tipped in.

TURN-IN: The extra length and width of cover material cut to overlap the head, tail, and fore edges of cover boards. It is folded over board edges and pasted to the inside surface. Also called Overlap.

VALLEY FOLD: The reverse of a mountain fold.

VERSO: The left-hand page of an open book. It usually carries even numbers.

WASTE PAPER: Paper used to keep the work area clean when pasting. Usually several sheets are stacked together on work area before pasting begins. Then as adhesive spreads, this paper is discarded. This is inexpensive paper, Kraft paper bags, plain newsprint, discarded computer printout paper, any strong paper that will not discolor the project with ink or dye.

WATERLEAF: A paper made without sizing, leaving it very absorbent.

WATERMARK: A design applied to the surface of a paper mold which causes less pulp to be distributed in that area so the design is transferred to the finished sheet.

BIBLIOGRAPHY

BOOKS

Brown, Margaret R. *Boxes For The Protection Of Rare Books: Their Design And Construction.* Washington: Library of Congress, 1982.

Burdett, Eric. *The Craft Of Bookbinding: A Practical Handbook.* Newton Abbot, U.K.: David and Charles, 1975.

Chibbett, David. *The History Of Japanese Printing And Book Illustration.* Tokyo: Kodansha International, 1977.

Collins, A.F. *Bookcrafts For Juniors*, 3d ed. Leicester: The Dryad Press, 1956. A practical guide designed for teachers with seven to eleven year old students. Many project ideas.

Dashi, Saryu. *Masterpieces Of Jain Painting.* Bombay: Marg Publications, 1985.

Diringer, David. *The Book Before Printing: Ancient, Medieval And Oriental.* New York: Dover Publications, 1982.

Ekiguchi, Kunio. *Gift Wrapping: Creative Ideas From Japan.* Tokyo, New York and San Francisco: Kodansha International, 1972.

Esin, Emel, Verliet, H.D.L., Ed. *The Book Through 5000 Years; Central Asia: Iranian, Tokharian, Tibetan, Nepalese, Turkish, Si-Hia, Mongolian, Manchu Written Records.* New York: Phaidon, 1972.

Gardner, Kenneth, Verliet, H.D.L., Ed. *The Book Through 5000 Years; The Book in Japan.* New York: Phaidon, 1972.

Gauer, Albertine, Verliet, H.D.L., Ed. *The Book Through 5000 Years; Manuscripts of India, Ceylon and South East Asia.* New York: Phaidon, 1972.

Gimm, Martin, Verliet, H.D.L., Ed. *The Book Through 5000 Years; The Book in China.* New York: Phaidon, 1972.

Hollander, Annette. *Bookcraft.* New York: Van Nostrand Reinhold, 1984.

Ikegama, Kokjiro. *Japanese Bookbinding.* New York, Tokyo: Weatherhill, 1986.

Johnson, Arthur W. *The Thames And Hudson Manual Of Bookbinding.* New York, London: Thames and Hudson, 1987.

Johnson, Paul. *A Book Of One's Own: Developing Literacy Through Making Books.* Portsmouth, NH: Heinemann Educational Books, 1992.

———. *Literacy Through The Book Arts.* Portsmouth, NH: Heinemann Educational Books, 1993.

Johnson, Pauline. *Creative Bookbinding.* Seattle and London: University of Washington Press, 1963, and New York: Dover Publications.

Johnston, Edward. *Writing & Illuminating, & Lettering,* 32d ed. London: Pitman, 1979.

Kyle, Hedi. *Library Materials Preservation Manual.* Bronxville, New York: Nicholas T. Smith, 1983.

Lewis, A. W. *Basic Bookbinding.* New York: Dover, 1957.

Lyons, Joan. Ed. *Artists Book, A Critical Anthology And Source Book.* Rochester, New York: Gibbs M. Smith, 1985.

Mason, John. *Bookcrafts And Bookbinding.* London: B. T. Bastsord, 1935.

Mayer, Ralph. *The Artist's Handbook Of Materials And Techniques,* Fourth Edition Revised and Updated. New York: Viking Press, 1981.

Meilach, Dona Z.. MACRAMÉ: *Creative Design In Knotting,* New York: Crown Publishing, 1971.

Museum of Fine Arts, Boston. *How To Care For Works Of Art On Paper.* Boston: Thomas Todd Co., 1977.

Roberts, Matt T. and Don Etherington. *Bookbinding And The Conservation Of Books, A Dictionary Of Terminology.* Washington D. C.: Library of Congress, 1982.

Shannon, Faith. *Paper Pleasures,* Weidenfeld and Nicolson, 1987.

Smith, Keith. *Non-Adhesive Binding: Books Without Paste Or Glue.* Fairport, New York: The Sigma Foundation, 1991.

———. *Structure Of The Visual Book.* Fairport, New York: The Sigma Foundation, 1992.

Tate, Elizabeth. *The North Light Illustrated Book of Painting Techniques.* Cincinnati: North Light Books, 1986.
A technique guide for painters. Many techniques are adaptable to paper decoration and patterned papers.

Watson, Aldren A. *Hand Bookbinding: A Manual Of Instruction,* New York: Reinhold Publishing, 1963.

Wilson, Adrian. *The Design Of Books.* Salt Lake City and Santa Barbara: Peregrine Smith, 1974.

Young, Laura S. *Bookbinding And Conservation By Hand: A Working Guide,* New York: R. B. Bowker, 1981.

Zeier, Franz. *Books, Boxes, And Portfolios: Binding, Construction And Design Step By Step.* New York: Design Press, 1990.

ARTICLES

Grass, Patricia. "Chicago 1983: Making A Manuscript Book" *Portland Society for Calligraphy Newsletter* no. 3, Portland OR, 1983.

Chaika, Betty Lou. "Visible Bookbinding Structures" *Fine Print* 12, no. 1, San Francisco, l986.

Johnson, Judy. "Hand-Stitched Chapbooks" *Northwest Book Arts* no. 2, Seattle.

Kyle, Hedi. "Orihon's Triumph: Origin And Adaptations Of The Concertina Fold" *The Ampersand, Pacific Center for the Book Arts* 3, no 2, San Francisco, l982.

Lindsay, Jen. "Principles Of Bookbinding: Single-Section Binding" *The Scribe, Journal of the Society of Scribes and Illuminators* no. 32, London, 1985.

————. "Principles Of Bookmaking Ii: Fukuro Toji, A Japanese Binding" *The Scribe, Journal of the Society of Scribes and Illuminators* no. 34, London, 1985.

Schaleger, Gretchen. "Twisted Cords For Sewing Cards" *Valley Calligraphy Guild* January-February, Eugene, l983.

Sommerville, Sam. "Page Layout; Some Considerations" *The Scribe, Journal of the Society of Scribes and Illuminators* no. 27, London, 1983.

Spitzmueller, Pamela. "Long Stitch, Kettle Stitch Non-Adhesive Binding" *Workshop Notes,* Oxbow PBI, 1986.

Willmott, Jill A. "Simple Bookbinding" *Journal for the Calligraphic Arts* 3, no. 4, Wichita, Kansas, 1986.

CATALOGS

Daniel Smith, Inc. *"Materials And Information For Artists Reference Catalog"* Seattle, 1990.

————. *"A Catalog of Artists' Materials: Reference Catalog 1993"* Seattle, 1993.

————. *"A Catalog of Artists' Materials: Reference Catalog 1994/95"* Seattle, 1994.

New York Central Art Supply. *"Fine Paper"* New York, 1990.
They no longer produce this catalog; price list is available.

RECCOMENDED CATALOGS, MATERIALS, & RESOURCES

Daniel Smith, Inc. *"A Catalog of Artists' Materials: Reference Catalog"*. A thick catalog produced each fall; detailed information about all the papers they carry including clear, colored photographs of sheet corners. Very helpful in ordering supplies. Packed with useful information. Listed under Supply Sources, p. 275.

Connecticut Valley Calligraphers. *"The Ultimate Resource Guide For Lettering Artists"* Farmington, 1993. Wealth of information. Includes US and foreign resources; lists suppliers of books and book arts materials from vellum and archival to rubber stamps. Some museum and library rare book and manuscript collections and exhibits listed. Some bookarts schools/workshops listed. Brief notes on listings. Write to: Resource Guide, Connecticut Valley Calligraphers, Box 1122, Farmington, CT 06034.

SUPPLY SOURCES

We have listed sources who give prompt, reliable service and will ship out of the country. Generally, we have not listed art stores, handmade paper artists and marblers. Catalogs and samples are often available.

AIKO'S ART MATERIALS IMPORT:
Japanese papers and binding
supplies, paper sample book

3347 N. Clark Street
Chicago, IL 60657-1616
(312) 404-5600

BASIC CRAFTS COMPANY:
Binding supplies, catalog

1201 Broadway
New York, NY 10001
(212) 679-3516

THE BOOKBINDER'S
WAREHOUSE, INC.
Binding supplies, paper,
vellum/parchment

31 Division Street
Keyport NJ 07735
(908) 264-0306
Fax: (908) 264-8266

BOOKMAKERS
Binding and conservation
supplies, catalog available

6001 66th Avenue, Suite 101
Riverdale, MD 20737
(301) 459-3384
Fax: (301) 459-7629

BOOKMAKING NEEDS

665 Third Street, Suite 335
San Francisco, CA 94107
(415) 546-4168
Fax: (415) 546-1916

BRAUNWARTH und LUTHKE
Binding supplies, paper
ships worldwide

Ickstattstr. 3, Postfach 140 125
8000 Munich 5, Germany
089 2 10 08 56

CARRIAGE HOUSE PAPERMILL
Handmade papers and supplies
Donna Koretsky

79 Guernsey Street
Brooklyn, NY 11222
Tel/Fax: (718) 599-7857
(800) 669-8781

COLOPHON BOOK ARTS SUPPLY
Binding supplies and
practical advice

Attn: Don Guyot
3046 Hogum Bay Road N. E.
Olympia, WA 98506
(206) 459-2940
(206) 459-2945

CONSERVATION MATERIALS LTD.

340 Freeport Boulevard
Post Office Box 2884
Sparks, NV 89431
(702) 331-0582

CONSERVATION RESOURCES
INTERNATIONAL INC.

8000-H Forbes Place
Springfield, VA 22151
(703) 321-7730

COWLEY VELLUM & PARCHMENT
WORKS

97 Caldecote Street
Newport and Pagnell Bucks
MK16 ODB England
011-44-610038

DANIEL SMITH INC.
   Paper, books, and art supplies,
   excellent Reference Catalog
   printed each fall,
   ships worldwide

4130 First Avenue South
Seattle, WA 98134
(206) 223-9599
(800) 426-6740, orders, US. & Canada
(800) 426-7923, service
Fax: (800) 426-7923

FAULKNER, FINE PAPERS LTD.
   Handmade paper, book binding
   supplies

76 Southampton Row
London, WCIB 4AR, UK
011-44-71-831-1151

HARCOURT BINDERY
   Binding supplies

51 Melcher Street
Boston, MA 02210
(617) 536-5755

HOLLINGER CORPORATION
   Binding supplies

Post Office Box 8360
Fredricksburg, VA 22404
(703) 898-7300
(800) 634-0491

JOHN NEAL BOOKSELLER
   Papers, books, and
   calligraphy supplies

1833 Spring Garden Street
Greensboro, NC 27403
(919) 272-7604

NEW YORK CENTRAL ART
SUPPLY CO.
   Papers and artist supplies

62 Third Avenue (at 11th St.)
New York, NY 10003
(212) 473-7705
(800) 950-6111
Fax: (212) 475-2513

PAPER & INK BOOKS
   Papers, books, and
   calligraphy supplies

15309A Sixes Bridge Road
Emmitsburg, MD 21727
(301) 447-6487

PAPER SOURCE Inc.
  Papers

232 W. Chicago (corner of Chicago & Franklin)
Chicago, IL 60610
(312) 337-0798

PENDRAGON
  Papers, books, and
  calligraphy supplies

Post Office Box 1995
Arlington Heights IL 60006-1995
(708) 870-9988
Fax: (708) 870-9989
(800) 775-PENS

RUGG ROAD
  Papers and prints

Brickbottom Building
1 Fitchburg Street Unit B-154
Somerville, MA 02143
(617) 666-0007

RUSSELL BOOKCRAFTS

Bancroft, Hitchin
Hertfordshire, UK

SAN FRANCISCO ART INSTITUTE
  Papers, acid free board

Art Supply Store
800 Chestnut Street
San Francisco, CA 94133
(415) 771-7020

TALAS
  Jake Salek
  Binding supplies, papers,
  archival supplies

568 Broadway
New York, NY 10012-9989
(212) 219-0770
Fax: (212) 219-0735

T. N. LAWRENCE & SON LTD.
  Fine paper and art supplies

2 - 4 Bleeding Heart Yard
Greville Street, Hatton Garden
London, ECIN 8SL, UK
011-44-1-242-3534

TWIN ROCKER
HANDMADE PAPERS

Kathyrn & Howard Clark
100 East Third Street
Post Office Box 413
Brookston, IN 47923
(317) 563-3119 & 3210

WEAVING WORKSHOP
TEXTILE ARTS CENTRE
  Waxed linen cord in colors

The Galleria
916 West Diversey
Chicago, IL 60614
(312) 929-5776

WOOLFITTS ART SUPPLIES
  Art and binding supplies, and
  papers

390 Dupont Street
Toronto, Ontario
M5R 1V9 Canada
(416) 922-0933

INDEX

NOTES

We would love to see photos of the original keepsakes and treasures that this book inspires. If you would like to show us what you have made, and would be willing for a photo of your work to appear in a future printing of *Books, Boxes and Wraps,* you may send your photos or slides to the address below.
Your comments are also welcome! Write or FAX (206) 820-9031

Marilyn Webberley
Bifocal Publishing
P.O. Box 272
Kirkland, WA 98083-0272

NOTES

ABOUT THE AUTHORS

An award-winning painter, **Marilyn Webberley**'s drawings, paintings and calligraphy have appeared in museums, galleries and publications throughout the northwestern U.S., including the cover of a magazine receiving worldwide distribution. Marilyn has studied painting with the likes of William F. Reese, Lois McFarland, Ron Lucas, Ramon Kelley, Harley Brown and Carolyn Anderson, and studied portrait and landscape at Zhejiang Academy of

Photo by Edye Colello Morton

Fine Arts in Hangzhou, China. She has studied calligraphic scripts with a number of lettering artists including Jacqueline Svaren, Reggie Ezell, and Fran Sloan. Marilyn has taught university courses as well as private workshops on bookbinding, drawing, painting, design, and calligraphy and has been on the faculty at International Calligraphy Conferences in Portland, Oregon. A board member of Women Painters of Washington, Marilyn enjoys painting out in the open air in the Pacific Northwest and has also painted in India and China. Of her subject matter, Marilyn says, "I only work with heart-touching moments from my own experience – Landscape, portrait, still life, and visions of the inner heart. . . . I love watching the effect of light on color." Married 35 years, she has four children and four grandchildren. Marilyn has practiced meditation for twenty years.

Seattle calligrapher **JoAn Forsyth** has been a student of calligraphy for over twenty-five years. Her work has appeared at exhibitions and in publications throughout the US. Her calligraphic work appeared in *Florilège,* Alain Mazeran, Paris, France. Jo has taught calligraphy at two International calligraphy Conferences, at Bellevue Community College in Washington and for private groups in the Pacific Northwest region. Wherever she has roamed, Jo has always lived near the water: in California, in Hawaii, in Oregon (Lake Oswego), and in Seattle (Puget Sound). In keeping with her love of the waves, Jo and all her family love to sail. Married 43 years, her husband still makes her laugh! She has four grown children and three grandchildren. Swimming and gardening provide her time for creative thinking.

Books, Boxes & Wraps

Design and illustrations by Marilyn Webberley, Kirkland, WA
Cover calligraphy by Stan Knight, Mount Vernon, WA
Cover watercolor-marbled design by Eileen Canning, Lacey, WA
Color separation by Northwest Graphics, Mount Vernon, WA
Text composed in Adobe Optima
Printed and bound by Malloy Lithographing, Inc., Ann Arbor, MI
on 55# Glatfelter Authors Antique, acid free 85% recycled paper
Smyth sewn and bound in 12 pt. film laminated soft cover

"It's FANTASTIC! ... A marvelous book! ... comprehensive ... user-friendly ... "

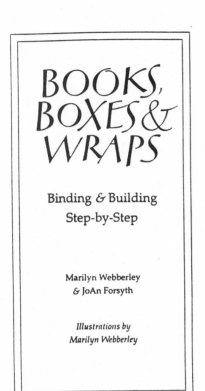

BOOKS, BOXES & WRAPS

Binding & Building
Step-by-Step

Marilyn Webberley
& JoAn Forsyth

Illustrations by
Marilyn Webberley

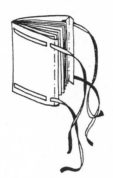

Within these covers are easy-to-follow directions
– as well as historical memorabilia – to help
you enjoy making palm leaves, scrolls,
accordion, and edge-sewn bindings,
single and multiple signature books,
and a variety of wrappings and boxes.

Projects suitable for everyone
from the novice handicrafter
to the seasoned artist
are included in designs ranging
from the simply rustic
to the elegantly complex,
with over 800 illustrations
that charm and inspire the eye.

An additional working tips section is
packed with useful information.

The first edition includes 124 projects, 304 pages,
is offset printed on – acid free paper,
Smyth Sewn, bound with colored
endpapers and a full color soft cover
that stays open when in use.

Library of Congress Catalog Card Number 94-96690
ISBN 1-886475-00-8

Fair warning: Opening this book may lead to the creation of many more!

BOOKS, BOXES & WRAPS $39.00 plus shipping and handling charges per book:

Washington orders: $46.00   includes shipping fourth chass and tax;
other US orders: $4.00   fourth class $6.50 priority
Canadian orders: $8.50   US funds, shipped first class air

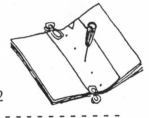

Make check payable to BIFOCAL PUBLISHING and send to:
Marilyn Webberley, PO Box 272, Kirkland WA 98083-0272

- -

BOOKS, BOXES & WRAPS

$39.00 plus shipping and handling charges per book given above:

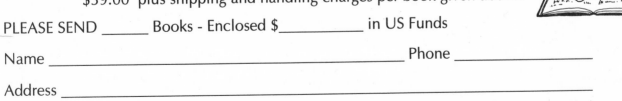

PLEASE SEND _____ Books - Enclosed $_____ in US Funds

Name _____ Phone _____

Address _____